SO-DTE-775

Graphic Standards Field Guide to Home Inspections

Also available in the Graphic Standards Field Guide series:

Graphic Standards Field Guide to Commercial Interiors
Graphic Standards Field Guide to Softscape
Graphic Standards Field Guide to Hardscape
Graphic Standards Field Guide to Residential Architecture
Graphic Standards Field Guide to Building Construction

Graphic Standards Field Guide to Home Inspections

STEPHEN GLADSTONE, ACI

John Wiley & Sons, Inc.

A special thank you to those who helped develop the Graphic Standards Field Guide series:
Corky Binggeli, ASID
Nina M. Giglio CSI, Assoc. AIA, SCIP
Dennis J. Hall, FCSI, FAIA, SCIP
Leonard J. Hopper, RLA, FASLA

This book is printed on acid-free paper. ♾

Published by John Wiley & Sons, Inc., Hoboken, New Jersey

Published simultaneously in Canada

Limit of Liability/Disclaimer of Warranty: While the publisher and the author have used their best efforts in preparing this book, they make no representations or warranties with respect to the accuracy or completeness of the contents of this book and specifically disclaim any implied warranties of merchantability or fitness for a particular purpose. No warranty may be created or extended by sales representatives or written sales materials. The advice and strategies contained herein may not be suitable for your situation. You should consult with a professional where appropriate. Neither the publisher nor the author shall be liable for any loss of profit or any other commercial damages, including but not limited to special, incidental, consequential, or other damages.

For general information about our other products and services, please contact our Customer Care Department within the United States at (800) 762-2974, outside the United States at (317) 572-3993 or fax (317) 572-4002.

Wiley also publishes its books in a variety of electronic formats. Some content that appears in print may not be available in electronic books. For more information about Wiley products, visit our web site at www.wiley.com.

Library of Congress Cataloging-in-Publication Data:

Gladstone, Stephen, 1949–
 Graphic standards field guide to home inspections / Stephen Gladstone.
  p. cm. — (Graphic standards field guide series ; 4)
 Includes index.
   ISBN 978-0-470-54291-0 (pbk.); 978-0-470-92156-2 (ebk); 978-0-470-92157-9 (ebk); 978-0-470-92158-6 (ebk); 978-0-470-95128-6 (ebk); 978-0-470-95147-7 (ebk) 1. Dwellings—Inspection—Handbooks, manuals, etc. I. Title.
 TH4817.5.G59 2010
 643'.12—dc22
                          2010025483

Printed in the United States of America

10 9 8 7 6 5 4 3 2 1

Contents

Introduction

Welcome to Wiley's Graphic Standards Field Guides!

We know that when you're on a job site or in a meeting, questions come up. Even the most seasoned professionals may wish they could look up that one piece of information that is just outside their instant recall or just beyond their current experience. There is a real need to make immediate on-site decisions—to access information on the spot, no matter where you are.

Graphic Standards Field Guide to Home Inspections is designed to be a quick and portable reference for busy professionals like you. It focuses on just the information you need away from the design desk, wherever you are.

Who This Book Is For

We have tried to give you a good mix of required information, easy on-site reference, and some common sense and direction, both for the new inspector and for those with years of experience under their belts. If you're actively inspecting homes, you will find much of this information helpful, and perhaps it will steer you to a better understanding of some inspection topics. We hope it will allow you to find new ways to deal with this ever-expanding business, which entails both knowledge of construction and solid detective work. If you are interested in becoming a higher-functioning inspector, and looking to increase your inspection and environmental menu of services, this book is for you. This book contains the critical core information you'll need when working away from the office. It's like having the jobsite knowledge of your firm's most experienced professional in your pocket. In addition, it has some tips and common-sense ideas from the author's years of experience.

How This Book Is Organized

The content of this book is organized according to a logical path that a home inspector might follow taking into account state requirements and the standards of practice of the American Society of Home Inspectors (ASHI®) standards of practice. Each chapter covers a specific component of a residential building, and includes topics appropriate to home inspection. Use the chapter's opening pages to find a specific topic, or refer to the index to find exactly what you need.

Information on specific topics is presented in lists and tables, making it easy to find and reference quickly. Architectural details and drawings, coupled with photographs, demonstrate standards and help you evaluate what you may encounter on-site.

Each topic contains the following sections:

Description—A brief overview of the topic, to provide some context.

Assessing Existing Conditions—Key things to look for when you're in the field that will help guide your decisions.

Acceptable Practices—Keys to what constitutes good-quality work and references to industry standards.

Reporting—What should be noted in the inspection report.

Practices to Avoid—A quick list of what to look out for.

Look to the References section at the end of each chapter to learn where to find more information about the topic, within this book or in other sources.

This symbol ● indicates things you may see in the field that are good rules of thumb or acceptable practices.

How to Use This Book

The *Field Guides* are meant to go anywhere you go. You can keep one in the office to refer to, or keep one in the glove compartment, just in case—the book is a convenient reference to have on hand whenever you are away from needed information and out of the office. We are often asked about specifics on an inspection, and having a handy reference can instantly provide an answer or another way of analyzing the situation.

Use the *Field Guide* to:

- Help a client evaluate a prospective property.
- Find information on unexpected on-site conditions.
- Remind yourself of possibilities and alternatives.
- Create a checklist to make sure you asked all the right questions during a site visit.
- Expand your expertise on the home inspection process.

About the Author

Stephen Gladstone, ACI, has been inspecting homes since 1983. His inspections are comprehensive and very thorough, but his emphasis has always been on helping his inspection clients by teaching them about their new home. His philosophy has been to provide a higher level of service and to make sure that, at the conclusion of the inspection experience, his clients will have enough good information and insight to make solid decisions and feel assured that they are buying the home of their dreams, and not a nightmare. Stephen has been a contributing author for many years, a very active member of the American Society of Home Inspectors, and a national seminar presenter, educator, and radio personality. He brings his unique experiences as well as a sound basis of expertise to this book.

About Graphic Standards

First published in 1932, *Architectural Graphic Standards (AGS)* is a comprehensive source of architectural and building design data and construction details.

Now in its eleventh edition, *AGS* has sold more than one million copies and has become one of the most influential and indispensable tools of the trade for architects, builders, draftsmen, engineers, students, interior designers, real estate professionals, and many others. The entire family of *Graphic Standards* resources is ready to help you in your work. In recent years, the franchise has expanded to include *Interior Graphic Standards, Planning and Urban Design Standards*, and the most recent publication, *Landscape Architectural Graphic Standards*. Each of these major references follows in the tradition of *Architectural Graphic Standards* and is the first source of comprehensive design data for any design or construction project. Explore what these products have to offer, and see how quickly they become an essential part of your practice.

Visit www.graphicstandards.com for more information.

Chapter 1

Beginning an Inspection

Introduction

A home inspection is a search through the obvious that looks for subtle signs and symptoms, to better identify the condition of the home, for a buyer. The process of honing your inspection skills takes time and experience, but also can be aided by some careful mentoring. This book is designed as a field guide to help you choose a logical path to follow, as you perform your inspections. The tips and information included should make this incredibly important job a bit easier.

The professional home inspection business is barely 40 years old at this printing. As a result, it has changed greatly from its simplistic beginnings, when tradespeople would give homes a quick once-over, and offer blanket approvals based on hunches and feelings. The evolution that has brought us to today encourages the inspector to be highly educated, use more sophisticated testing equipment, and focus on a whole gamut of building science information and environmental issues.

Figure 1.1 Regardless of architectural style or condition, your inspection is meant to look for signs and indicators of potential problems, maintenance needs, and safety issues.

Figure 1.2 Pictured here are some popular moisture meters used to detect higher levels of moisture in building products.

New ways of looking at ventilation and energy consumption, newer building components, and diagnostic tools such as infrared cameras and moisture meters are all changing the analysis of a home's condition.

The public relies on the knowledge and skills of the inspector to protect them from less obvious dangers, poor building products, and inadequate or faulty installation techniques. They expect us to warn them when unexpected risk or substantial expense is projected.

This field guide is written specifically for inspectors. It is an aid to assist them as they follow the routine of an inspection, and to provide a resource that is dependable and proven. In addition, the text may help inspectors to see the trees through the forest, or at the very least, help establish a path toward more successful inspections.

I have put my 27 years of experience into this guide for two reasons. First, it is to no one's advantage to repeat the mistakes I have made over the years. The second reason is my desire to help guide future inspectors by sharing. With the hope that you will do the same for the next generation of inspectors, I offer my compass so that you may guide all those who follow.

Figure 1.3 This new technology can pinpoint water leaks and heat loss for those with a high-quality infrared camera and knowledge of the techniques required to operate the equipment and analyze the information found.

Figure 1.4 Structural movement may be significant or not. Only years of experience and an understanding of construction can give you a degree of comfort when diagnosing structural problems.

Before Beginning an Inspection

- Try to prepare before you go. Obviously, intensive training, attending seminars on related subjects, and plenty of field training are critical to learning the required skills. If you are not ready to fly solo on inspections, work with someone else until you are.
- As the Hippocratic Oath for doctors says: Do no harm. The people buying your services expect you to have the skills and knowledge to protect them. Don't let them down.
- Be professional. Arrive early. Do your best. Follow through. Don't cut corners.

Tools

Gather the tools you will need before you need them. Use a good canvas bag to carry the more important tools into the home.

Here are some of the inspection tools that I believe are critical:
Assorted screwdrivers—Flat-head, Phillips, Robertson (square head), and stubby screwdrivers
Some good pliers—Pump pliers and a locking vise grip
Sharp knives—Razor and pocket type

Figure 1.5 As you set up your tools and vehicle, some thought should go into what you will need, what you might need, and what would be helpful if something goes amiss.

Figure 1.6 A large, easy-to-carry bag can be brought into the home with the tools and materials you might need.

Flashlights—I use rechargeable types, but you will need a few good bright lights
A digital thermometer
Water-sampling bottles from a water lab
Business cards and marketing materials
A moisture meter (preferably with probes as well as nonintrusive radio waves)
Some dye tablets for septic systems
A small first-aid kit (with tweezers and adhesive bandages)

On my belt I carry a pouch with the following:
Five-way ratcheting screwdriver
Compass
Microwave tester
All-purpose combo tool (e.g., Leatherman®)
Electrical testers—Two-prong outlet tester, three-prong, and ground fault circuit interrupter (GFCI) tester, and voltage sniffer
Jimmy tool for opening locked closet doors
Business cards
Thermometer
A small knife
Pens and a laser pointer

Figure 1.7 Tools I need next to me at all times during the inspection

Pepper spray for aggressive pets or wildlife
Smaller-size screwdrivers
Flashlight

In my vehicle I keep the following:
A ladder (I have found that a 22-ft Little Giant® works the best)
A telescopic ladder (I use the Telesteps® heavy-duty wide-rung 18-ft model)
A carbon monoxide meter (Bacharach's Monoxor® or Snifit®)
A combustible gas detector (TIF 8800®)
A good termite probe
Radon machines (I use Femto-Tech® continuous monitors)
A 12-volt cooler (for water samples)

Bins

I have five full-sized bins in my truck to keep items clean and organized. They are each labeled.

Figure 1.8 Good ladders can save your life or help reduce your risk. Looking at a roof from a ladder can change the whole roof perspective.

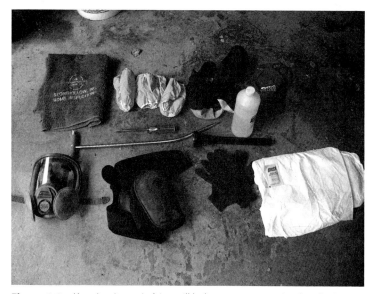

Figure 1.9 Keeping items in bins will help you stay organized, make it easier to find things, and look more professional.

1. Crawlspace bin:
   Tyvek® suits
   Gloves (heavy work type and latex disposables)
   A bump cap (baseball cap)
   A full-face respirator (3M N95®)
   Surgical shoe booties (disposables)
   Kneepads
   Two plain sheets (blue–colored ones show less dirt) for closets
   A good rechargeable lantern
   Safety glasses
   Towels

2. Papers bin:
   Extra reports and contracts
   Extra pages for my reports
   Information sheets on various subjects (radon, asbestos, wells,
      septic systems, pools, mold, etc.)
   Maps of my area
   Phone books
   Code Check® books
   Extra writing pads
   Bilingual information sheets

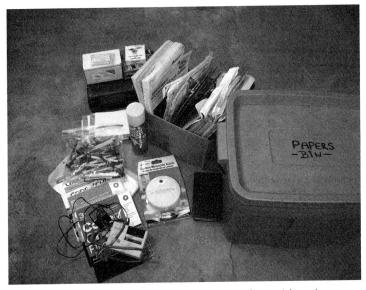

Figure 1.10 Keeping cards, brochures, promotional materials, and giveaways in a clean bin will allow you to present items that are desirable and in good condition when you need them.

Pens/pencils
Markers
Radon notification sheets
Printer and charger for radon machine

3. Clean-up bin:
   Small 1-gal. wet/dry vac
   Paper towels
   Clean rags/towels
   Bottle of isopropyl alcohol (to clean respirator)

4. Miscellaneous bin:
   Bug repellant
   Wasp spray
   Dog biscuits
   Vehicle safety—Flares, cables, first-aid kit, fire extinguisher, flat fix
   Referral gifts

5. Marketing/Promotional materials bin:
   Newsletters, coloring books and crayons
   Stickers, tape measures with your logo, brochures and thank-you
     cards (marketing)
   Flyers, promotional materials

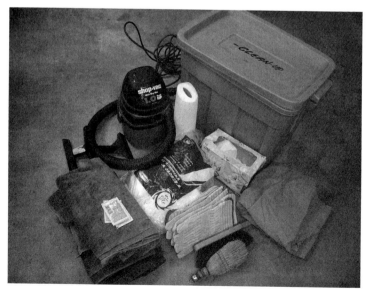

Figure 1.11 There will always be a leak, a moment of inattention, or a
clogged drain. Plan for the worst, and carry what you need to bring the home
back to the condition you found it in.

Glove Compartment

Personal & Company Identification
Copies of licenses
Business cards
Electric tape
Pens
Important phone and email list
White glue, rubber cement, and crazy glue

Center Console

Phone charger
Laptop power inverter
Gum or mints
Sunglasses
Change for parking meters
Digital camera
Calculator
Cell phone
GPS

Figure 1.12   Important materials that I keep in the glove compartment

Getting Organized

When I leave in the morning, I have my appointments ready with directions and the reports for each job. I check to make sure that all my equipment is in the vehicle and that any items on chargers are fully charged.

Arrival on Site

- Give yourself enough travel time to arrive 15 minutes early. No more than that.
- Arriving too early is usually not wise. Park up the road and wait, if you are too early. Use that time to get organized.
- Prepare by looking at the homes on the street, looking for similarities, building style, components, etc. Look at drainage issues and common characteristics. Note hydrants, street lighting, storm drains, private roads, and so forth.
- When you park, find a place near the house, but preferably where you are not in anyone's way, or apt to be blocked in. Get your vehicle in a position that allows you to escape, even if others decide to remain.
- Always avoid parking near storm drains to avoid losing items that can fall out of your car accidentally.

Figure 1.13   Your vehicle should allow you to easily stow ladders, bins, and necessary tools in an organized and professional manner.

- Size up the home. Make sure it is the right address and that the description matches your notes.
- Is it the right age and square footage? Is there a discrepancy? Look for outbuildings, cottages, garages, barns. Will you need more time? Or will you have to return because of the size of the home? Will you need to renegotiate your fee? The only time you can renegotiate your fee is in the first few minutes of the inspection.
- If you take photos, take a shot of the front view. This can become your report cover.
- Knock on the door and/or ring the bell. If someone is home, ask if you can just start on the outside before the Realtor® and client arrive.

This procedure allows you some time to meet the seller to ask questions. It also allows him or her to put away the dogs. This is often the time you find out that the address is incorrect or that the inspection was canceled—now you may need those 15 minutes to find the right house!

Questions to Ask the Homeowner

- How long have you lived here?
- What improvements have you made?
- Is there a buried fuel tank?
- How old is the roof? Is it a replacement? Were old layers removed?
- Is there a basement water problem?
- Is there a radon issue?
- Is the home on a termite- or ant-control contract?
- Are there some areas that are not accessible, or one that shouldn't be entered?
- Is anything broken, disconnected, or winterized?
- Has the home been inspected or tested recently?

When you have the time, begin your exterior inspection—but when the client or realtor arrives, **stop** and go meet with him or her. You must be polite but you must also "control" the inspection process.

Proper Client Relations

Remember whom you are working for. The client should have your full attention, and any information you gather is confidential and not to be shared without the client's permission. In some states, this is law; in others, it is simply common sense.

- First impressions are made in seconds, so dress properly for the inspection and make sure you, your team, and your vehicles transmit the message of professionalism. Clients should feel they have hired the right company to perform the inspection.
- Build confidence and take control of the inspection. A firm handshake, good eye contact, and a practiced introduction will be important. Let clients know what the scope of the inspection will encompass and how they can participate.
- If you are delayed, or know you are going to be late, call the client and/or the Realtor® to let them know you are on your way.

Once you have introduced yourself, I recommend that you follow a prepared orientation speech. You should let clients understand what your logical path entails. Do not allow them to lead you in a disorganized manner. Let them know that by following your lead they will ensure that all the necessary inspection elements are covered.

I am an advocate of making sure your clients understand what you have been hired to do. They must understand what the scope of the inspection will include from the very beginning. The wild expectations of an inexperienced client can set you up for disaster.

Having a small chat initially that lets clients know what to expect can smooth the whole process, build confidence in your relationship, and help explain their role in the inspection.

Opening Speech

The speech should be well rehearsed and must touch on all of the important elements in order to be successful and reduce your liability. Practice. After shaking hands and acknowledging the client, ask him or her to join you in a warm spot away from distractions, and out of the hearing of the homeowners. Then go over the touchpoints of the opening speech.

> "It's important that I explain what we are planning to do here today, for you, and with you if you choose to participate, and I encourage you to participate as much as you wish. Please follow me around, ask questions, and learn as much as possible about your new home.

> Today, during this three-hour window of opportunity, we are going to go around the outside and inside, looking at the visible and accessible elements and systems of this home, to see the conditions as they are today. We are looking for water stains, bulges,

cracks, leaks, and items that are improperly installed or just not right for the age of the home. If we come upon problems, I will explain them to you, answer your questions, and write them in your report.

As we go around, I am looking for signs and symptoms of potential problems that may cost more than $500 to repair or replace—not minor dings or damages that are cosmetic, or of lesser importance. It's important for you to remember that my eyes work just like yours; I cannot see through the walls or see the future.

You should also remember that telephone consultation with me is free forever. If you are confused or need more information—or if someone tries to sell you a service you are not sure you need—you can call me to discuss it before you spend money or get ripped off. Unfortunately, there are plenty of scammers who will try to sell you services you may not need.

Please be aware that what you are buying from me today is opinion; I am very happy to share my opinion with you, but it is not a warranty or guarantee. We offer two guarantees: one you won't like, one you will. The first is that, in time, everything will break and cost more than you want to spend . . . so budget for some things to go wrong and for needed repairs. Second, we have a satisfaction warranty on the inspection. If you do not feel we met or exceeded your expectations for the home inspection, you need not pay for it.

But I promise you, we will look as carefully as possible at this home, and you will be so happy with the thoroughness of our inspection that you will indeed be pleased with our services today.

I like to offer this medical analogy: If you had limped up to me when we first said "Hi," or if your pants were ripped or stained, I would have asked, "What happened?" to gather some information about the recent damage.

If you trusted me to lift your pants leg and I saw a scar or a bruise, I would ask you for some history of your past injuries. With houses, sometimes we can gather this same history from the owners, and sometimes there is little information to work with.

If you trusted me to x-ray your leg, I would know better about the structure under the pants and skin, and whether you were able to hold yourself up for an extended period of time or not. With houses, it is often difficult to see the structure, with finished walls and ceilings, floor coverings, and furniture in the way.

If you trusted me with a scalpel, I could open your leg and better understand how you were put together, but then you would need me to have the skills to put you back together! Your homeowner will not be happy if we do any destructive evaluation of the home, but if we see areas of concern, we will ask for more information, to try to better understand any existing or chronic problems.

But you will have to do your part as well. On the morning of the closing, you need to carefully make sure that the home is substantially in the same condition that it's in now, or better. If it is not, you will have to wave a flag at the closing to discuss this. Also, you should watch for movement damage or leaks over the time you are living here, and call us if you have questions about such things. And don't forget that you will have to budget some money to pay for things that get broken over time.

Does this all make sense to you? Are you okay with what I am explaining? Before we begin, do you have any immediate concerns or worries about the property?"

Usually, clients will mention a couple of issues, and I'll let them know that we will focus on those when we get to them. If everyone is okay, I tell them I'd like to begin on the outside, and we will go over the report and sign the contract papers when we are inside, in a few minutes.

Adjusting client expectations is probably the most critical discussion a home inspector can have. This speech readies the client for the process, places the inspector in charge with the client tagging along, and clearly explains the inspection's scope and limitations. The speech is given verbatim every time, because it is a critical verbal disclaimer—to keep the client on track, and keep you out of court.

The Inspection Begins

As you follow this guide and examine the photos and charts, remember that homes and components may change. Products in use today may become problematic or create a health concern in the future. The most critical element will always be the service you provide to your clients and the relationship of trust you establish with them.

Chapter 2

Exterior Components

Siding (Cladding)

Description

Exterior facets of a home inspection are important because each element helps to keep drafts and moisture out, while helping to keep the heat and cooling in. Clearly, deterioration of the siding or poor installation technique will reduce its ability to meet required comfort levels and energy efficiencies. The result can be additional damage that allows air infiltration, water intrusion, and infestation by insects and vermin. The resulting mold growth and unhealthy conditions can cause illness.

Definitions

Bulkhead — Basement stair and metal-covered doors.
Efflorescence — Salts left on masonry and stone when moisture containing the salts evaporates into the air.
Exterior insulation finishing system (EIFS) — Synthetic stucco made with polystyrene board, which has been very problematic in the past because of moisture build-up.
Grading — The way the water naturally flows on the property.

Figure 2.1   Weep holes in veneer siding allow moisture trapped behind the brick or stone to drain without causing damage.

Gutters — Troughs that catch water from the roof and direct it to leader piping to drain on the grade or through underground drains.
Kickouts — Flashing details that divert water away from areas of concern.
Lintel (header) — Metal or wood support above windows, doors, and openings.
Spalling — Crumbling, cracking, and delaminating of masonry from trapped moisture.
Weep screed — A metal stop that is installed at the base of stucco to allow water to exit.
Weep holes — Openings in the veneer that allow drainage from moisture entry and condensation.

Assessing Existing Conditions

Most exterior components are installed in such a manner as to shed water off the surface of the components toward the ground. Caulking and sealants can keep some water and air out of details, as can flashings around penetrations both in roofs and siding. When these are

Figure 2.2 Clapboard siding was used in early homes both for its look and because it created a tighter, wind-resistant home. Watch areas where splashing may rot lower boards.

designed and installed properly, moisture should not easily enter the home.

Inspection Concerns

- Regardless of the type of siding, the inspector is always looking for any gaps, openings, or damage that can allow water, air, or insects and vermin to enter. Recommending the filling of cracks and openings is a given.
- Areas of greatest concern are flashing points (chimneys, skylights, penetrations of roof and wall surfaces). All penetrations can contribute to gaps that can degrade surfaces or allow infiltration over time.
- Assess all areas around such penetrations and openings on the walls and foundation where electrical, utility, or refrigerant lines enter or exit the home.
- Closeness to grade can cause splashing and surface deterioration. Desired minimum distance from masonry to grade is 4 inches. For other sidings, the minimum should be at least 6 inches.
- Remember that mice can enter through a nickel-sized hole.
- Seams, side edges, and top flashing details are critical to check with most siding, as well as the proximity to the soil, adequate drainage, and clean weep holes.
- Note water stains, damages, and insects; see if fasteners have degraded.
- When siding is next to a roof surface (as found with dormers), roofing should be minimally 1–2 inches from the siding.

Cedar/Wood Clapboard

As with any wood siding we are looking for signs and symptoms of the siding going bad, poor installation, and other items that can degrade the siding, (i.e., moisture, poor installation technique or leakage).

- Examine all seams for soft areas; examine nails for adequate attachment.
- Note splits, stains, damages, and nail deterioration.
- Note previous damage caused by painters (swirl marks, sandblasting damage, thin material, etc.).
- Moldy conditions can often be cleaned but may have caused physical damage.
- Recommend that unnecessary plant life growing on the surfaces (ivy, trellises, vines) be removed.

Figure 2.3   Cedar clapboard siding

Figure 2.4   Cedar shingles. Any plants growing on the siding will hold moisture and block visibility. Paint deterioration, rot, and mildew can follow, as well as insect damage.

Inspection of Cedar/Wood Clapboard Siding

Wood siding expands and contracts with weather conditions, temperature changes, and moisture content.

- Clapboards must be properly nailed to prevent movement.
- Ends and seams should be backed with house wrap or building paper to prevent moisture from accumulating behind siding.
- Butted seams should have a scarf miter and be sealed with sealant, to reduce the chance of moisture getting behind siding.
- Wood clapboard should be stained, painted, or coated with wood preservative on all sides, to better protect and stabilize it against the weather.
- Nailing should be no farther apart than every 24 inches.
- Nails should be at least an inch from the ends and an inch from the edges.
- Predrilling nail holes may prevent cracking, especially at the edges.

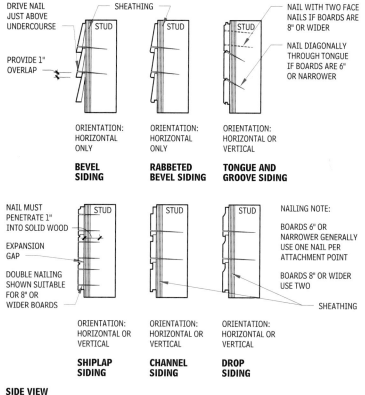

SIDE VIEW

Figure 2.5   Horizontal wood siding

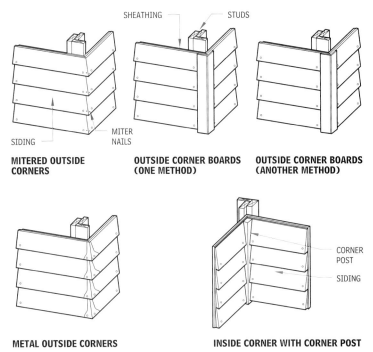

Figure 2.6 Inside and outside corners

Figure 2.7 Older homes (built before 1978) are more likely to have paint layers that contain lead and other heavy metals. Preparation and alteration will require special care.

Exterior Clapboard Inspection

- Examine wood, edges, and end for deterioration, soft wood, and any visible damages. Swirl marks or sandblasting or even aggressive power washing can damage the wood surfaces.
- Loose pieces and cracked or missing sections should be reported.
- Peeling paint surfaces will require prep and repainting.
- Older homes (those built before 1978) may have lead paint concerns. New Federal programs require lead safe practices, testing, and alterations be made by certified contractors.
- Rusting nails may indicate that the wrong type of nail has been used.
- The greater the exposure to the weather (amount of face wood exposed), the more deterioration may result.
- Boards wider than 8 inches are more apt to curl or warp.

Exterior Wood Shingles and Shakes

- Cedar, redwood, cypress, and pine shingles are tapered thin pieces of wood of random widths that can be used—depending on exposure and pitch—for both roofing and siding. They are sold in 16-, 18-, and 24-inch lengths, depending on the desired exposure to the weather.
- Shakes are thicker and more random in variation. They are generally 18 or 24 inches in length.

Figure 2.8 Very popular on all styles in the Northeast, cedar shingles are apt to be stained or painted and will last a lifetime if properly maintained.

Figure 2.9   Offering thicker protection and texture, shakes are very durable and weather resistant. These are worn and deteriorating at the roof line.

- Installation can be blind nailed (that is, the shingle above the lower shingle covers the nail by approx ¾ inch), or galvanized nails can be used toward the lower part of the wood and may be visible.
- Shingles and shakes are minimally nailed with two galvanized nails at least ¾ inch from the edge, and the overlap of the next shingle should be at least 1½ inches.
- Cracks in the wood can let water in, so the seams must be staggered when installed. Care must be taken not to damage the material and to make sure all flashing details are correct.
- Head flashings on doors and windows can help divert water away from the top of the window and reduce the chance of water entry.

Inspection of Wood Shingles and Shakes

- Examine the wood for damage, weathering, insects, and signs of warping.
- Shakes are typically thicker and need at least a ⅛- to ¼-inch gap between shingles to allow for expansion and contraction.
- Examine seams and overlap to make sure nails (if blind nailed) are covered by the shake above.
- Nails should be galvanized.
- Look for head flashings above doors and windows.
- Probe wood for soft spots and rot. Split boards or shingles should be noted in your report.

Figure 2.10 Asbestos added to concrete created an inexpensive siding that offered the added advantage of being flame retardant. Now we know that it can cause lung cancer if the fibers are inhaled.

Concrete Asbestos Shingles

- Although asbestos has been shown to cause lung diseases, there are still many homes across the country that have been sided with composite concrete asbestos material. Its popularity as an excellent siding material was due to its flame resistance. The asbestos is only a problem if the shingles are damaged, and it is a concern when they are to be removed and disposed of.
- These shingles by their nature are brittle and are often damaged by impact from ladders, tree limbs, and lawn mowers.
- They were commonly blind nailed with aluminum nails and finished with aluminum corners or wood corner-boards.
- This siding could be painted or not, and may have been manufactured with or without a textured pattern. Some had straight edges, and some were wavy-edged.

Inspecting Concrete Asbestos Shingles

- Look for damages, cracks, and holes. Ascertain whether shingles are properly nailed.
- Look at flashing details around windows, doors, and edges.

Figure 2.11 Older homes may have both asbestos and lead issues on the exterior of the home. Lead was used for durability, asbestos for fire resistance.

- Report damages; add warning about possible asbestos content being a health concern.
- Cracked/damaged pieces can be replaced with new non-asbestos-containing concrete siding.

Figure 2.12 Newer concrete composite siding is proving to be very durable and weather resistant, without the asbestos safety issues.

Figure 2.13 Board and batten siding is made of planks and strips. The strips cover the gaps. It is a more rustic look, and the nails are exposed.

Inspecting Composite Concrete/Non-asbestos Siding

- Newer-technology siding made with concrete and cellulose fibers has been quite well accepted by builders over the last 10 years. Products such as HardiePlank® and CertainTeed WeatherBoards®, among others, offer good durability without the environmental risk.
- These materials are heavy and require more labor to install, so watch for nail pops and waviness that may result when back surfaces are not properly sealed.
- This type of material may have a 50-year warranty on materials but only 15 years on the painted finish.
- This material is brittle and should not be installed wet.

Inspecting Board and Batten Siding

- Although the look is a wood barn style, many homes have this type of siding that comprises planks installed vertically and a piece of thinner board that is used to cover the seams.
- Without adequate sealant, drafts, insects, and moisture can enter. Thin wood may warp or twist.

Aluminum and Steel Siding

- Metal siding lost favor in the late 1980s because of the denting and chalking issues, and its price versus that of vinyl.

Figure 2.14 Metal siding requires proper grounding and is prone to oxidation. Repainting over time may help restore the look, but only if the old surface is not chalking. Look for damages and missing parts. Note that your ladder can dent it.

Figure 2.15 Aluminum-sided home with grounding

- Metal siding can conduct electricity and should be grounded and bonded all the way around the home.
- Although metal siding can be cleaned and painted, aluminum oxides (chalking) can make painting more difficult.
- Newer powder-coated materials are much more likely to promote easier maintenance.

Inspecting Steel or Aluminum Siding

- Look for loose pieces, corrosion, or damage.
- Look for trim details that are improper, missing, or damaged.
- Usually these are blind nailed, or screwed to the subsurface.
- Two-inch galvanized steel nails are typically used, 16 on center and never closer than 6 inches from the siding overlaps. There should be a $\frac{3}{4}$-inch space at the edges to accommodate corner trims.
- Note peeling, chalking, or paint issues.
- Make sure corners are grounded around the corner boards and connected to a ground rod.

Stucco Siding

- Concrete stucco is usually manufactured in the field by mixing and creating three distinct layers. Each layer is installed and allowed to dry.
- The stucco is applied over a base of house wrap or building paper and the metal or plastic lath; then a $\frac{3}{8}$-inch base or scratch coat is applied first, followed by a second coat called the brown coat, about the same thickness, and a finish coat that is at least $\frac{1}{8}$ inch.
- At the bottom of the stucco is a metal drip screed, which is designed to allow moisture to escape from behind the layers onto the exterior foundation wall.
- In some applications, especially in Tudor-style homes, pieces of wood are set into the stucco as a designed look. Sealing around the wood is problematic, and alternative composite trim use is increasing to reduce rot and water-entry problems.

Inspecting Stucco Siding

- While fractures and cracks are not unusual, especially superficial hairline cracking, cracks can indicate movement and water-entry issues.
- Crumbling may indicate poor-quality materials or unseen rusting of the metal lath.
- Where there is evidence of patching, moisture issues should be carefully evaluated.
- If there are wood trim pieces, check carefully for rot, soft areas, insects, and/or water entry.

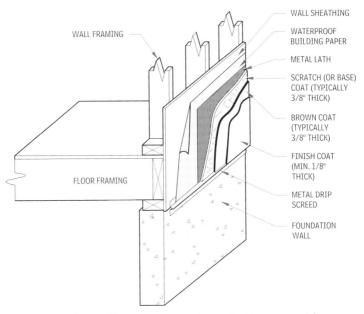

WALL FRAMING

WALL SHEATHING

WATERPROOF BUILDING PAPER

METAL LATH

SCRATCH (OR BASE) COAT (TYPICALLY 3/8" THICK)

BROWN COAT (TYPICALLY 3/8" THICK)

FINISH COAT (MIN. 1/8" THICK)

METAL DRIP SCREED

FOUNDATION WALL

FLOOR FRAMING

Figure 2.16 Stucco: Three-coat process for application on wood-frame walls

Figure 2.17 Hard-stucco-sided home. Tapping on the material will help you determine hard stucco or EIFS.

Figure 2.18 Make sure details and penetrations around windows, doors, and trim are properly sealed with caulking.

- Examine the ground areas near the grade for drainage concerns and deterioration of the finish.
- Though hard stucco is a strong finish, it can be damaged by wear and tear, by vehicles (tractors and lawn mowers) bumping it, by recreational equipment (basketballs, baseballs, and hockey pucks), and from shrubs or trees rubbing against the surfaces.
- Peeling paint may be a sign of trapped moisture or just bad paint adhesion.
- Trim details around windows and doors must be properly flashed or sealed. These areas are more prone to physical damages.
- Bulging areas may indicate that the mechanical attachment to the lath has been damaged or lost.
- Be aware that there are premanufactured hardboard panels that can be used to imitate stucco. They may be difficult to identify except for their uniformity (typically 4x8, 4x9, or 4x10 sheets).[*]
- Watch for incompatible flashings near concrete. Aluminum and steel should not be used on cement stucco, as both will corrode.

Synthetic Stucco

Originally a European product, made for covering masonry buildings, synthetic stucco came to this country in the 1980s and became very

[*]*Principles of Home Inspection*, Carson Dunlop & Associates, 2nd edition.

Figure 2.19 Although it provides high efficiency and a unique look, there is nationwide concern that synthetic stucco traps moisture and often rots out interior wood framing as a result. Some states have banned its use.

popular in the 1990s. Similar to concrete stucco, it starts with house sheathing and wrap, which is covered with a layer of polystyrene bead board. Then a fiberglass mesh is applied, with a final coat of a light mortar coating that is troweled or sprayed on. The look is very much like that of regular stucco, but it is more vulnerable to holding moisture within its layers and rotting any wood in the building envelope. Newer upgrades may include a spun plastic backer installed beneath the polystyrene to help create a drainage plane that allows the water to safely flow out of the siding. Some states have banned the use of synthetic stucco, and others have minimal regulations about it.

Testing to figure out which is synthetic, versus regular hard coat, is done by tapping and evaluating the sound and brittleness of the material. Synthetic sounds hollow and is a softer material.

Inspecting Synthetic Stucco

- Any hole, penetration, caulking detail, or weep hole is capable of allowing water to enter. Water damage that is completely concealed by the synthetic stucco has been found to have completely rooted away interior framing and allowed mold growth.
- When the polystyrene boards get wet, they suck in water like a straw.

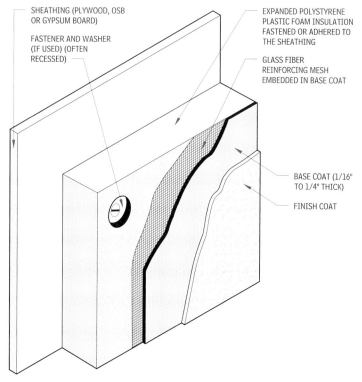

SHEATHING (PLYWOOD, OSB OR GYPSUM BOARD)

FASTENER AND WASHER (IF USED) (OFTEN RECESSED)

EXPANDED POLYSTYRENE PLASTIC FOAM INSULATION FASTENED OR ADHERED TO THE SHEATHING

GLASS FIBER REINFORCING MESH EMBEDDED IN BASE COAT

BASE COAT (1/16" TO 1/4" THICK)

FINISH COAT

Figure 2.20   Synthetic stucco (EIFS)

- Water will rot wood and window attachments and grow mold.
- Interior sheathing and framing can quickly degrade.
- Be careful—it can look great, and still be a mess underneath.
- Sometimes it takes less than a year to develop significant damages.
- Although synthetic stucco is manufactured by several companies, it is considered by many building authorities to be a defective and potentially faulty system.
- The best way to test is with high-quality surface moisture meters, infrared cameras, and intrusive probe moisture measurements.
- The inspector is strongly warned to refer potential purchasers and realtors to Internet sources so they can better understand the long-term costs and problems with this type of material.
- Because of the polystyrene (if it remains dry), the insulation factors of this type of siding can be very cost-effective.
- High wind conditions can drive rain into details that are difficult to see.
- Manufacturers often recommend that foam weather-stripping be installed in voids around windows and doors before caulking.

Figure 2.21   Look for sealant around all windows and kick-out flashings, and examine penetration areas carefully. Moisture issues can become a large concern after as little as two to three years.

Figure 2.22   Texture 1-11® or exterior-grade plywood panel can warp, pull away from the sheathing, and rot in corners around doors and windows. Look for soft wood or insect evidence.

Figure 2.23 Examine edges, nails, and z flashing at horizontal joints.

Texture 1-11 (T-1-11®) Siding

- Exterior paneling siding became popular in the 1970s, mostly for outbuildings, sheds, and garbage-can holders. It was used on contemporary homes and less-expensive homes as a dramatic change from other types of siding.
- Flashing of the seams, warping caused by nails popping, and weather were problematic.
- Edge deterioration and accessibility to wood-destroying insects and bees create problems.

Inspecting T-1-11®

- Examine edges, seams, and corners for damage and openings.
- Note fasteners and any popping nails.
- Warping of loose boards can allow water to enter.
- Z flashing is required on horizontal seams and joints.

Bevel and Plank Siding

- Shaped strips of vertical planking became very popular in the 1960s through the 1980s. Milled wood, often with tongue and grooved edges, gave a barn-board look to homes.
- The siding was installed over house wrap or building paper and nailed in place.

Figure 2.24 Beveled sidings and tongue-and-groove sidings move quite a bit seasonally; make sure gaps do not open, allowing water to enter behind the siding.

Inspecting Bevel and Plank Siding

- Look at all edges and check for damage on the tongue and groove areas.
- Look for cracks, warping, or knotholes.
- Expansion and contraction seasonally is normal but may cause problems when seams open or when the wood swells in warmer/wetter months.

Vinyl Siding

- Using vinyl siding on new construction adds a new dimension to the idea of maintenance-free homes. Vinyl is touted as never needing painting and requiring very little maintenance.
- Vinyl is light, easy to install, and can be installed over old siding and over additional insulation used as a backer.
- Details around windows and corners are able to lock out the weather and trim the siding in a reasonable manner, and the whole process is affordable and energy-efficient.

Inspecting Vinyl Siding

- Because of its vulnerability to high winds, its brittleness in cold weather, and damage caused by lawn mowers, weed whackers, and

Figure 2.25 Cold plastic siding can crack if a ladder hits it too hard. Use caution.

Figure 2.26 Damage from heat, caused by a barbeque. This can easily happen to vinyl.

Figure 2.27 Veneers give the look of brick or stone without being a structural element of the home. Look for cracks, damage, and moisture issues.

projectiles, the inspector must look carefully for penetrations and damages that can allow water, air, and insects to enter.

- Flashing details, corners, and window trim are usually interlocking and may be held in position by friction. Bumping or pulling on a piece of trim may release it and cause problems.
- Look for insulation under the siding (often found easily by using a mirror to look at the edge of the bottom course).
- Penetrations need sealant where pipes and wires run into the home.
- Inspectors should use caution when laddering the home so as not to crack or damage the siding.
- A frequent damage we see is from barbeque grills too close to the plastic, causing melting damage.
- Another damage to look for is missing rake board trim details because of high winds.
- Seams are directional, and installers should take this into account.
- Nailing is blind and loosely done to allow some expansion and movement of the siding.

Brick and Stone Veneer

Veneers offer the look of brick, stone, or tiles to the home without the need to structurally support the home with materials that are more costly than concrete block and wood framing.

Figure 2.28 Stone veneer gives the look of stone without the full weight and complexity of a stone building.

- Regardless of the applied masonry product, the most common means of installing a veneer is to create a shelf on the foundation for the material to rest on and strapping attachments every few inches to the sheathing secured by the mortar.
- The anchoring system is important and should be moisture-protected.
- With the home sheathed and house-wrapped first, the veneer is installed with a void between the veneer and the wrap, allowing moisture to run down and drain through drainage weep holes. Newer materials like spun nylon mesh seem to work quite well when combined with this system in new construction.
- Contractors and homeowners need to keep weep hole drains clear for proper drying.
- Masonry waste should be prevented from filling the void and blocking the natural drainage.

Inspecting Veneer Siding

- Cracks can be a strong indicator of problems.
- Sealant details are critical to keep out water that can cause heaving when ice conditions are created.
- Flashing details need to be carefully evaluated.
- Check weep holes.
- Edges that are exposed to the weather need to be properly sealed or protected.
- Efflorescence salts may indicate trapped water.

Figure 2.29 Natural stone homes are rare because they were very expensive to build and heat, and they can wick moisture in. Watch for cracks, efflorescence, and settling issues.

Figure 2.30 Bowing brick can indicate structural issues.

Actual Brick and Masonry Buildings

- While brick-constructed buildings are still out there, it is rare—because of cost and labor intensity—to find new-construction actual brick homes. Newer construction is often poured concrete or masonry block with a veneer of brick or stone.
- Early brick homes were susceptible to shifting, expansion and contraction, and cracking; deterioration of mortar and spalling were very typical.
- Structural issues with brick can be serious and expensive to fix.

Inspecting Brick and Masonry Buildings

- With brick and masonry, it's all about cracks and determining the severity of the cracks.
- The rule of thumb is that if a crack is large enough to insert a pencil into, it should be pointed out.
- We always recommend documenting cracks with photographs and monitoring them for additional movement or water intrusion over time.
- Continued movement can create considerable concern, and the next step is to have a professional engineer develop a cure.
- Water entering through a foundation can cause damage and create health concerns. Monitoring water entry is critical to determine whether waterproofing may be needed or lesser repairs are required.

Figure 2.31 There's no stone here! Here's easy-to-clean vinyl siding that looks almost like stone from the street.

- Check mortar conditions because, over time, mortar may become degraded for many reasons, requiring the addition of more of the original material or newer sealants to better protect it.
- Look for spalled brick (caused when moisture is absorbed and trapped within the brick, damaging the brick when it turns to ice).
- Examine penetrations; homeowners should add sealants to better protect areas where plumbing and wiring enter or exit the home.
- Climbing ivy, trees too close to the home, or overgrown shrubs can harm all types of siding, but on masonry surfaces they are more prone to be ignored—or worse, nurtured—by homebuyers. Because these plants hold moisture and grip into the brick, additional damage can result.
- Also, plant life on the home can limit the inspector's ability to see cracks and damages.

Inspecting Vintage and Problematic Older Sidings

- Hardboard siding made from composite materials tends to get soft at the edges, cut sections, and nail holes. This material may become wavy and may rot at bottom edges, over time.
- Asphalt shingle tile is rarely used anymore. It is a dated look and creates a fairly watertight barrier around the siding that does not allow vapor to breathe through it.

Plastic shingles and plastic made to look like other types of siding have undergone many changes, including improvements in the materials that make them more resistant to sunlight and traffic. Fashion and design still influence what people will wrap their homes with. The inspection remains the same, however. Look for damage, water entry, poor energy efficiency, and cosmetic deterioration.

Exterior Doors

Description

Entry door systems provide energy efficiency, security, and beauty to the home. Locksets, weather-stripping, and materials need to be examined. Door operation should be easy and yet secure. Materials need to be weather resistant and low maintenance.

Assessing Existing Conditions

- Note materials. Wood, metal, fiberglass, and plastics are commonly used.
- Note weathertightness features. Weather-stripping, insulation, positive latching in several locations, thermopane glass, and door sweeps will help improve the efficiency.
- Note security. Locksets, deadbolts, and viewing holes all add to the personal security of the home.
- Note any damage.
- Test operation. Doors should open smoothly, not rub on other surfaces, stick, or be warped or out of plumb.

Figure 2.32   Wood door. Check weather-stripping gaskets and locksets, and look for settling. Glass should be tempered on newer doors.

Figure 2.33 Make sure doors close properly and latch. Look for torn magnetic gaskets and sweeps. Some thresholds are adjustable.

- Look for damages to the door, door trim, and door frame.
- Note storm doors and conditions.
- Note catches, spring closers, and other hardware.
- Slider doors should roll smoothly and lock positively.
- Note sagging or lack of bearing headers.

Acceptable Practices

- Open, close, latch, and unlock each door, noting conditions found.
- Open operable windows and accessory doors; check saddles, sweeps, and gaskets.
- Test spring closers and auto-closers.
- Check for trip hazards, drip details, and adequate support below the threshold.
- Note any damaged glass.

Practices to Avoid

- Do not slam or force doors that are rubbing or difficult to open.
- Note deadbolts that are keyed on both sides as a potential hazard.
- Note nontempered glass or damaged glass as a potential hazard.

Windows

Figure 2.34   Wood double-hung six-over-one thermopane windows.

Description

Windows allow fresh air and light to enter and help regulate temperatures. Screens can keep out insects and fine airborne particulates. Condensation on the glass is often an indicator of humidity levels. Security and latching locksets help to make the home more secure.

Assessing Existing Conditions

- Note materials. Wood, metal, fiberglass, and plastics are commonly used.
- Note weathertightness features. Check for weather-stripping, insulation, positive latching, thermopane glass, and hinge details.
- Note security. Look for locksets, windows that tilt in for cleaning, and any other special features.
- Note any damages.
- Test operation. Windows should open smoothly, not rub on other surfaces or stick, or be warped or out of plumb.
- Look for damage to the sashes, muntins, putty, glass, operators, cranks, and window, window trim, and window frame.

Figure 2.35 New construction requires egress windows from sleeping areas in basements.

- Note storm windows, screens, caulking, and weep holes.
- Note catches, latches, springs, closers, and other hardware.
- Note moisture between the glass panes.

Figure 2.36 Jalousie windows were very popular in the 1950s–1960s in the "Florida 3 season" room. These windows typically have very poor energy efficiency and low security. They are rarely tempered glass and can shatter easily.

Acceptable Practices

- Look for damage. Open, close, latch, and unlock each window, noting conditions found.
- Open operable windows, and check sills and gaskets.
- Open skylights; examine operators, lens conditions, and gaskets.
- Whenever possible, examine skylight from rooftop, where you can see any damages and flashing details.
- Head flashings can be critical to windows and doors; make sure they have been installed properly.
- Basement windows should be up from the grade or placed in a window well.

Practices to Avoid

- Do not slam or force windows that are rubbing or difficult to open.
- Do not open or leave open skylights in bad weather when damage is possible.
- Note nontempered glass as a potential hazard.
- Do not open windows by moving dividers (plastic or wood), as they can break.

Figure 2.37 Be careful opening basement windows. Many have not been opened for years. They may have very fragile old glass, and they may have lead paint.

Exterior Stairs

Figure 2.38 Steps are dangerous enough without varying riser heights and missing handrails.

Description

Stairs are important because they allow access to different areas around the home, and yet unsafe stairs can be both a danger and a liability. Checking for safety is critical with stairs because they are a major source of accidents, injuries, and deaths in and around the home. Exterior steps should be lit, should have good drainage, and should be designed for safe use with appropriate hand and guardrails.

Assessing Existing Conditions

- Are the treads damaged? Are there cracked, loose, or broken treads?
- Are risers equal and tread widths consistent?
- Are handrails oval or rounded ones that are graspable, with returns at each end for safety? Are they secured with good hardware?
- Are landings properly sized for comfort and safety?
- With masonry stairs, is the mortar intact? Are there cracks that will allow moisture entry and ice issues?

Figure 2.39 Railings too open, guardrail unsafe, no grippable handrails, platform unsafe from door—warning!

- Are there guardrails to prevent someone from falling through the railings or off the sides of the stairs?
- Are the railing openings larger than 4 inches?

Acceptable Practices

- Examine and report on conditions and safety hazards.
- Check railings for shape, and see if they are loose.
- Monitor rise and run for comfort and consistency.
- Make sure there are necessary guardrails on stairs and platforms.
- If stairway is roofed, make sure there is adequate headroom (minimally 7 ft) and that there are no projections that someone might walk into.

Practices to Avoid

- Do not lean on railings; instead, shake them. Nails and hardware will corrode over time, and wood can rot sufficiently to put the inspector in danger.

Porches, Decks, and Balconies

Description

Decks, patios, and balconies provide homeowners with leisure spaces for all kinds of activities. Safe conditions on each may be conducive to fun and safe recreation.

Assessing Existing Conditions

- For covered porches, look for signs of damage, water stains, and wear and tear.
- Look at structure to evaluate if the construction looks appropriate—that is, does it look typical and have headers, normal-sized supports, and spans?
- If construction looks substandard, an engineer's referral may be warranted.
- Check the base for materials and workmanship; check window and door operation for normal function.

Figure 2.40 Updated Colonial with wraparound porches. Remember to look below if accessible.

Figure 2.41 This home on the water had plexiglass panels on the balconies rather than railings so as not to block the view.

- Probe structural elements to ensure that insects, rot, and mold have not caused the materials to deteriorate.
- Examine siding elements and flashings.
- Look for signs of insects and wildlife.

Acceptable Practices

- Probe all wood for insects and soft areas from rot. Examine all structural areas.
- Look for physical damage and water stains.
- Look for peeling or blistering paint, or plaster damages.
- Note window and door issues and damaged glass and screens.
- Examine all hardware.
- Note safety concerns, outlets, and lighting, and note any heat source.

Practices to Avoid

- Do no more damage than needed when probing.
- Do not open windows by moving the divider grills.
- Many porches are add-ons that may now have baths and dryers venting into the living space. These should be vented to the outside.
- Note uneven floors, but be aware that the structure may have been built to self-drain rain and snow and may not be level.

Patios, Walkways, and Driveways

Description

Concrete, asphalt, stone, slate, fieldstone, flagstone, paver stones, Belgium block, and brick are popularly used alternatives to create safe walkways and surfaces that cars can be driven and parked on.

Assessing Existing Conditions

- Cracked materials can cause moisture issues and trip hazards.
- Settling and heaving can be an indicator of problems.
- Retaining walls may need repairs.
- There may be drainage concerns.
- Driveways may need sealant or crack repair.
- Gravel driveways may need annual relocation of gravel.

Figure 2.42 Walkways should be wide enough and far enough away from shrubs for safe access. Watch for trip hazards and poor drainage.

Figure 2.43 Look for loose pavers or bricks, trip hazards, settled areas, and uncemented treads.

Figure 2.44 Driveways should drain away from the garage, have minimal damage, and provide safe access.

Acceptable Practices

- Walk the patio, looking for uneven areas and damage.
- Check walls and retaining walls for mortar needs and cracks.
- Examine exterior drainage for low spots and discharge on patio or too close to the home.

Practices to Avoid

- Be careful when vehicles, furniture, or grills block your view.
- Moving planters, grills, and the like is beyond the scope of the standards, but is often a wise decision that can catch deficiencies.

Chimneys

Description

Checking the exterior of a chimney requires getting up close to it or using a good set of field glasses or a zoom lens on a camera. Spalling, cracks, and loose material can worsen as moisture enters. Adding caps and screens will reduce crown and flue damage.

Assessing Existing Conditions

- Chimneys should extend out of the roof at least 3 feet.
- Chimneys should be 2 feet higher than anything within 10 feet.
- Chimneys should have a liner for safety.
- Flues should have caps and screens to avoid water and wildlife entry.
- Cracks and damages should be noted and repairs recommended.
- Chimneys larger than 30 feet on a roof plane should have a cricket to divert water away.
- Flashing and counterflashing must be properly done.

Figure 2.45   Shine a light down each flue, being careful to examine inner flue conditions—and do not drop flashlight!

Figure 2.46   Small cracks will allow water to enter and cause heaving and spalling (bricks exploding) in winter.

- Exterior fireplace chimneys usually have three sides exposed to the weather, and as a result are harder to start in colder climates.
- When there are multiple flues, their heights where they extend out of the crown should vary.

Acceptable Practices

- When possible, a careful examination for cracks and openings should be done. However, limited visibility and accessibility may require you to exclude the chimney from the full inspection.
- Recommend caps and screens, and be sure to check damper operation and clean-out and vent doors.
- Dirty clean-outs should be swept.
- Sooty conditions may require further investigation and cleaning.

Practices to Avoid

- Remember to leave damper in the position found, or leave a visible note that it has been changed from the original position.
- Be careful with loose bricks on the top courses. They can fall and damage other surfaces.
- Do not nudge or test chimney stability by pushing or shaking it.

- Be wary of antennas, guy wires, and tripping hazards when on the roof.
- Do not get roof tar on your shoes, and use care when walking on a hot roof, because you can burn yourself and damage the finish.
- Do not drop your flashlight down the flue.

Gutters and Leaders

Description

Wood, metal, and plastic troughs have been used since early construction to divert water from upper roof surfaces to the ground and away from the home. Depending on the look desired and the homeowner's budget, the inspector may find any number of rain-collection devices. Most are aluminum, which is popular because it is light, inexpensive, easy to extrude, and able to last for many years. Copper and zinc are typically used for their look, and are much more expensive. Plastic is more problematic because of cracking and other damages, and is less popular. Wood gutters have been largely phased out because of the required maintenance and cost. Leader pipes lead water away from the gutters, and leader drains route the water away from the building foundation. Some home drains expel the water on the ground, while others are subterranean and drain to dry wells or to lower areas.

Figure 2.47 Gutters and leaders allow water from rain and snow to be carefully diverted off the roof to controlled drainage.

Figure 2.48 Leader pipes can easily become clogged, undergo damage, or fall off if maintenance is less than required. Often this will place water in undesirable places close to the home.

Assessing Existing Conditions

- View the conditions of the gutter and leader system, and report on any damages, leaks, or areas needing securing.
- Pitch is important, and in order to drain properly, gutters need at least a $1/4$ inch-per-foot pitch.
- Debris build-up is a concern, especially in homes with lots of trees and leaves.
- Gutters need frequent cleaning, especially in fall. Drains should be evaluated as well.
- Most systems will have all pieces screwed together to maintain good alignment.
- Water should not be pooling in the gutters.
- Many types of gutter leaf-protection systems exist. Some work, and others help to block the inspector's visibility.
- Unless it is raining during the inspection, it may be difficult to more fully assess the gutter and leader system's ability to control and discharge large amounts of water.

Figure 2.49 Route water away from the foundation, away from walks and driveways, and away from the garage.

Acceptable Practices

- Check for loose connectors, clogged outlets, and loose fasteners.
- Look for damaged units or those pulling away from the home.
- Check drains for debris and clogging.
- Look at transition couplings (where drains go underground) and for extensions to rout water away from the foundation.
- Eyeball pitch and look for pooling water.
- Internal or Yankee gutter systems are more built into the roof. Watch for deterioration of the roofing and the soffit and fascia, or for stains and mold.

Practices to Avoid

- Watch for service wires lying on top of or near the gutters.
- Do not lean on gutters or push them off the home.
- Be careful of sharp edges.
- Do not do damage with your ladder.
- Do not assume that underground drains work.

Soffit and Fascia/Columns, Posts, and Piers

Description

Wood and composite trim will ultimately deteriorate from being exposed to the elements. The inspector should look at the signs and symptoms of damage to wood and composite trim materials, whether they are load bearing or not. As water splashes, pools or dampness may get around them, causing damage.

Assessing Existing Conditions

- Probe all wood for soft spots, deterioration, and wood-destroying organisms.
- Note any damages or repair needs.

Figure 2.50 Look for soft wood, insect damage, paint needs, and environmental hazards such as lead paint.

Figure 2.51 Look for low-quality or missing footings, poor connections, posts that are out of plumb, and sagging or crushing of materials.

- Obviously, load-bearing posts are particularly important, because sagging, settling, and possible collapse must always be considered.
- Recommend an engineer when those conditions are found.

Acceptable Practices

- Probe and do soundings in wet locations, looking carefully for soft wood, termites, and mold conditions.
- Look for out-of-plumb, settling, or crushed conditions.
- Check under floor support to make sure the load is carried.
- Look for splitting, checking, and any signs that the posts are under stress.

Practices to Avoid

- Do not do any more damage than necessary.
- Do not perform engineering.

Figure 2.52   Make sure that deck railings are not too open, paint is not lead, trim is intact and clean, and insects and birds are not doing damage.

Finishes, Paints, and Stains

Description

Although cosmetic in nature, stains and paints and their condition directly relate to hidden damages and suggest lack of maintenance. Damages to the exterior surfaces will quickly transfer to additional damage that may or may not be visible.

Assessing Existing Conditions

- Check paint for chipping, peeling and flaking, sagging, and general deterioration.
- Note if water is getting through to the inside.

Figure 2.53 Proper preparation, good paint or stain, and caulking will keep the home in good condition and prevent weathering.

Figure 2.54 Watch for wood-boring bees, woodpeckers, and carpenter ants close to the home. Dampness and too much shade will encourage mold, lichen, and rot.

Acceptable Practices

- Visually inspect all painted surfaces and note conditions found.
- For buildings older than 1978, caution clients about potential lead paint issues.
- Recommend preparation and repainting to keep materials protected from the weather.

Practices to Avoid

- Do not probe or do more damage to surfaces than necessary to show the problem.
- Do not peel paint off the home.

Resources

ALSO IN THIS BOOK:

- See Chapter 12 Inspector Safety

OTHER RESOURCES:

- Carson Dunlop & Associates. *Principles of Home Inspection:* Systems & Standards. Chicago, IL: Dearborn Real Estate Education, 2003.
- Casey, Michael. *Mechanical Inspection.* Inspection Training Associates, 2004.

Chapter 3

Structure

Foundation Types

Description

Foundations are composed of several elements that result in a system we call the building structure. The elements of this system consist of soil, footings, foundation wall, framing, and sheathing. If construction is done properly, they work together to transmit the live and dead loads to the ground and will stand the test of time. If it is done improperly, they may shift, twist, sag, deflect, or possibly collapse.

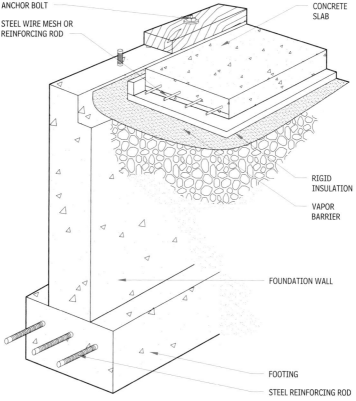

Figure 3.1 The bottom part of a foundation is called a footing (or footer). The footing is generally wider than the foundation wall and is located about 12 inches below the frost line (the average depth at which soil freezes, year after year). The footing distributes the house's weight to prevent future settling or movement.

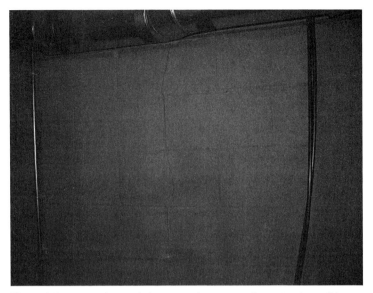

Figure 3.2 Even when visibility is at its best, some determination will be required as to the significance and extent of damage caused by the crack. Drawing upon experience will increase your comfort level over time, but calling in an engineer when you are not sure is a good policy to follow.

Definitions

Dead load—The weight of the building materials and sometimes the soil around the structure.

Live load—People, possessions, and weather conditions (ice, snow, etc.).

Frost heaving—Pressure resulting from water freezing and expanding. As a result, homes in frost areas must have footings placed below the frost line of that area.

Floating slab—One that is supported by the dirt below it and not by any perimeter foundation. A slab on grade is usually poured at grade level.

Monolithic slab—One that, when poured, creates a foundation and the slab at the same time.

Assessing Existing Conditions

Foundation Conditions

- Note the physical condition of the visible components. Are there signs of damage, movement, or unusual conditions that might indicate substandard conditions or materials?

- Is the construction unusual, unconventional, or amateurish-looking?
- Is the foundation problematic?
- Are there indications that the supports are too small or poorly attached?
- Are cracks or movement obvious to see?
- Are there signs of moisture intrusion?
- Are there signs of previous repairs?

Acceptable Practices

- Look carefully at all foundation walls. While footings are rarely visible, the result of a bad or too shallow footing may show itself with signs of settling, such as cracks or larger movement.
- Look for bowing or horizontal cracks in the basement.
- Look for sheathing that has bulged or bellied at the edge of platform-framed sections.
- Try doors and sliders for operation, and open windows to be sure they have not twisted or racked.
- Because problems may telegraph throughout the home, look at rafters and collar ties, connections, and obvious separations at connectors/fasteners.
- On engineered wood, look for alterations that might cause weakness and truss uplift.
- Look for shims under girders and lack of proper bearing.
- Look for evidence that bearing points may have been moved.

Practices to Avoid

- Do not force or pry open a door or window that will not open normally.
- Do not blame others for faulty or substandard work; just state that there are issues of concern.
- Do not assume that workmanship has the blessing of an architect, engineer, or knowledgeable contractor.
- Do not offer a cure or practice engineering, unless you are one.

Definitions

Beams or girders—Horizontal structural members (usually made of wood or steel) that carry and distribute a load from the floor, walls, or roof to the foundation or columns, posts, or piers below.
Pad footings—Footings that support central posts or columns in the center of a span (for example, the middle of a garage post).

Figure 3.3 Step cracks often indicate damage or movement as a result of uneven settling. These may require monitoring over time or immediate repairs, depending on severity.

Pilasters—Foundation walls thickened in order to better hold back pressures or stop or slow movement.

Piles—Piles may be substituted for footings when the soil is of such poor quality as to suggest that no reasonable depth will be able to stabilize the structure.

End-bearing piles—Piles that can be driven into the ground until they reach a sound substrate.

Friction piles—Piles that can be driven down far enough to resist farther downward movement.

Settlement Cracks: Patterns and Diagnosis

Description

Cracks are often misunderstood. Most foundations built from concrete or concrete masonry units are by their very nature stiff and not resilient. As a result, when this material cures, there's a certain amount of shrinkage; until the material is sufficiently cured, it is vulnerable to damage and movement, if proper care is missing or if poor design is applied. Cracks show us that there are significant stresses and allow the concrete to relieve that stress. So sometimes the crack solves the problem, and at other times it is evidence that a problem exists that may need repair.

Figure 3.4 Many cracks are the result of expansion and contraction ripping the drywall paper because different materials move at different rates. This is not unusual in most homes. It may also indicate poor framing.

Figure 3.5 Hydrodynamics teaches us that wet goes to dry—wet soil transfers to dry block or concrete to dry basement. Improving drainage is a good way to slow moisture entry into the home.

Definitions

Cold joint—If there is a delay between deliveries when a foundation is being poured, or if it is done in two or more parts, the seam that develops is called a cold joint or a cold pour. The significance of a cold pour is that the foundation is not monolithic and may allow movement or water to enter.

Cracks—Separation damages to the foundation as a result of pressure, damage, movement, or inferior materials. Some cracks may be significant, others may not.

Cut lot—A property that had dirt removed under the foundation to make it level. If the soil below is undisturbed, this is preferred.

Differential cracks—Usually indicated by vertical cracks or stairstepped cracks.

Fill lot—A property that has had soil added under the foundation to make it level. If soil is not properly compressed, settling is often an issue.

Foundations—The foundation supports the weight of the building and transfers the load to the footings, and they in turn transfer it to the soil. Built from poured concrete, concrete block, cinderblock, brick, stone, clay tiles, wood, or new materials that can support concrete and insulation materials.

Heaving—Upward movement of the home or foundation components. All footings must go below the frost line to avoid heaving in cold climates.

Figure 3.6   Concrete may crack for many reasons. Make sure you look carefully, and note your concerns in the report.

Honeycombing—Voids that are created when concrete has too much air or bubbles in the mix. This can create weak areas in the concrete that can fail.

Joist hangers—Steel hangers that are specifically engineered for holding wood of different dimensions. The inspector should check if they are sized properly and adequately nailed with the correct nails.

Piers—Support columns that may or may not have footings. Typically end bearing.

Settlement cracks—These indicate movement and in most cases will be wider at the top.

Transitional lot—A property where soil may be partially removed and/or partially filled. The result may be unequal or uneven settling and cracks.

Assessing Existing Conditions

- Look for cracks and damages.
- Settling cracks. Normal settling is typical of all homes, and if the home settles slightly there may only be a cosmetic issue.
- Significant settling will require repairs that should be referred to a soils expert or an engineer.

Figure 3.7 This settling was noted above a front porch, where the footings were not adequate.

- Because the house has moved, it is important for the inspector to think of the home as a system in motion. As a result, areas such as bearing points, connections, flashings, and supports need to be examined particularly well.
- Realistically, many of these elements may have moved in subtle ways, and damage may not be obvious to the inspector.
- Limitations of your inspection must be understood by your client and explained in your report.
- Be careful how much emphasis you place on crack size. Analyze all movement and signs of damage; the width of the crack may not be as important as other reactions to the crack, such as movement, distortion, and damage.

Acceptable Practices

- Most home inspection organization requirements and state statutes require that the inspector probe structural components, looking for wood that is damaged. This will often identify rot, mold, and damage from wood-destroying insects and structural issues.
- Probing and soundings should be done whenever possible.
- If the sills are inaccessible, or there is limited visibility, note this in your report.

Figure 3.8 Termites can stay in one area or demolish joists, box beams, and wall framing. Often there is no telling the extent of the damage without "destructive" investigation.

- Noting foundation cracks, movement, and additional damages should be performed as the inspector tours the home.
- Recommend documentation with photos to time-stamp any movement or periods of water entry.
- Note drywall and plaster cracks, and doors and windows that are racked or difficult to open or close.
- Floors that are out of level or areas that feel wrong should be noted.
- Cracks in slabs that are load bearing should be noted if there is evidence of settling.
- Always look for signs of smoke, soot, or actual charring from fire damage. Previous fires may not have been disclosed, and replacement of burnt or damaged structure may not have been reported.

Practices to Avoid

- Don't skip or hurry—look carefully. Remember, this is what separates the inspectors worth their salt from the rest. When you are doing your exterior walk-around, look for lines that are off, look for unevenness, variations, and any signs of cracks. When inside, examine all rooms (all walls, floors, and ceilings), and try the doors and windows. In attic spaces, check rafters, framing, and collar ties. Carefully examine

Figure 3.9 Sometimes, noting what's missing can be really important. Make sure spans are supported with posts, piers, or columns. Sometimes the homeowner will remove a much-needed support to accommodate furniture or a pool table.

staircases and stairwells. In basements and crawlspaces, look for damages, cracks, and evidence of problems.

- Do not push, shake, or "test" chimney strength. It may fall, or damage may worsen. Note loose brick, flashing gaps, and so forth.
- Do not underestimate damages simply caused by rot—they can be substantial.

Reporting: Crack Diagnosis

- Types of movement are vertical, rotational, and horizontal.
- Some rough parameters: Vertical foundation movement of $^1/_2-^3/_4$ inch in 20 feet is not considered a big concern. But look for movement and damage.
- In bowed walls, determine if the wall center of gravity extends outside the middle third, which would be considered unstable.
- Forces on the foundation may be caused by soil pressure, hydraulic pressure from surface water or groundwater, vegetation (trees and root systems), traffic vibration, and point load. Many dynamics may not be obvious during the inspection.

Figure 3.10 While there is rarely any evidence of a footing below a pier, look for cracks or physical evidence that can compromise its strength.

On concrete foundation walls that are higher than 4 feet tall, cracks within 4 feet that are $\frac{1}{8}$ inch to $\frac{1}{4}$ inch can be a concern. Greater than $\frac{1}{4}$ inch can be more serious.

- Horizontal cracks are often caused by pressures against the crack from tree roots, expanding ice, physical damage (a backhoe hitting the uncured wall), and the like.
- Vertical cracks typically are the result of variation in the side-to-side forces.
- Stairstepped cracks usually suggest settling.

Assessing Existing Conditions

If a crack has been "repaired," the repair may be a combination of those noted in the following list, or it may be insufficiently repaired. It is not likely you will be able to make any call except to recommend that an engineer do the calculations. Foundation repairs may include:

Vertical repairs—Concrete underpinning, steel piers, helical piers, and mud jacking.

Horizontal repairs—Buttresses or steel I-beams or actually rebuilding all or part of the foundation walls/footing.

Figure 3.11 Sometimes temporary repairs are added, and the real, more permanent fix may be forgotten.

Acceptable Practices

- Look at all wall surfaces for any signs of distress, damage, or stains. Photograph or describe findings in your report.
- Any cracks of substance should be noted. Movement may indicate structural issues and require an engineer's opinion.

Practices to Avoid

- Level and plumb are desirable in a home but rarely found after a few years as a result of normal settling, shrinkage, and movement. If the conditions found are compromised, do not assume that there is a chronic problem.
- The inspector should remember and remind the client that the inspection is a snapshot in time and that conditions may change.
- Excessive movement should always be reported and an engineer consulted.

Figure 3.12 Retaining walls with inadequate drainage behind them, or those without weep holes, may not be able to hold back forces when water turns to ice.

Basements: Dampness, Seepage, and Waterproofing

Description

Interior water damages can cause significant health and structural issues if the conditions are allowed to continue. The inspector should note any waterproofing that is visible and accessible, from exterior coatings to interior sealants, sumps, pumps, and interior coatings. If there is a sump pump, or some form of under-slab waterproofing system, every effort should be made to have the client find out what has been installed and why.

Increased moisture can create rot and mold, which may attract termites or create indoor health issues. Excessive moisture levels may show themselves with damp walls and building materials, condensation, visible mold, dripping water, and water stains.

Figure 3.13 Water may enter a basement in many ways. Look carefully at the evidence before you make a diagnosis.

Figure 3.14   Seepage may require excavation around the exterior, or water-proofing within. Both can be expensive.

Assessing Existing Conditions

- Look for dehumidifiers, sweating pipes and tanks, water stains, condensation on windows, and generally damp conditions.
- Try to gather some disclosure about previous water stains or newly painted areas.
- Use your nose. Mildew smells may be a clue to unsafe areas requiring a respirator and personal protection gear.
- Moisture may be the result of leaks from plumbing or fixtures.
- Look at pumps and waterproofing equipment to try to determine if they are a back-up or needed more than seasonally.
- Make sure equipment is working, or report that it was not tested and that this should be done before the closing.
- Stained baseboard trim or mold at the base of basement drywall indicates potential issues—don't miss the clues.

Acceptable Practices

- Look carefully for any signs of moisture entry.
- Test sump pumps where accessible and safe to do so.

Figure 3.15 Wet wood will rot over time and attract insects and mold.

- Note where it drains to. Many municipalities do not allow clean wastewater to be sent to sewage treatment. Instead, it should be routed to the grade.
- Look for any signs of moisture intrusion, pooling water, or signs of leakage.
- If water is entering the foundation, it may require sealants or exterior excavation to reseal. Waterproofing the interior, even partially, may be more cost-effective.

Practices to Avoid

- Do not test sump pumps that are ungrounded or look dangerously installed.
- Do not assume that anything has been fully repaired.
- Do not assume that the system can keep the home dry.
- Battery back-ups are not tested in a home inspection.

Crawlspaces

Description

Crawlspaces add an interesting dynamic to home inspection. Usually these areas are designed to allow uncomfortable access to equipment and framing, when it was not cost-effective or desirable to dig a full basement. In many cases, the home inspector will need access to these areas in order to better determine the existence of rot, insects, or good structure. Unfortunately, this area may be moist, moldy, loaded with rodents or fecal material, and hazardous. Personal protection equipment should always be worn in unsafe environments.

Assessing Existing Conditions

- Look for soft, rotted, wet, or damaged wood framing. Probing and soundings of the sill, box beam, girders, posts, and joists should be performed.
- Any bearing issues should be noted (see Bearing Chart on pages 83-84).

Figure 3.16 Simply put—if you don't get in there, you will miss clues to the conditions of this home. And remember, personal protection equipment is a must, even if the crawlspace looks clean.

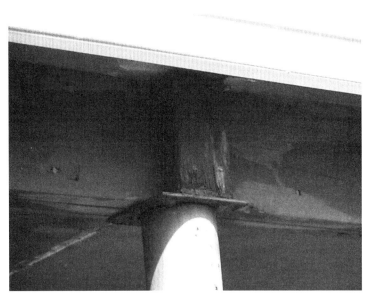

Figure 3.17 Look for temporary repairs and bad house science. Obviously, there could be a better way to fix this.

- Girders or beams that do not have sufficient air around them should be noted in your report.
- Loose posts, those without proper mechanical connection, and those with physical damage or signs of insects or moisture should be noted.
- Inadequately shimmed posts or bearing should be noted in the report.
- Cracks, movement, damages, or insufficient support should be noted.
- Spans that are too long or structures not rated for their use should be noted.
- Unusual or insufficient posts, columns, or supports should be noted.
- Any engineered wood that has been compromised by cutting, notching, boring, or alteration from its original design or plan for use should be noted if visible and accessible for review.
- Look for sagging, deflection, or visible damage of all weight-bearing components. Note bouncy flooring.
- Use of a bright flashlight and closely evaluating the perimeter edges may define subtle, less visible signs of damage or movement.

Bearing Chart

Steel or wood should rest on flat, full-width bearing surfaces.

Steel beams should be supported by steel shims and welded in place.

Wood beams can be shimmed with wood shims, which should be glued or mechanically fastened. They should have full bearing and be as hard and dense as the wood they are being used to shim.

Beams resting on masonry should have a depth of at least 3 in. and rest only on solid masonry, not hollow block.

Where beams rest on masonry, there should be at least $1/2$ in. of airspace around the sides and top, to allow the beams to dry and climatize to avoid rot.

Wood bearing on wood should be at least $1\frac{1}{2}$ in.

Wood overlap on girders or beams should be at least 3 in. on each side (6 in.).

Span Chart

For #2 grade spruce 16 oc with a live load of approx. 40 psf and 20 psf dead load:

  2x6 spans about 9 ft

  2x8 can span about 11.5 ft

  2x10 can span about 14 ft

  2x12 can span about 16 ft

If spaced closer (12 in. oc):

  2x6 spans about 10 ft

  2x8 can span about 13 ft

  2x10 can span about 16 ft

  2x12 can span about $18\frac{3}{4}$ ft

From *Principles of Home Inspection* (Carson Dunlop, Systems & Standards series, Dearborn).

Acceptable Practices

- This is purely a visual assessment, and in most cases the inspector will not be using instrumentation or sophisticated measuring devices to test.
- A careful systematic look at the crawlspace will establish conditions and the need, if any, for further evaluation.
- If there are any signs of concern, additional evaluation by an architect, professional engineer, or competent contractor should be recommended.

Practices to Avoid

- When inspecting crawlspaces, personal protection and suspicion of potentially unsafe conditions should not be taken lightly. Crawlspaces present one of the more dangerous elements of an inspection. The inspector may be breathing unsafe air or crawling through unsafe materials and over unsupported vapor barriers that can have fatal results. Wet conditions can conduct electricity, and being alone and hurt in a crawlspace can put an inspector in a compromised situation. Make sure others know where you are, and maintain communications with them.

Figure 3.18 Sometimes, personal protection equipment isn't enough!

- Use care with damaged or altered framing. Do not probe too hard, because you may start a collapse that was waiting to happen. Use your common sense when you see evidence of substandard workmanship, and do not put yourself or your client at risk.
- Do not remove personal protection clothing in the living space of the home, because you may be leaving unsafe particulates where others may come into contact with them. Placing disposable gloves, booties, and Tyvek® suits into a sealed plastic bag as you exit the crawlspace or basement will protect the residents from contamination. Think safety.
- Do not make contact on wires and any metal in crawl areas without the use of a voltage sniffer to determine if contact with them could be dangerous. Watch wet areas.

Dehumidification vs. Humidification

Description

In many parts of the country, dehumidification is a very important ingredient of achieving a comfort level within the home that reduces the opportunity for mold growth and allergies. Dehumidifiers can effectively lower water content throughout the home if regularly emptied and monitored. Reduction of the humidity level will help stop condensation, dripping from uninsulated piping and tanks, and mold growth in areas prone to dampness.

If the home is too dry, however, static electricity can become annoying, furniture may crack, and mucus membranes can dry, and personal discomfort may be noted.

Many homes have central humidification working alone or in tandem with a forced air heating/cooling system. Most of these units will become dirty and unhealthy over time if not kept scrupulously clean. Because they are often out of sight (usually located in basements, crawlspaces, closets, and attic spaces), they are largely ignored when it comes to the weekly maintenance and cleaning required by most manufacturers for safe operation.

As a result, we recommend that they be disconnected and/or removed from service and replaced with room humidifiers, if needed. We also recommend using distilled water instead of tap or well water. This will remove minerals and other contaminants from the water before it wets the air. Locations around the home where moisture is desired can be more easily monitored and kept clean, as required, with room units.

Assessing Existing Conditions

- Look for signs of dampness, slick walls, condensation or static electricity, dry wood, and the like. Based on your inspection, you may wish to recommend additional dehumidification, or recommend that humidification equipment be cleaned, altered, or removed.
- Look at window sills and sashes for condensation stains.
- Look at tanks and piping, and check for signs of basement or crawlspace condensation.

Figure 3.19 Water flows over the grid, and water vapor is drawn into the circulated air.

Figure 3.20 Removing excess levels of moisture will reduce condensation issues in the basement.

- Attic spaces with poor ventilation or substandard insulation may also exhibit water stains from condensation on windows, nails, and chimney flashings.

Acceptable Practices

- Note dampness levels as you inspect.
- Report wet conditions, stains, and signs of mold or rot.
- Recommend dehumidification if the conditions seem too damp.
- Note leaks, stains, or damages for repair.

Practices to Avoid

- The use of instrumentation (moisture meters and infrared cameras) is beyond the standards; however, it can establish conditions that can pinpoint a problem. If you use instrumentation, be aware that you are increasing your liability.

Brick and Brick Veneer Issues

Description

Although brick is used more today as a veneer for the "look" of brick, inspectors may occasionally find structurally built brick homes. These homes must be carefully evaluated for damages. Chimneys and fireplaces should be carefully evaluated for signs of damage, and structural columns or posts may be brick and should be looked at for evidence of structural deterioration.

Assessing Existing Conditions

- Check mortar for degradation. Mortars were often different concentrations of sand, water, and Portland cement. Over time, chemical action, acidic rain, and vibration can degrade them.
- Bricks, depending on their manufacturing, might be more or less able to absorb moisture and resist the weather.
- Spalling, caused by moisture, freezing, and expanding, can cause serious damage to brick.

Figure 3.21   Watch for mortar deterioration on load-bearing columns.

- Chimney mortar can develop small cracks in the upper courses or crown that allow moisture to enter them and cause damage.
- Mortar serves two purposes when used as a construction system. It becomes the glue or adhesive that holds the CMU's or bricks together and then it is itself an element of the construction that must stand the test of time for both strength and resilience. When inspecting a chimney or masonry siding veneer it is critical to evaluate that the mortar is holding the materials together properly and that it is not deteriorating from the weather, excessive drying or freezing. Mortars used should always be softer than the materials being bonded to avoid damage to those materials. Older mortars are typically softer than newer more plastic mixes, and will need pointing more often using the right materials.
- Watch also vulnerable areas, where gutters and leaders overflow, flashing details that are prone to drip, or where water washes over a surface. Note any substantive deterioration of the mortar.
- When patching or repairing, the mortar mixed should be similar to the original formula to avoid spalling and allow for proper drainage and drying.
- Remember that most masonry products absorb large amounts of moisture and they need to get rid of it just as quickly by interior drainage systems, heat and/or proper airflow. Blocking or sealing these products can trap the water within and cause serious damage.
- Additionally there are chemicals in the environment and in some masonry products that can cause chemical reactions creating additional damages (e.g. acid rain, salt water, efflorescence salts).

Acceptable Practices

- This is purely a visual assessment, and in most cases the inspector will not be using any instrumentation to test.
- Carefully look at brick areas for missing units and soft or weathered mortar.
- Look for damaged brick, crown, or corbelled areas.
- Look at edges of veneers to see if they maintain weathertightness.

- Look for weep screeds or weep holes to provide a way to route water from behind the brick, and note when these holes have been foolishly filled in.

Practices to Avoid

- Examine carefully, but do not push against, shake, or stress-test a chimney.
- Do not damage the mortar.

Interior Structural Framing

Description

Within the scope of the inspection, elements of the structural components not already mentioned may come into play, such as sheathing, rafters and joists, collar ties, and platform vs. balloon systems. The inspector should understand the terminology and the problems inherent with different products used.

Assessing Existing Conditions

- Look for soft, rotted, wet, or damaged wood framing. Perform probing and soundings of the rafters, collar ties, purlins, and struts.
- Look for water stains, rot, or insect damage.
- Any bearing and mechanical connection issues should be noted, especially in heavy storm areas.

Figure 3.22   The switch to platform rather than balloon framing compartmentalized construction, making it stronger and more fire resistant.

Figure 3.23 New-technology-engineered lumber is stronger, is less wasteful, and allows longer spans for safe loads.

- Look for girders or beams that do not have adequate fasteners (if visible).
- Look for cracks, damaged wood, and evidence of fire or charring.
- Look for notching or boring that might affect the strength of the wood.
- Spans that are too long or structures not rated for their use should be noted.
- Unusual or insufficient bracing or supports should be noted.
- Any engineered wood that has been compromised by cutting, notching, boring, or alteration from its original design or plan for use should be noted if visible and accessible for review.
- Look for sagging, deflection, or visible damage of all weight-bearing components. Note bouncy flooring.
- Use of a bright flashlight and closely evaluating the perimeter edges may define subtle, less visible signs of damage or movement.

Acceptable Practices

- Just as with every other aspect of the inspection, look carefully for what is there and—just as important—for what is missing.
- Try to assess what loads are in the home and how each load is transferred down.
- Note areas that are hidden from view and not fully evaluated.
- Note doorways and window header space for adequate headers or lintels.

Figure 3.24 Taking away the strength of the supporting structure because the trap needs to be installed below the tub sets up a situation in which the tub could become an elevator—going down.

- Note rusted steel lintels.
- Look for rafter spread, which may indicate weak or damaged wall-roof connections.
- Look for "H" clips on sheathing where nailing is not possible.
- Look for alterations on trusses or damage.

Practices to Avoid

- Do not lean on items in attic spaces that may not be nailed or fully supported.
- Do not walk on unfloored attic spaces.
- Avoid being hurt by opening pull-down and fold-down ladders carefully. Note loose hardware and missing insulation above these.
- Avoid loose attic flooring, flooring that is too thin, and areas where the plywood is not attached to a joist.

Previous Repairs and Disclosure

Description

Although disclosure is required in many jurisdictions, the inspector may or may not be offered this information, and information offered may not be complete. It is recommended that the inspector request disclosure information and be allowed to request additional information from the seller that might influence conditions.

Assessing Existing Conditions

- Check available disclosure forms.
- Ask about modifications, alterations, and upgrades of the home that have been performed.
- Look for evidence of compliance with traditional building requirements. (Obviously, your inspection is not a code compliance inspection, but it may be clear that certain items do not comply, and this alone may raise suspicion about the quality of work and lack of inspection and permits.)
- Because quality of workmanship and expense play an important role in any renovation, the inspector must tread carefully with his or her evaluation of the work.

Acceptable Practices

- Look carefully to determine deficiencies.
- Look for clues to compliance with codes, such as ground fault receptacles, handrails, egress windows, proper ventilation, and so forth.
- Note in your report any substandard workmanship noted in the visible aspects of your inspection that might indicate substandard work in the nonvisible aspects of the inspection.
- Note temporary, incomplete, or emergency repairs.

Practices to Avoid

- Do not place blame. Just urge caution and further investigation.
- Do not question legitimacy or legality. Urge additional evaluation and repair if necessary.

Reporting

When applicable, these comments should be attached to photos or diagrams.

A conventional perimeter foundation, shown, has a poured concrete wall supported by a poured concrete footing. Both are strengthened by steel reinforcing rods (also called rebar). This type of foundation is used in connection with both raised floors and slabs.

Cracks often occur at corners, windows, and large slabs.

An outer and usually thin coat over a foundation wall is called parge coat. Because it is a thin cosmetic veneer, it can crack. Cracks in the veneers may not reflect that the blocks below are also cracked.

Settlement cracks often are paired to a matching crack on another side of the foundation. Settling can be caused by poorly supported loads, noncompressed soils, voids, and low-quality cement.

Remember, some cracking or shifting can be caused by the homeowner, or by a contractor adding to the load or taking away the strength (removal of a post, cutting structural members, shims slipping, adding a piano or a water bed, etc.).

Some cracks can occur over time, from a member failing, shrinking, or twisting. Lack of bearing can cause collapse.

New construction may have thinner walls that may be more prone to cracking.

Repairs are often made to cracks with new enhanced caulks that have more resilient chemicals that allow some ongoing movement.

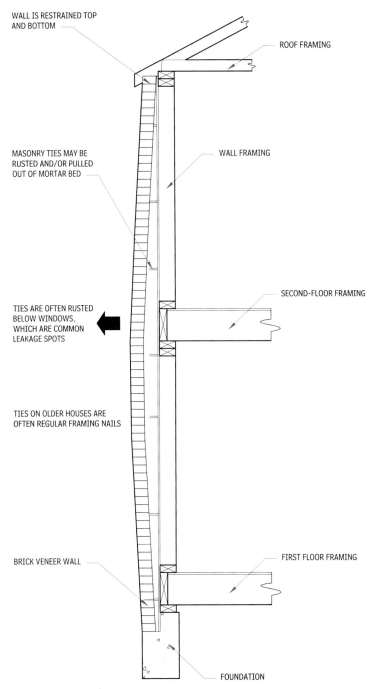

WALL IS RESTRAINED TOP AND BOTTOM

ROOF FRAMING

MASONRY TIES MAY BE RUSTED AND/OR PULLED OUT OF MORTAR BED

WALL FRAMING

TIES ARE OFTEN RUSTED BELOW WINDOWS, WHICH ARE COMMON LEAKAGE SPOTS

SECOND-FLOOR FRAMING

TIES ON OLDER HOUSES ARE OFTEN REGULAR FRAMING NAILS

BRICK VENEER WALL

FIRST FLOOR FRAMING

FOUNDATION

Figure 3.25 Brick or stone veneer issues

Chapter 4

Roofing

Roofing

Description

Safety is critical when inspecting roofing. While many inspectors like to assess the roof system from the outside—often before gaining access to the home—we recommend strongly that the attic be checked first. Look for indications of a weak structure or holes in the sheathing that may not be obvious from the outside. The weight of an inspector may exceed that of delaminating sheathing and old roofing. This could be a bad thing.

Climbing the roof before the client or realtor arrives, or when the owner is not home, could be a disaster if a ladder slips, the inspector get hurt, or the roof surface is too weak to hold the inspector.

When looking inside, look at conditions of the sheathing, rafters, and collar ties. Look for evidence of water entry, previous fire damage, and delamination of sheathing materials. Look for nailing, poor ventilation, insulation, and signs of wildlife and mold.

How many layers of roofing are obvious? Is the roof showing signs of duress?

A Note about Ladder Safety

Home inspectors use ladders daily for gaining access to many areas of a home. Make sure that your ladders are rated for your weight, that they are clean and undamaged, that they have slip-resistant feet, and that you use them safely. A 70 degree angle for climbing is usually safest; it can be approximated by placing your toes against the base of the rails of the ladder and extending your arms straight ahead of you. If the angle is correct, your fingertips should just touch the rung in front of you. Remember, an overextended ladder may tip when you climb on the unsupported part. Tying the ladder to a gutter or part of the building may save your neck, or help you avoid an embarrassing moment. Be safe with ladders. Ask your client or the broker to "foot" your ladder.

Do not place a ladder in front of a door or window, and especially not in front of a garage door. A driver may not see the ladder or expect it to be set up there. Make sure the ladder is locked and that it cannot easily shift while you are on it. Do not allow your client or others to climb up with you—you may have to carry them down when they realize they are afraid. And finally, do not leave unattended ladders against the home; put them away to avoid problems.

Figure 4.1 Mushroom fan removed and roofed over.

Figure 4.2 Moisture in the attic, poor ventilation, leaks on the roof, wind-blown rain, and ice damming can all contribute to sheathing delamination and mold growth.

Many inspectors feel that walking a roof is not necessary to evaluate the roof. Others have shared stories about deficiencies that were obvious to them only when they had climbed onto the roofing. Regardless of your philosophy, roofs need to be checked from as close as possible, especially areas where projections, flashing details, and elevations change.

Use of a good set of binoculars or a zoom lens on a camera may get you close enough to look for deterioration (granular loss, curling, and warping), damages (such as rips, popped nails, and missing shingles), or poor installation. Inspectors are encouraged to get as close as practical to the roofing to determine conditions.

Table 4.1 Life Expectancies of Roofing Materials

Roofing Type	Life Expectancy	Walk on it?	Notes:
Asphalt 3 Tab Shingles	17–20	If pitch is safe, yes.	Best if old layers are removed and ice shield added.
Asphalt Laminated Shingles	20–40	If pitch is safe, yes.	Best if old layers are removed and ice shield added.
Asphalt Overlay (2nd layer)	15–20	If pitch is safe, yes.	Not a great idea other than saving removal fees.
Wood Shingles	10–40	no	Make sure there is good ventilation, mount on.
Wood Shakes	30	no	Require interlayment felt paper.
Rolled Roofing	10–15	If pitch is safe, yes.	Typically used on sheds and outbuildings.
Low Sloped Built up	20–40	yes	May be layered over insulation.
Modified Bitumen	17–21	yes	Difficult to determine modified vs. rolled.
EPDM	14 average	yes	Very thin … easy to puncture. Usually over insulation.
Most Membranes	10–20	yes	Type often determined by usage, environment, and cost.
Concrete Tile	50–75	no	Heavy. Requires engineers stamp for framing requirements.
Terra Cotta	20–50	no	Fragile. Bees like to nest in it.
Copper	50	Usually not a good idea	May dent or bend with hail or discolor roofing.

Continued

Table 4.1 Life Expectancies of Roofing Materials

Roofing Type	Life Expectancy	Walk on it?	Notes:
Slate	100	no	Heavy. Requires engineers stamp for framing requirements.
Synthetic Slate	50+	no	See manufacturer's installation notes.
Metal Roofing	20–40	Usually not a good idea	
General Note:			Life expectancy also depends on climate, weather conditions, mechanical damage, fasteners, sheathing, ventilation, gauge & installation.

Asphalt/Fiberglass Shingles

Description

The most popular and cost-efficient types of roof coverings is three-tab and architectural laminated shingles. Easy to install and very weather resistant, these materials typically last at least 20–25 years and have proven to be an effective water-shedding system on roofs with a 4:12 pitch or better.

Manufacturers will allow a 2:12 pitch as long as the underlayment has been doubled up. Newer products such as Ice and Water Shield® (W. R. Grace) and Deck-Armor™ (GAF) decrease the ability for water to get into the sheathing and attic.

Figure 4.3   This roof has one layer of cedar shake and two layers of asphalt shingles. Nailing into old material is rarely a good idea. Removal of old materials gives you an opportunity to examine the sheathing and add ice shield membrane.

Figure 4.4 Placing any penetration so close to the valley will have issues that may end up with chronic leaking. This is three-tab asphalt fiberglass shingles.

Assessing Existing Conditions

- The three most popular forms of asphalt/fiberglass shingles are three-tab, laminated, and rolled material. Over the last 20 years, the laminated, though more expensive per square, have proven themselves to be an excellent improvement over three-tab shingles, because they eliminate some of the exposure to the weather and the frailty of three-tab slotted shingles. Rolled materials (used for low sloped and shed-type ancillary buildings) have a very short life expectancy. Modified bitumen and membranes are becoming a longer-lived and more durable alternative to rolled roofing.
- The inspector should be looking for granule deterioration, rips, cuts, and obvious signs of surface damage. Curling, puffiness, or a baked look indicates ventilation and heat issues. Color variation may result from granule loss. Ventilation is critical as well. Good shingles will not last if the attic has poor ventilation. See ventilation pages (Chapter 9).
- A curled roof shingle may not leak, but it may be vulnerable in situations where wind-driven rain or gusts of snow conditions exist.
- Be aware that most asphalt roof problems result from improper nailing and may not be visible. Shingles that slide out of position may

Figure 4.5   Laminated architectural shingles with a ripped roof boot on a plumbing stack. This roof is very durable and long-lasting, but the boot should be replaced and the front edge sealed with mastic to avoid water entry.

be the result of improper nailing, popped nails, or staples that have ripped through the individual shingles.

- Most jurisdictions will not allow more than three layers of roofing.
- Be sure to check for delaminating plywood in the attic, which can indicate ventilation, leakage, or poor-quality materials.
- Check bounciness of the sheathing.
- Look for cracks in the material or missing granules.
- Look for swelling, curling, or missing shingles.
- Lift edge of roofing and determine number of layers. New roofing when nailed into multiple layers may not properly anchor, and with expansion and contraction it may pull out. Remember, each layer will probably reflect 20 years of service.
- Look for ice shield membrane and aluminum edge flashing.
- If it is visible, look for nailing pattern (most shingle manufacturers require six nails per shingle on the nailing line now). In previous codes only four were required.
- Most municipalities do NOT allow staples for fasteners because they can easily rip the roofing. If allowed, staples must be horizontal and not rip the shingle.
- Nails and/or staples should be ½ inch below the glue line and at least 1 inch in from the edges of the shingle.
- Check for cracks on cap shingles and damages to ridge vent materials.

Figure 4.6 The more layers, the more wavy it will look. Use caution—previous layers may be hidden by flashings.

Acceptable Practices

- Identify in your report how you evaluated the roofing (i.e., from the ground, from the attic, walked, with binoculars, with a zoom lens, etc.).
- Note areas NOT inspected and not accessible.
- Identify weather conditions, temperature, and time of day.
- If the evaluation of the roof can be done from several edge locations around the home, that may suffice. Checking nailing and flashing, and looking for ice shield membrane can provide a good deal of information that the inspector can offer to the client.
- Look inside for deficiencies before you walk on the roof.
- Only walk a roof if it is safe, and cool enough not to damage the material. Note conditions found, report number of layers, and try to estimate the age.

Practices to Avoid

- If the roof is too steep to walk or too dangerous to stand on, or if you believe that conditions exist that will do damage or be risky to an inspector, do not climb on it. Remember to note the circumstances in your report.

Figure 4.7 As the sun cooks the shingles and the granules wash away, the look and projected life of the shingles are reduced.

- In colder or wet weather, never use a ladder without having someone foot it, to avoid unexpected movement.
- Avoid unsafe ladder techniques. Ladder safety requires additional discussion, but minimally we want about a 70 degree angle and at least two or three rungs above the gutter/roof edge for safety. Angles and fulcrum balance points are important to understand as well as weight ratings and capacities for certain ladders.
- Do not let a ladder extend too high above the edge; it may kick out when the inspector steps off, and become a hazard.
- Never assume that all roof surfaces are the same vintage. Patching or section replacement is practical when the homeowner is trying to save money.
- Do not estimate projected life expectancy.

Wood Shingles

Description

Wood shingles, if installed properly, can last 25–35 years. Typically manufactured of cedar, they come in different grades and can be smooth or striated. When installed on skip sheathing or nylon matting, the shingles breathe, and having good airflow around them can help extend their life. Shingles can be coated with wood preservative and fire-retardant materials, but are vulnerable to blown rain in wet locations and to forest fires in dry, wildfire-prone locations.

Desired for their wood look and texture, these shingles are found minimally on 4:12 roofs and greater. The material can expand and contract with temperature and moisture levels, and can crack or warp over time.

Figure 4.8 Watch wood-shingle roof exposures to the weather. Sunny sides may warp and split, while the shady sides may grow moss and lichen.

Figure 4.9 Ice shield membrane, when properly installed, will add an extra layer of protection from leakage at the overhangs, around the penetrations, and at edges.

Assessing Existing Conditions

- Do not walk these roofs. Even if the pitch is walkable, the material can crack underfoot.
- When viewed from inside, water and stain marks may indicate false signs of leakage. Tannin stains are not unusual where chemicals and sap have leached out, looking like a leak.
- Nails used for installing shingles should be galvanized ringed nails.
- Ice shield membrane should be installed under the first 3 feet (or more if there is a larger overhang) to prevent ice damming.
- If shingles are mounted on plywood, additional venting is usually recommended.
- Adequate attic venting is critical to roof longevity.
- First courses should be tripled.
- Look for curling, cracking, lifting, or openings that will allow water to enter.
- No more than two seams should be lined up in repetitive courses.
- Nails should not be closer to wood edges than 1 inch. There should be at least two nails per shingle. There should be a ¼-inch gap between shingles to allow for expansion.
- The overlap at the roof edge should be 1½ to 2 inches. (1½ in. if there are gutters).

- Missing or broken shingles may indicate previous tree-limb damage. Any deficiencies or vulnerable areas should be reported.
- Mold and mildew can damage the cedar. Often, installation of copper or zinc strips on the peak of the roofing can help reduce mold, algae, lichen, and moss build-up.
- Exposure to the weather should be a little less than one-third of the length of the shingle.

Acceptable Practices

- Identify in your report how you evaluated the roofing.
- Identify weather conditions, temperature, and time of day.
- Look inside for deficiencies in the sheathing before you walk or ladder any roof.
- View the shingle from the edge, second floor windows and attic areas. Do not walk a wood-shingle roof; they can be slippery and put you in danger.

Practices to Avoid

- Do not get talked into walking on shingle roofs; they are often slippery, and your weight can crack them. There is no benefit to walking on one and being blamed for the resulting leakage.
- Don't forget to note how the roof was inspected in your report and the limitations of your inspection.
- Avoid just reporting on one access point of the roof. If the evaluation of the roof can be done from several edge locations around the home, that will give you a larger picture.
- Checking nailing, flashing, and any visible underlayment will clue you in to conditions.
- Be careful with the ladder against shingle tips, if there are no gutters.
- In colder or wet weather, do not use a ladder without having someone foot it to avoid unexpected movement.
- Never assume that all roof surfaces are the same vintage. Patching or section replacement is practical when a homeowner is trying to save money.
- Shakes and shingles do not mix. If different materials are used in the same plain, call it out, as a leakage concern.

Table 4.2 Maximum Wood-Shingle Exposure Chart

Shingle Length	3:12 to 4:12 Slope	4:12 and Greater Slope
16 inch	3³/₄ inch	5 inch
18 inch	4¹/₄ inch	5¹/₂ inch
24 inch	5³/₄ inch	7¹/₂ inch

Wood Shakes

Description

Wood shakes, if installed properly, can last 30–35 years, or more. Typically manufactured of cedar, they come in random widths and thicknesses. Shakes give the roof a very textured, random look. They are installed on skip sheathing (wood slats, with felt or a breathable membrane interlayment). You should be able to see the interlayment from inside the attic.

- Shakes can be sprayed or brushed with wood preservative and fire-retardant materials, but can be vulnerable to blown rain in wet locations, and to sparks from fires.
- Desired for their random wood look and texture, these are found minimally on 4/12 roofs and those with a greater pitch. The material expands and contracts with temperature and moisture levels, and can crack or warp over time like any other wood roof.

Figure 4.10   Wood shakes create a very thick textured look and over time may warp or allow water to be blown in.

Assessing Existing Conditions

- Be careful walking on shakes. They may be slick, or may crack if dry. Although they may look strong enough to hold your weight, they may not be, or the underlayment or skip sheathing may break.
- When viewed from inside, water and stain marks may indicate false signs of leakage. The interlayment should be visible.
- Nails should be galvanized ringed nails.
- Ice shield membrane should be under the first 3 feet, to prevent ice damming, or more if there is a larger overhang.
- If the roofing is mounted on plywood, additional venting is usually recommended.
- Adequate attic venting is critical to roof longevity.
- Look for curling, cracking, lifting, or openings.
- No more than two seams should be lined up in repetitive courses.
- Nails should not be closer to wood edges than 1 inch. There should be at least two nails per shingle and a $3/8$–$5/8$-inch gap between shingles. Nails should be approximately $3/4$ inch from the shake edge.
- Overlap at the roof edge should be $1 1/2$ to 2 inches (without gutters) and $1/2$ to 1 inches (with gutters). Nails should be $1 1/2$ inches above the bottom edge of the shingle covering them.
- Missing or broken shakes may indicate previous tree-limb damage.
- Exposure on a 24-inch shake is usually 10 inches or less.
- A double starter row is required.
- Mold and mildew can damage the cedar.

Acceptable Practices

- Identify in your report how you evaluated the roofing.
- Identify weather conditions, temperature, and time of day.
- Look inside for deficiencies before you put any weight on the roof, but we do not recommend that you walk on the roof—walking a wood-shake roof can be slippery and put you in danger.

Practices to Avoid

- If the pitch is extreme, we encourage you not to walk on these roofs; they are often slick, and your weight can crack them. There is no benefit to walking on one and being blamed for the resulting leak.
- Don't forget to note how the roof was inspected in your report, and list any limitations of your inspection.

- Avoid just reporting on one access point of the roof. If the evaluation of the roof can be done from several edge locations around the home, that may be adequate to evaluate the roofing. Checking nailing, flashing, and any interlayment visible in the attic will clue you in to conditions. Be careful with the ladder against shake edges, if there are no gutters.

- In colder or wet weather, do not use a ladder without having someone foot it, to avoid unexpected movement.

- Never assume that all roof surfaces are the same vintage. Patching or section replacement is practical when a homeowner is trying to save money.

- Shakes and shingles do not mix. If different materials are used in the same plain, call it out as a concern.

Slate Tiles

Description

Slate tiles, if installed properly, can last 50–80 years, sometimes longer. Manufactured of stone, slate comes in different quality grades and from various quarries. Installed on a reinforced deck that requires an engineered design, slate roofs are very heavy. Slates can be coated with sealant to make them very weather resistant, but some delamination can still occur, and annual reinspection of the materials is encouraged.

Slate is naturally a fire-retardant material, and this adds to its desirability in finer homes.

Because of its rich look and texture, a slate roof is considered one of the best roofs to have. Slates can be installed on a roof that is minimally a 4:12 pitch or greater. The material sheds water but can crack or delaminate over time.

Figure 4.11 Natural slate roofs require annual reinspection to make sure the slates are in position and are in good shape.

Figure 4.12   Slate roofs require an engineering plan to make sure the framing is able to carry the weight of the stones.

Assessing Existing Conditions

- Do not walk these roofs. Even if the pitch is walkable, the material can crack underfoot.
- When viewing from inside, look for water and stain marks, which may indicate leakage.
- Nails should be copper.
- Ice shield membrane should be under the first 3 feet to prevent ice damming, or more if there is a larger overhang.
- Slates are often mounted on tongue-and-groove fir or a plywood subbase.
- Adequate attic venting is critical to roof longevity.
- Look for cracking, lifting, or delamination or loose or damaged hardware.
- No more than two seams should be lined up in repetitive courses. There should be at least a $\frac{1}{8}$- to $\frac{1}{4}$-inch gap between slates.
- Nails should not be closer to slate edges than 1 inch. There should be at least two nails per slate.
- Overlap at the roof edge should be $1\frac{1}{2}$ to 2 inches.
- Missing or broken slates may indicate previous tree-limb damage.
- Mold and mildew rarely cause a problem.

Figure 4.13 While broken edges may not mean the roof is leaking, slate repairs can be expensive because the roofs cannot be walked.

Acceptable Practices

- Identify in your report how you evaluated the roofing.
- Identify weather conditions, temperature, and time of day.
- Look inside and out for deficiencies.

Practices to Avoid

- Do not get talked into walking on these roofs; they are often slippery, and your weight can crack them. There is no benefit to walking on one and being blamed for the resulting leak.
- Don't forget to note how the roof was inspected in your report, and list the limitations of the inspection.
- Avoid just reporting on one access point of the roof. If the evaluation of the roof can be done from several edge locations around the home, that may suffice. Checking nailing, flashing, and valley metal deterioration will clue you in to conditions.
- Be careful with the ladder against slates.
- In colder or wet weather, do not use a ladder without having someone foot it, to avoid unexpected movement.

- Never assume that all roof surfaces are the same vintage. Patching or section replacement is practical when a homeowner is trying to save money.
- Many repair systems have been developed for installing loose or repaired slates.

Concrete and Terra Cotta Tiles

Description

Terra cotta (clay) tiles and concrete tiles, if installed properly, can last 30–50 years. Typically manufactured of clay, they can be manufactured in many colors and shapes. Some newer materials are actually made of concrete. Installed typically on a reinforced deck that requires an engineered design, these roofs can be very heavy. Because of the shape, flashing details, and the way the tiles are secured are important details to check.

- Annual reinspection of the materials is encouraged. Look for cracks and damages from shifting, and impact damage from trees and debris.
- This type of roofing is naturally a fire-retardant material, and this adds to its desirability in finer homes.
- Desired for their "Mission"-style look and texture, these tiles are found minimally on 4:12 roofs and greater. The material sheds water and can crack or become damaged over time.

Figure 4.14   Perfect to protect a home from bright sunlight and glaring heat, these tiles actually are a roof over a membrane below.

Figure 4.15   A picture of workers laying out the tiles for installation

- Often a membrane is the actual roofing system below, with the clay tiles above it.
- Flashings are usually made of copper.

Assessing Existing Conditions

- Do not walk these roofs. Even if the pitch is walkable, the material will crack underfoot.
- When viewing from inside, look for water and stain marks, which may be signs of leakage.
- Nails should be copper. Older fastening was done with nails and a dollop of cement. Newer installations use spray adhesive foam.
- Ice shield membrane should be under the first 3 feet or more, if there is a larger overhang to prevent ice damming. Most roofs apply membrane under all areas first.
- If tiles are mounted on plywood, additional venting is usually recommended; membranes are very typically installed below the tiles. The tiles then protect the membrane from harsh weather and sun.
- Adequate attic venting is critical to roof longevity.
- Look for cracking, lifting, sliding, shifting, or missing tiles.
- Edges and roof details are installed with pan flashings.
- Tiles and concrete molded shingles should be installed according to the manufacturer's requirements.

Figure 4.16 Superficial damages may not show up as leaks, but look for storm and poor-fastening damages.

- Overlap at the roof edge should be 1½ to 2 inches.
- Mold and mildew rarely cause a problem other than cosmetic.
- Bees and birds like to nest in damaged nooks and crannies.

Acceptable Practices

- Identify in your report how you evaluated the roofing.
- Identify weather conditions, temperature, and time of day.
- Look inside and out for deficiencies.

Practices to Avoid

- Do not get talked into walking on these roofs; they are often slippery, and your weight can crack them. There is no benefit to walking on one and being blamed for the resulting leak—and you may get hurt sliding off one to the ground.
- Don't forget to note how the roof was inspected in your report, and list the limitations of the inspection.
- Avoid just reporting on one access point of the roof. If the evaluation of the roof can be done from several edge locations around the home, that may better indicate problems and existing conditions.

Figure 4.17 When setting your ladder, be careful not to break tiles, and watch for bees and wasps.

- A quick look may miss nailing issues, flashing problems, and valley metal deterioration. A longer look will clue you in to important conditions.
- Don't get stung. Be careful with the ladder against brittle tiles, and watch for bees and birds nesting.
- In colder or wet weather, do not use a ladder without having someone foot it, to avoid unexpected movement.
- Never assume that all roof surfaces are the same vintage. Patching or section replacement is practical when the homeowner is trying to save money.

Synthetic Materials

Description

Synthetic tiles made from various materials—from composite plastics to concrete and fiberglass—can last 50–80 years, if installed properly. Typically, they are manufactured to look like other roofing materials, but they can be less expensive or more durable, if installed following manufacturer's recommendations. It is important to let your client know that these tiles are unusual and may be experimental.

Annual reinspection of unusual materials is recommended.

Assessing Existing Conditions

- Do not walk these roofs unless the manufacturer says that this will not damage the tiles. Even if the pitch is walkable, some materials can crack underfoot.
- When viewing from inside, look for water and stain marks, which may be signs of leakage.

Figure 4.18 These are synthetic slate tiles that look very impressive from the ground, and carry a 50-year manufacturer's limited warranty.

- Nails should be whatever the manufacturer recommends.
- Ask about adequate attic venting, which is often critical to roof longevity.
- Look for cracking, lifting, or delamination and loose or damaged hardware.
- No more than two seams should be lined up in repetitive courses. They should be at least ³/₄ inch apart.
- Overlap at the roof edge should be 1¹/₂ to 2 inches.
- Missing or broken roof pieces may indicate previous tree-limb damage.
- Look for evidence that mold or mildew is causing a problem.

Acceptable Practices

- Identify in your report how you evaluated the roofing.
- Identify weather conditions, temperature, and time of day.
- Look inside and out for deficiencies.
- Do not walk a synthetic roof surface unless you know the manufacturer says that this will not do damage.

Practices to Avoid

- Do not walk on these roofs, unless you know it is okay to do so. There is no benefit to walking on one and being blamed for the resulting leak.
- Don't forget to note how the roof was inspected in your report, and list the limitations of the inspection.
- Avoid just reporting on one access point of the roof. If the evaluation of the roof can be done from several edge locations around the home, that may suffice. Checking nailing, flashing, and valley metal deterioration will clue you in to conditions. Be careful with the ladder against synthetic tiles.
- In colder or wet weather, do not use a ladder without having someone foot it, to avoid unexpected movement.
- Never assume that all roof surfaces are the same vintage. Patching or section replacement is practical when a homeowner is trying to save money.

Metal Roofing

Description

Inspectors will find several forms of metal roofing that are popular on residential homes. There are sheet goods attached in various manners and individual tiles or preformed shingles. Care should be taken because these roofs may be prone to denting and bending. Also, they may be very hot to the touch and can become slippery in rain and ice situations. Metal roofing is often light, and though it can be expensive, it can often outlast some other types of roofing.

Assessing Existing Conditions

- Do not walk these roofs unless the manufacturer says that it won't do damage. Even if the pitch is walkable, some materials can dent underfoot.
- When viewing from inside, look for water and stain marks, which may indicate leakage.

Figure 4.19   If the pitch is okay, remember that you can dent metal roofing and that it can be blazing hot in the sunshine.

Figure 4.20   Watch around penetrations, and look carefully in the attic areas. Don't slam a door during a snowstorm!

- Nails or fasteners should be whatever the manufacturer recommends.
- Check for adequate attic venting, which is often critical to roof longevity. There can be condensation issues under metal roofing.
- Pitting can be caused by acidic rain or chemicals.
- Hail can damage the roofing.

Acceptable Practices

- Look at materials from the ground and edge to determine conditions, deficiencies, and signs of weathering or improper installation.
- Many metal roofs carry very long warranties and are usually fire resistant in nature.
- Minimum slope for metal shingles is 3:12. Sheet goods that are soldered can be applied on almost any pitch.
- If the roofing is held in place with clips, look for missing or damaged clips. If interlocking or snap locking seams are used, look for open or damaged seams.

Practices to Avoid

- Walking on metal roofing can dent, bend, or damage it.
- Metal roofs can become hot and/or slippery.

Fibrous Shingles

Description

Composition materials made to look like other materials were very popular from the early 1900s to the 1970s. Concrete and fibrous additives were mixed, trying to formulate a strong, flame-retardant, and inexpensive alternative material. Asbestos fibers were often added to increase fire retardance. In the 1970s, the asbestos was identified as cancer causing and was banned. Fiberglass and other fibers are now used instead. Older materials may require lab analysis to determine asbestos content.

Assessing Existing Conditions

- Do not walk these roofs.
- When viewing from inside, look for water and stain marks, which may be signs of leakage.

Figure 4.21 This material seems to encourage moss and lichen growth. Cleaning it may kick up asbestos fibers. Disposal can be expensive.

Figure 4.22 Slippery and brittle. If you break a fibrous tile, none is available to replace it.

- Nails or fasteners should be whatever the manufacturer recommends (usually aluminum).
- Check for adequate attic venting, which is often critical to roof longevity.
- This type of roof seems to attract moss, lichen, and mold.

Acceptable Practices

- Look at materials from the ground and edge to determine conditions, deficiencies, and signs of weathering or improper installation.
- Shingles typically had nail holes drilled through the material and were installed with aluminum nails.
- Minimum slope for fibrous shingles is 4:12. Shingles should be installed over type 30 felt.

Practices to Avoid

- Do not walk on the roof as it can damage the shingles.
- Do not make light of asbestos-containing materials as they can be health concerns and, just as importantly, very expensive to properly remove and dispose of. Always explain the health concerns to your client, to avoid liability.

Figure 4.23 This section needs mowing! Remember to note limited visibility to attic in your report.

Low-Sloped Roofing

Description

Used on homes with relatively flat roofs and commercial buildings. Low-sloped roofing requires a minimum of $\frac{1}{4}$ inch per foot for drainage. Many materials have been used over the years to try to keep buildings with relatively flat roofs dry. The measure of success usually comes down to following the manufacturer's installation guidelines and following good working guidelines. Low-sloped roofing covers built-up roofing (BUR), modified bitumen (mod-bit) roofing, roll roofing, spray foams, EPDM, PVC, and other newly formulated rubberized and elastomeric materials. Almost all will be sunlight resistant or can be coated or covered with ballast or painted with chemicals to protect them and extend their life.

Figure 4.24 Low-sloped roof made of EPDM membrane roofing

Figure 4.25 Rolled roofing was a popular material to use on less radical roof pitches up until the 1970s with the advent of modified bitumen. It was inexpensive but also had a short life expectancy (5–10 years).

Assessing Existing Conditions

- Look carefully at the details. Make sure you walk the entire roof and examine various areas of concern. List areas of limited visibility or accessibility.
- When viewing from inside, look for water and stain marks, which may indicate previous or current leakage.
- Examine stains, and when possible test moisture content.
- Blisters or rips may indicate moisture intrusion. Seams that are open or damaged may allow water to enter.
- Make sure cant strips have been used to avoid hard angles on the roofing.
- Note environmental and weather conditions that could influence the potential for deterioration (bird activity, cooking grease exhaust, proximity to an airport or body of water, etc.).
- Note shady areas and sunny areas.
- Try to determine the system used and the age of the materials.
- Try to get additional history from the owner.
- Note gravel stops and other flashing details.
- Note drains and penetrations (vents, ducts, vent pipes, skylights, hatches, etc.).

Figure 4.26 Improper sealant and flashing details may defeat a perfectly good roof by leaving edges vulnerable to temperature changes that may let water enter around the tar or the flashing edges.

- Gutters, drains, scuppers, and the like should be clean and clear-flowing. Check attachment and pitch.
- In most cases, tar is used as a temporary seal. Rarely will it last longer than a few months when weather changes are radical. Check caulking and sealants around all penetrations.
- Where there is roof-mounted equipment (antenna, cable dishes, solar panels, evaporative coolers, service masts, HVAC units, etc.), check mountings and penetrations.

Acceptable Practices

- Look at materials closely. When walking these roofs, you will have to be cautious and careful. Some may be weak, some may be hot, and some sealants may be damaged by simply walking on them.
- Look for damages and signs of weathering or improper installation.
- Look for blisters, rips, open seams, damages, and signs of physical or chemical damage.
- Look for sharp objects on the roof that could cause damage (furniture, grills, tools, equipment).
- Look for pedestrian traffic damages.
- Examine parapets, drain areas, and scuppers. Look for damaged or problematic coping.

Figure 4.27 Carefully examine all edges, penetrations, and seams of low-sloped roof materials.

Practices to Avoid

- Walking on icy roofs can be a hazard. Hot roofs can be damaged.
- Do not walk backwards on a roof. Watch for wiring, guy wires, and antennae.
- Do not push against parapet walls, coping, or chimneys.
- Do not step on blisters or soft-looking areas.
- Do not walk on valley flashings.

Additional Reporting Items

Description

Flashings

Flashing details must be carefully evaluated by the inspector, while evaluating the roof. Flashings can be made of copper, aluminum, zinc, plastic, and galvanized metal. Some materials may interact with other materials, and manufacturers' requirements must prevail. Flashings and counterflashings around windows, doors, chimneys, and other building penetrations should be evaluated for moisture intrusion and deterioration.

Figure 4.28 Along chimney sides and sidewalls, we use step flashing covered by counterflashing to keep water out. Counterflashings need to be cemented into the brick but often are not.

Figure 4.29 Poor sealant may allow water to get around the flashings.

Figure 4.30 Uncontrolled water entering the home can start a chain reaction of expensive repairs.

Figure 4.31 Head flashing, when properly done, will keep water from running down the siding and into the top of the window unit.

Definitions

Valley flashings—The type of flashing detail that is used where two roof surfaces meet or come together. Valleys by their nature end up receiving more water than almost any other flashing detail, so they must be done properly to avoid leaks. Unfortunately, they are often not very visible to the inspector. Whenever possible, checking conditions below the valley in the attic can be very helpful.

Metal open valleys—These are flashings that are exposed to the weather from top to bottom on a roof surface. Most are 24 inches wide with at least 4 to 6 inches of roofing overhang on each side. Obviously, upper sections of the valley flashings must be placed over the lower units so water flows onto the lower one. A crease may be bent in the center of the metal to slow water and try to prevent it from going under the opposing side.

Closed valleys—These may be made with ice shield membrane, rolled roofing, felt paper, or metal and then covered with a weave of the regular roofing being used. It is critical that no nails be used when the shingles are woven in the area near (approx. 6 in.) the center line on each side of the valley flashing.

Chimney flashings/counterflashings—These are often done improperly; many inspectors report leaks around chimneys on a daily basis.

Crickets are required on most chimneys, and definitely on those that are wider than 30 inches. Chimney flashings include step flashings, apron flashings, cricket flashing, and counterflashing. When grouted in, the flashing should go into the mortar cut at least $1\frac{1}{4}$ inch.

Pipe/stack flashings—Usually a molded aluminum or copper flange with a specifically sized stretch neoprene gasket for the pipe to go through. Look for damages and ripped or missing gaskets.

Pan or channel flashings—Used on tile and concrete roofs, these act as a gutter diverting water away from sidewalls, skylights, and chimneys. Pan flashing should be at least 4 inches high at the chimney and at least 6 inches wide.

Edge flashings—Inserted at the edge of surfaces, these metal or plastic flashings help to prevent wind-driven rain from getting in and causing roof edges and rakes to deteriorate.

Gravel stop flashings—Special edge flashing that is designed to hold gravel ballast on a roof and limit erosion.

Skylight flashing—This should be at least 4 inches for less than 3:12 pitched roofs.

Attic Space Access

Attic access may be nonexistent, or as easy as climbing a staircase to the next floor. Many homes have pull-down stairs that fold down or roll down, allowing fairly easy access, and some homes have access panels that may be in a central hall or a closet, often requiring a ladder and acrobatics to get up there. Accessibility must be reported, and limitations that block visibility should be described.

Most jurisdictions require a 30-by-22-inch minimal opening into an attic. If there is a heating system in the attic, they often require a 24-inch-wide walkway to the equipment, a light above or near it, and an electric outlet for test devices. Heating systems are not supposed to be more than 20 feet from the access, and a serviceman's safety cutoff switch should be within eyesight of the unit.

The inspector is not required to traverse unfloored attic spaces or those where the floor is covered with insulation. In attics where the temperature is excessively high, the inspector may determine if it is too hot to safely enter.

Wearing a respirator may be a good idea in attics that are dusty or those that have fecal evidence of animals, rodents, or insects living there.

Figure 4.32 Be very careful on pull-down stairs. Hardware may be missing, rungs broken, or ends cut at the wrong angle.

Trusses and Conventional Framing

Whether the home is framed with dimensional lumber or uses trusses and engineered lumber or a combination of the two, the inspector should be looking for deficiencies and noting how the building has been built.

Any evidence of chords on trusses being cut or altered, of missing collar ties, or of damaged rafters should be reported.

Definitions

Live load—Temporary loads such as wind, snow, accumulated water, or the weight of people in the home.
Dead load—Weight of the roofing materials and any permanent attachments made to the roof structure.
Truss uplift—A phenomenon caused by trusses flexing and dimensionally changing during hot and cold seasons and by expansion and contraction caused by temperature and moisture content.
Truss bracing—Additional struts added to compensate for snow loading on a roof.
Purlins—Horizontal supports often supported by struts in a diagonal attached to a ceiling joist. These can help handle additional snow loading.

Figure 4.33 Light and economical trusses can be installed quickly and efficiently by two people. For the inspector, looking for damages and alterations is the key.

Figure 4.34 Altering the trusses by cutting or notching may render them unable to handle the weight that they were originally designed to handle.

Acceptable Practices

Trusses and Conventional Framing

- Look for any damages, alterations, cuts, breaks, or cracks in the materials.
- Check connectors and metal cleats for damages, separation, corrosion, or alterations.
- Look for trusses showing signs of excessive weight or movement (bowing, sagging, etc.), which could mean that additional loads have shifted, or that damages have affected the weight on certain pieces.
- Rot, dampness, mold, or insect activity should be noted.
- Look for sagging or evidence of over-spanned areas (not unusual in garages with loft storage).
- Look for unacceptable notching or boring.

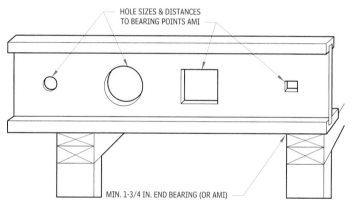

PREFABRICATED I-JOISTS

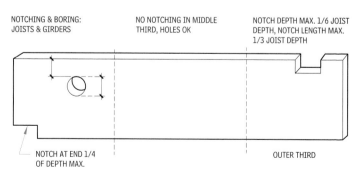

Figure 4.35

Figure 4.36 Check gutters for cleanliness, damages, and loose connections. Look for proper venting (photo shows ridge and soffit vents).

Chapter 5

Plumbing

Water Entrance Piping

Interior and Exterior Plumbing Inspection

Water Entrance Piping

Description

When it comes to damage in a home, water leaks—whether from a roof leak, blown-in rain through the siding, or seepage in the basement—can have catastrophic results. Water on organic matter can rot it, melt it, and grow mold on it. No less important are interior leaks caused by plumbing fittings, fixtures, and malfunctioning drains or supply piping. When a water heater leaks, rarely is a homeowner prepared for the replacement, and as a result damages can quickly mount up. For an inspection of plumbing, you must carefully examine miles of pipe and all kinds of kitchen, bath, laundry, and cleaning fixtures. Each has its own inspection logical path, and failing to see the signs of potential problems can increase your liability or make you look foolish when something lets go.

Figure 5.1   Locating the water service entry, determining the meter location, and making sure there is a main shutoff are requirements of most national standards. Operating the valve is not. Many valves require a heavy pipe wrench or lubrication. We recommend upgrading valves when they are older and less likely to positively shut the water down in an emergency.

Definitions

Cross-connection—A situation where the clean water supply is affected by a potential for contamination from dirty water, bacteria, or germs through a connection to the wastewater or other systems.

DWV—Drain, waste, and vent system.

Galvanic reaction or *electrolysis*—When metals that are dissimilar are placed together, a chemical reaction with the moisture in the air or the water in the pipe can cause corrosion.

Functional flow—The approximate normal water flow expected when operating several fixtures at the same time for a period of time.

Functional drainage—The average amount of water and waste that the drainage/waste system is expected to accept down the drain/waste pipes over a period of time.

Galvanized pipe—Steel pipe with a zinc coating.

Listed—All plumbing fittings that are to be used in a home must go through a process whereby they are evaluated and then listed by an approved listing agency. In theory, you should never use a fitting or appliance that is not approved or listed for the specific

Figure 5.2 Homes with wells will have either a jet pump system in a utility area or well room (shown) or a submersible pump located at the very bottom of the well.

designed use. Listed fittings are typically stamped or labeled as being listed.

Listing Agencies—Uniform Plumbing Code (UPC), International Association of Plumbing and Mechanical Officials (IAPMO), Underwriters Laboratories (UL).

O.D., I.D—Outer diameter and inner diameter. These are measurements for measuring pipe.

Potable water—Water that is safe to use for drinking, cooking, and any other domestic use.

Static pressure—When no fixtures are being used, the water pressure in a home should be at least 15 psi and less than 80 psi.

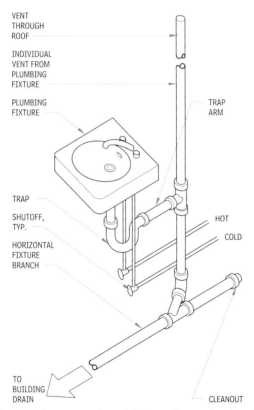

Figure 5.3 Typical water supply and drainage from a plumbing fixture.
Source: AIA, *Architectural Graphic Standards*, 11th Edition. Copyright 2007, John Wiley & Sons, Inc.

Assessing Existing Conditions

Municipal-Type Water Service Entry

Water service is typically a water pipe, which may be subterranean, entering the home via a curb box, possibly with an exterior shutoff, leading to a meter in a basement, crawlspace, or location in a closet. The meter area should have a main home water shutoff valve. While the inspector may not be willing to manipulate this valve, a visual inspection should evaluate the material it is made of and the conditions found, and a notation of location for safety should also be placed in the report.

- Note older materials such as lead, galvanized pipe, brass, or any sign of deterioration, leakage, or electrolysis.
- Meters should have a #6 to #8 sized ground wire properly clamped to metal piping on both sides of the pipe holding the meter. This

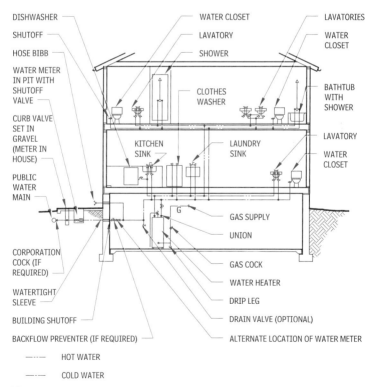

Figure 5.4 Water supply piping
Source: AIA, Architectural Graphic Standards, 11th Edition. Copyright 2007, John Wiley & Sons, Inc.

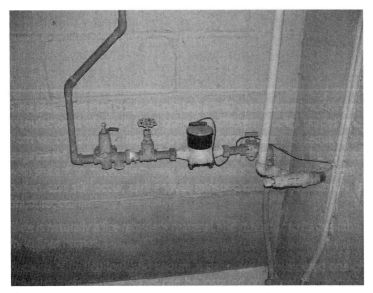

Figure 5.5   The wire from the water meter goes outside to a sensor unit at which a reading of water use can be received. During the inspection, buyers are often relieved to know that electric, gas, and water meters are mounted outside, so they can avoid scammers pretending to need to enter the home to read the meters.

Figure 5.6   The electrical grounding system historically has been done with both a driven rod outside and a wire clamped to the water service. The ground (or bond) wire should be clamped to both sides of the meter; if the meter is removed, the home is thus still bonded to the street plumbing.

allows the ground to remain constant even if the meter is removed for service.

▪ Note if the equipment and piping are vulnerable to freezing in colder climates.

▪ The minimum pipe size for water entry pipe is ¾ inch.

Well-Type Equipment

▪ Jet pumps are usually located in the home or a well room. This type of pump pushes water down into the shallow well and develops a siphoning effect that causes the water to be pumped into the home. The water is then sent into a pressure tank with a regulator.

▪ Submersible wells are usually deeper than shallow wells using jet pumps. These wells have a pump located at the bottom of a shaft that pushes the water up and through plastic piping into a pressurized tank. The tank will have a pressure regulator to tell the pump when to build pressure or turn off. Some tanks will have a valve on both sides of the tank, for ease of servicing. The valve on the house side of the tank is usually recognized as the most desirable main shutoff because turning off the pressure side can damage the pump.

Figure 5.7 These storage tanks should be insulated with plastic bubble-wrap insulation to avoid excessive condensation.

Figure 5.8 When inspecting older homes, we often find the well in or close to the home. This presents problems when there are insect infestations or leaks that can contaminate the well.

- Community wells (shared equipment) are usually not on the property, but expenses among the participants are shared. These would be treated as municipal systems, but a recommendation to do a water-quality test on any well system is always prudent.

Service Entry Plumbing

- The service entry piping in most homes from a municipal system will be copper, but, depending on its age, it may be any material from threaded iron pipe to lead to plastic. Many municipal water providers urge homeowners to purchase insurance on the piping from the curb box to the home, because this is considered to be the responsibility of the homeowner.
- Service lines from wells are typically plastic.
- Evaluation of the pipes entering the home should focus on age, condition, and sleeving. Material that is sleeved is protected from rubbing against concrete or from chemical reactions from building materials.
- Valves should look okay and not have telltale signs of leakage or corrosion.
- Water meters, when inside the home, may have a sensor sending a signal to an exterior terminal to allow the water company to "read" the meter without entering the home. The meter should be in good repair with no sign of damage or leakage.

Table 5.1 Pipe Support Distances

Material	Vertical	Horizontal
Cast iron	Every floor	5 ft (1)
IPS		
Up to ³/₄ in.	Every floor	10 ft
Over ³/₄ in.	Every floor	12 ft
Copper		
Up to 1¹/₂ in.	Every floor (2) 6 ft	
Over 1¹/₂ in.	Every floor (2) 10 ft	
PVC	Every floor	4 ft (3)(and at each change of direction)
ABS	Every floor	4 ft (3)(and at each change of direction)
PEX		

Notes:
(1) Hub-type cast iron in lengths greater than 5 ft may have supports every 10 ft.
(2) There should not be more than 10 in. between pipe supports.
(3) There should be a strap at every change of direction.

- The electrical system should be grounded to the cold water supply within a few feet of the service entry, if it is metal piping.
- Cold water piping goes through an environment where there is apt to be warm, moisture-laden air that can create condensation issues. The pipes should be insulated and properly supported every so many feet, per Table 5.1.

Piping

Copper Supply Pipe

- Type L (blue label) has a medium wall thickness, and is most commonly used for plumbing. Type K (green label) is the thickest, and most often used for underground applications.
- Type M (red label) is less often used for plumbing. It is more often found in baseboard radiators for quicker heat exchange.
- Copper, steel, and plastic pipe in contact with concrete must be properly protected from damage or abrasion with sleeving, insulation tape, or foam.
- Drainage system cleanout plugs should be brass, PVC, or ABS.
- Cleanouts must be gas-tight and watertight. They should be at every change of direction of 135 degrees or more and at every 100-foot run of pipe below the first floor.

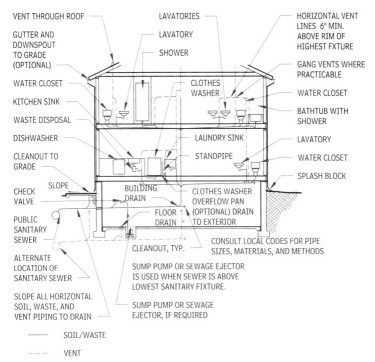

VENT THROUGH ROOF

GUTTER AND
DOWNSPOUT
TO GRADE
(OPTIONAL)

WATER CLOSET

KITCHEN SINK

WASTE DISPOSAL

DISHWASHER

CLEANOUT TO
GRADE

CHECK   SLOPE
VALVE

PUBLIC
SANITARY
SEWER

ALTERNATE
LOCATION OF
SANITARY SEWER

SLOPE ALL HORIZONTAL
SOIL, WASTE, AND
VENT PIPING TO DRAIN

LAVATORIES

LAVATORY

SHOWER

CLOTHES
WASHER

LAUNDRY SINK

STANDPIPE

BUILDING
DRAIN
         CLOTHES WASHER
         OVERFLOW PAN
FLOOR   (OPTIONAL) DRAIN
DRAIN   TO EXTERIOR

CLEANOUT, TYP.

SUMP PUMP OR SEWAGE EJECTOR
IS USED WHEN SEWER IS ABOVE
LOWEST SANITARY FIXTURE.

SUMP PUMP OR SEWAGE
EJECTOR, IF REQUIRED

HORIZONTAL VENT
LINES 6" MIN.
ABOVE RIM OF
HIGHEST FXTURE

GANG VENTS WHERE
PRACTICABLE

WATER CLOSET

BATHTUB WITH
SHOWER

LAVATORY

WATER CLOSET

SPLASH BLOCK

CONSULT LOCAL CODES FOR PIPE
SIZES, MATERIALS, AND METHODS

——— SOIL/WASTE

– – – VENT

Figure 5.9   Drainage and vent piping
Source: AIA, *Architectural Graphic Standards*, 11th Edition. Copyright 2007, John
Wiley & Sons, Inc.

- All piping used for DWV should be smooth internally, and drainage
  slope should always be at least ¼ inch per foot.
- Galvanized piping cannot be used underground and should be
  raised off the soil a minimum of 6 inches.
- Sewage ejectors must have a 2-inch discharge pipe with a check
  valve and a gate valve after the check valve. (Note: The gate valve
  requirement is often not followed and should be noted as missing
  in those situations.)
- Ejector tanks must be sealed with a watertight cover and vented
  with minimally a 1½ to 2-inch pipe.
- Air gap drains must have no less than 1 inch between the drain termination and the rim.
- Laundry standpipes should be 18–30 inches in height and preferably 2 inches or larger in diameter.
- All fixtures must be provided with a trap. One trap may serve a maximum of three sinks.

Figure 5.10 Sewage ejectors need electric macerator pumps to grind and lift the effluent. Do not use basement bathroom's feeding ejectors during a power outage.

Figure 5.11 Standpipes should be 18–30 inches if freestanding. This one is built into the wall.

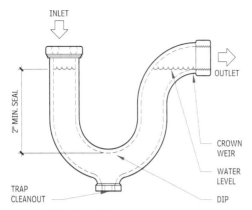

Figure 5.12   Typical plumbing fixture trap
Source: AIA, *Architectural Graphic Standards*, 11th Edition. Copyright 2007, John Wiley & Sons, Inc.

- Tailpipes on traps should not exceed 24 inches in length.
- Trap water seals must be 2–4 inches (minimum and maximum).
- Double trapping is prohibited; all traps must be protected with an approved vent pipe.

Figure 5.13   This contraption will work, but it is unlikely that it meets the plumbing code.

Interior and Exterior Plumbing Inspection

Description

Using your logical path, you will inspect the plumbing in all baths, kitchens, laundry areas, attics, and basements. During this process, you will note materials used, conditions found, and deficiencies that may require repair or replacement. Water pressure should be above 30 psi and below 80. Temperature pressure relief (TPR) valves should be set to drain at 150 psi.

Bathrooms

Toilets

- Is it flushing properly?
- Is it loose to the floor?

Figure 5.14   Follow a logical path as you do a bathroom. Flush the toilet, run the sink, look at lighting, test functional flow and drainage, check the venting/window, look at tile and floor, and test the electrical outlet.

- Are there damages to the china or the mechanism?
- Does it flush improperly, or run?
- Are there stains or discoloration?

Sinks

- Is the faucet operation good? Is the aerator working?
- Is there functional flow and drainage?
- Check for attachment to the wall or vanity. Examine vanity cabinet (if present) for damage and stains.
- Check drain mechanism controller.
- Look for valves and check for leaks. Make sure hot and cold are labeled and that hot is on the left.
- Crazing (cosmetic surface deterioration), actual cracks, or rusting would initiate a recommendation for the appliance to be replaced.
- Examine the condition of trap and waste lines.

Bidets

- Examine as you would a sink.
- Check external valve and feed for leaks.
- Make sure it is secured to the floor.
- Try valve in rim and sprayer positions.
- Look for leaks and physical damages to the china.

Figure 5.15 Crazing is a cosmetic cracking of marble dust sinks that indicates deterioration of the sink surface. This typically requires replacement.

Figure 5.16   An old-style bidet can become a cross-connection as the fountain/sprayer in the center can be submerged in gray water.

Showers

- Check shower walls for loose tiles or veneers and bad sealant.
- Look for loose soap dishes, shelves, and accessories.
- Note condition of grout/sealant along seams.
- Note water pressure and volume (functional flow and drainage) individually and with multiple fixtures running.
- Check operation of sliding glass tub doors and surrounds. Look for damage and adjustment needs; check gaskets, rollers, and handles.
- Look for tempered glass where required (glass walls, windows, glass doors, transoms, etc.). Make sure valves have hot and cold properly labeled, and that hot is on the left.

Bathtubs

- Examine fittings and valves. Note drips, leaks, and loose parts.
- Check functional flow and drainage.
- Check for an overflow or cross-connections.
- Look for damages (cracks, dings, leaks, signs of reglazing).
- Remember to look in basements and areas below bathrooms for signs of active or previous leakage.

Figure 5.17 Neo-angle showers are usually placed in a corner when room space is tight, with the door on the angle. Check for good door operation and water stains around floor and wall tiles.

Figure 5.18 These bathtubs look great in a retro bathroom, but great care is required to control where water ends up.

Whirlpools

- Check fittings and jets.
- Look at the drain cover for compliance with local safety regulations.
- Look for GFCI safety controlled circuitry.
- Make sure outlets, switches, and lighting are out of the bather's zone.
- Check for an access panel for servicing the pump.
- When running the water, listen for vibration and odd noises.
- Look for damages and leaks.
- Smell for mold or dampness.

Steam Generators

- Examine fittings and timers in the shower or on the wall of the bathroom; look for sealant around those that are in the shower.
- At the steam generator, examine conditions. On living floors, the generator should be in a tray to contain accidental leakage.
- Report that there is a temperature pressure relief valve (required equipment for safety).
- Examine valves and look for leakage.
- If you run the steamer, stay in this area until you turn it off. Generally steam will flow after about 5–10 minutes.

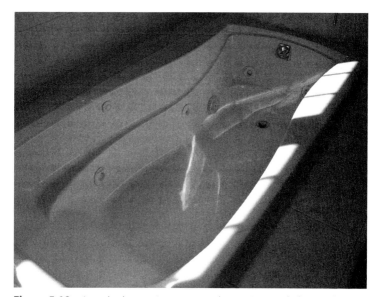

Figure 5.19 Jetted tubs require access to the equipment below and need to be wired with GFCI circuit protection. They require careful regular cleaning and sanitizing to avoid skin rashes and bacterial infections.

Figure 5.20 Steam generators need a temperature pressure relief valve that is piped exactly like a water heater and may require a pan and drain setup installed on a second floor.

Laundry Rooms

Sinks

- Is the faucet operation good? Is the aerator working?
- Is there functional flow and drainage?
- Check for attachment to the wall or vanity. Examine vanity cabinet (if present) for damage and stains.
- Check drain mechanism controller.
- Look for valves and check for leaks.
- Crazing (cosmetic surface deterioration, actual cracks, or rusting) would initiate a recommendation for the appliance to be replaced.
- Examine condition of trap and waste lines.
- Check pitch on drain piping. Check for pump-up systems or sewage ejectors.
- Listen for venting problems.

Washers

- Examine drain piping for damage, size, and functional drainage.
- Examine hoses for quality, construction, and deterioration.
- Look for water stains around the machine.

Figure 5.21 Examine drain and trap. Many basement sinks have pump chambers and check valve setups.

Figure 5.22 Check hoses at connectors and machine. Look for damage, water stains, and corrosion.

- If it is on a second floor, look for a tray or tile base with a floor drain. As these would typically not drain to a waste line, try to determine the termination point to warn clients where this water would discharge.
- Check supply valves, looking for corrosion, damage, or leaks.

Dryers

- Examine unit for damage and cleanliness.
- Examine wiring for safety and grounding. If the unit is gas-fired, look at gas fittings.
- Look at lint discharge line for plastic hose, wrong diameters, or distances that are too long.
- Look at dryer vent flapper termination. Is it working? Is it near the air conditioner, where lint will clog the coils?
- Does it vent into a porch, attic, or garage?

Kitchens and Food Preparation Areas

Cooktops

Sinks

- Is the faucet operation good? Is the aerator working? Test for operation, and test spray wand.
- Is there functional flow and drainage?

Figure 5.23 The perfect solution to a loose connection. I wonder what the other sneaker is doing?

Figure 5.24   Make sure older gas connections look safe and that flex connections are of newer materials.

Figure 5.25   Check downdraft unit below cooktop. Make sure it is ducted appropriately to the exterior.

Figure 5.26   Be aware that sinks glued from below the countertop areas can have voids around edges where germs and bacteria will grow.

- Is there an extendable hose for filling pots? Does it catch on items or plumbing below the sink? Is it leaking?
- Check for attachment to the wall or vanity. Examine sink cabinet for damage, water stains, and damage to the shelving.
- Check the strainer for function.
- Look for valves and check for leaks.
- Sink damages, crazing (cosmetic surface deterioration), actual cracks, or rusting would initiate a recommendation for the appliance to be replaced. Note dents, scratches, and the like.
- Examine condition of trap and waste lines.
- Check pitch on drain piping.
- Listen for venting problems.

Prep Sinks and Bar Sinks

- Is the faucet operation good? Is the aerator working?
- Is there functional flow and drainage?
- Check for attachment to the counter or base cabinet. Examine base cabinet for damage and stains.
- Check drain mechanism controller.
- Look for valves and check for leaks.
- Crazing (cosmetic surface deterioration), actual cracks, or rusting would initiate a recommendation for the appliance to be replaced.

Figure 5.27 In many homes there are non-GFCI-protected outlets near these sinks. Recommend that outlets be upgraded to GFCI type.

- Examine condition of trap and waste lines.
- Check pitch on drain piping. Check for pump-up systems or sewage ejectors.
- Listen for venting problems.

Waste Disposal Equipment (Grinders/Macerators)

- Check conditions. Look in the unit with a flashlight before you turn it on.[*]
- Look at internal conditions and contents to make sure it is safe to turn the unit on.
- Examine drain lines for loose fittings (vibration issues). If the dishwasher drains through a tailpiece, look for leakage or loose connections.
- Examine ring attachment below sink strainer for leaks or staining. (Do not turn, tighten, or try to move unit by hand. If it is loose, just report it.)
- Check wiring for inappropriate wiring, lack of strain relief connectors, and improper termination.
- Look for an under-counter, backsplash, or in-cabinet disconnect.

[*]Although many inspectors do not include some appliances as part of their inspection, examining the plumbing aspects of a disposal is recommended. Also check for GFCI outlets near damp locations.

Figure 5.28 Look for leaks, water stains, and disconnect (can be as simple as a plug or a box with a switch).

Dishwashers

- Examine the interior of the dishwasher, because this can give you a good idea of the water conditions within the home. Sediment, staining, and rusty conditions may be obvious or subtle.
- Make sure the dishwasher is secured to the countertop or the cabinets to avoid tipping issues.
- Check for physical damage, noisy operation, and odors.
- Examine trays, water arms, and towers.
- Follow drain line to waste connection and see if there is an anti-siphon device on the counter or a high loop of pipe in the cabinet. We do not want water from the sink to be siphoned into the dishwasher.
- Examine valves, and look for stains or damage around and below the unit.
- Look for an electrical disconnect in the sink cabinet or on the back-splash.

Ice Makers and Refrigerator Water and Ice Service Doors

- When possible, try to examine valves and lines leading to or below the refrigerator location.
- Signs of leakage or previous stains should be noted.
- Examine ice maker for physical damage, and carefully try water, ice, and crushed ice functions.

Figure 5.29   Pictured is a two-drawer-type dishwasher. These drawers function independently of each other.

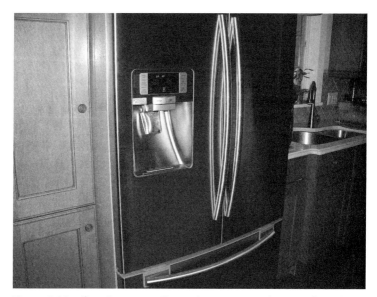

Figure 5.30   If you inspect appliances, be sure to test the water function and ice delivery to ensure good operation. Refrigerators should be approximately 44 degrees F and freezers 4 degrees F, so remember fours.

- You may wish to advise clients that lines and fitting behind the unit are not being examined and that care should be exercised when they move the unit.
- Note odors or odd noises.

Basement and Utility Areas

Water Heaters (Regular, Tankless, and Solar)

Stand-alone water heaters are generally fueled by gas, oil, or electric. The gas can be propane or natural gas, depending on availability. The water tank is usually a steel tank lined with glass, and most have a

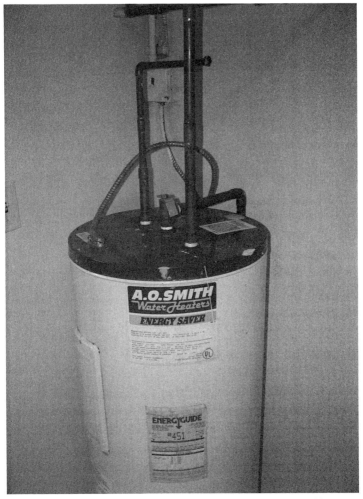

Figure 5.31 This is a 40-gallon electric water heater. Their projected life expectancy is approximately 7–13 years, depending on the quality of the water.

projected life expectancy of 7–13 years. Older copper- and stone-lined tanks had longer designed lives, but newer tanks generally rotate out around 10 years. The pH and mineral content of the water may affect this as well. No water heater (except sealed combustion chambers and electrically heated) may be located in a bedroom, bathroom, clothes closet, or a closet accessible from a bedroom.

Gas-Fired Water Heaters

- Examine the entry pipes for corrosion and/or leaking.
- There should be unions for easy replacement on the plumbing lines, and valves to turn off the supply (cold) and contain the hot water in the lines if there is a service need. If the second valve is not in place, the system will require draining for replacement.
- Examine the TPR valve. The TPR should be piped within a few inches of the floor, with $3/4$-inch piping. The valve should be installed within 6 inches of the top of the tank. If mounted on the living floors, there may be additional requirements for pans and drain lines in case of leaks. Termination points are good to determine, but may not be visible.
- TPR restrictive practices are critical for the safety of the home. See Figure 5.32.
- Examine the tank for signs of corrosion, rusting, or leakage.
- Check temperature of the water at a sink to determine if the settings are too high.
- Flues should be secured with screws and have a pitch of $1/4$ per foot to the flue of the chimney.
- Gas stacks should be mounted higher in the flue if oil-burning equipment enters the same chimney.
- Examine the pilot, and raise the temperature temporarily to look at the burn chamber (if readily accessible). Determine the state of cleanliness of the chamber, which may indicate problems.
- Gas appliances have common ignition noises. Listen for unusual sounds that might indicate a malfunction.
- Check function and location of emergency switches.
- In garage applications, the ignition source must be 18 inches off the floor, so the unit may be configured that way, or it may be installed on a box.
- Vehicle protection using steel bollards is typically required.
- Gas piping should be grounded to discharge any stray voltage away from the equipment.

Oil-Fired Water Heaters

- Examine the entry pipes for corrosion and/or leaking.
- There should be unions for easy replacement on the plumbing lines, and valves to turn off the supply (cold) and contain the hot water in

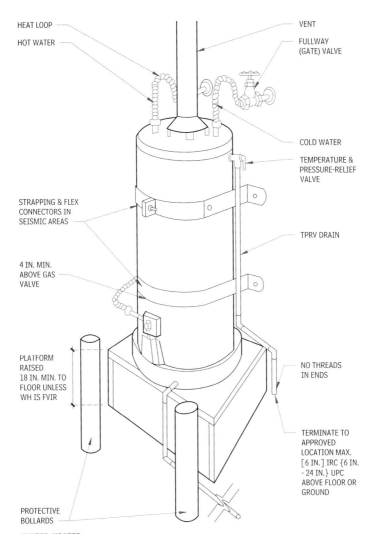

HEAT LOOP
HOT WATER
VENT
FULLWAY (GATE) VALVE
COLD WATER
TEMPERATURE & PRESSURE-RELIEF VALVE
STRAPPING & FLEX CONNECTORS IN SEISMIC AREAS
4 IN. MIN. ABOVE GAS VALVE
TPRV DRAIN
PLATFORM RAISED 18 IN. MIN. TO FLOOR UNLESS WH IS FVIR
NO THREADS IN ENDS
TERMINATE TO APPROVED LOCATION MAX. [6 IN.] IRC {6 IN. - 24 IN.} UPC ABOVE FLOOR OR GROUND
PROTECTIVE BOLLARDS

WATER HEATER

Figure 5.32 Listed above are many of the requirements for water heaters. Those located in a garage need to be on a platform with vehicle protection. Those in seismic areas need straps, and water heaters on upper floors should have pans and drains.

the lines if there is a service need. If the second valve is not in place, the system will require draining for replacement.

- Examine the TPR valve. The TPR should be piped within a few inches of the floor with ¾-inch piping. The valve should be installed within 6 inches of the top of the tank. If mounted on the living floors, there may be additional requirements for pans and drain lines in case of leaks. Termination points are good to determine, but may not be visible.

Figure 5.33 This is a 40-gallon gas-fired water heater. Look for rust stains, corrosion, and any signs of leakage.

Figure 5.34 Make sure flues are venting uphill, and pipe size is not reduced as it vents to the chimney.

Figure 5.35   Metal chimneys can easily be bumped or disconnect if not screwed together and properly fastened to the water heater. This can become a very hazardous situation.

- TPR restrictive practices are critical for the safety of the home. See Figure 5.32.
- Examine the tank for signs of corrosion, rusting, or leakage.
- Check temperature of the water at a sink to determine if the settings are too high.
- Flues should be secured with screws and have a pitch of ¼ per foot to the flue of the chimney.
- Oil stacks can be mounted in tandem with other oil-burning equipment where it enters the same chimney.
- Barometric dampers are usually required.
- Some oil technicians will measure the draft and, as a result, decide to close off the automatic damper. If you see this, recommend that a service technician verify the need for this action.
- Examine the burner and fittings, and raise the temperature temporarily to look at the burn chamber (if readily accessible). Determine the state of cleanliness of the chamber, which may indicate problems.
- Look for soot on and around the equipment, which may indicate a need for service.
- Oil appliances have common ignition noises. Listen for unusual sounds that might indicate a malfunction.
- Check function and location of emergency switches.

Figure 5.36   Look for burn marks, oil drips, and very hot water.

- In garage applications, the ignition source must be 18 inches off the floor, so the unit may be configured that way, or it may be installed on a box.
- Vehicle protection using steel bollards is typically required.
- Oil piping should not be plastic and should lead to a convenient point outside for delivery.
- Interior feed lines from the tank to the water heater should be protected from physical damages.
- Buried oil tanks can become an environmental nightmare. Make sure there are no signs of subterranean lines or upgraded lines and tanks.

Electric Water Heaters

- Check tank conditions, looking for leakage rust or damages.
- Examine the entry pipes for corrosion and/or leaking.
- There should be unions for easy replacement on the plumbing lines, and valves to turn off the supply (cold) and contain the hot water in the lines if there is a service need. If the second valve is not in place, the system will require draining for replacement.
- Examine the TPR valve. The TPR should be piped within a few inches of the floor with ¾-inch piping. The valve should be installed within 6 inches of the top of the tank. If mounted on the living floors, there may be additional requirements for pans and drain lines in case of leaks. Termination points are good to determine, but may not be visible.

Figure 5.37 Look carefully at subtle signs that might indicate a leak. Recommend an insulation blanket on electric units.

- TPR restrictive practices are critical for the safety of the home. See Figure 5.32.
- Check temperature of the water at a sink to determine if the settings are too high.
- Examine wiring into the unit. Look for strain relief, deterioration, and proper wire gauge. Check breaker or fuse location for water heater.

Tankless Water Heaters off a Domestic Coil
This type of hot water heater will flow clean (cold water) through a coil inside the boiler, absorbing heat as it passes through. It can be efficient as long as the water usage is not in great demand from multiple fixtures at the same time. Inspection is limited to examining the entry and exit fittings, the flange, and any temperature mixing valves.

Instantaneous Water Heaters
This is a newer technology that can be electric or gas-fired. There is no tank, but rather a valve and heat source. The unit senses that hot water is needed when a valve is opened, and the heating element turns on, heating the water, which is then released to flow to specific areas of the home. Units are sized for the area to be served, and can be mounted on a wall near the areas requiring the heated water. When there is no need for hot water, the unit is off.

Figure 5.38 Temperature pressure relief valves are a very important safety device. Make sure they are on the water heaters.

Figure 5.39 Inserted in a boiler, the tankless coil is heated by the boiler to a temperature set on the aquastat.

Figure 5.40 Newer capacity, higher-efficiency instant water heaters only heat the water on demand.

- Inspection requires an understanding of how the unit works; an examination for leaks, damages, and stains; and a temperature check to make sure the water is the right temperature.
- Some vent directly to an outside wall. Others may require a chimney.

Plumbing to the Boiler

- Examine supply lines to the boiler and applicable equipment.
- Look at pressure regulator and backflow protection for leaks, corrosion, and any signs of problems.

Figure 5.41 Look carefully for corrosion and leaks. Note also any sign of asbestos residual on piping.

- Check fittings, circulators, gaskets, and flanges, and look at the expansion tank and the boiler itself. Note any issues or service requirements.

Condensate Piping and Pumps

- Air-conditioning condensate lines can leak and dump lots of water in unexpected locations, resulting in damage and mold. Checking the piping for fractures, loose fittings, and previous evidence of leakage could take hours, and much could still be missed. During the heating season, these pipes rarely have much if any water in them, so the evaluation during that season will be limited.
- Look at accessible fittings and pipe for water stains and damage.
- Look around the equipment for signs of additional water damages.
- If the pump activates, try to determine where and if it is actually discharging. Often the discharge is piped in small-diameter plastic tubing to a drain or to the outside. Be looking for cross-connection potential.
- Pumps are often disabled when someone mistakenly unplugs them. Others may become damaged if someone bumps into them, or if they are not level.

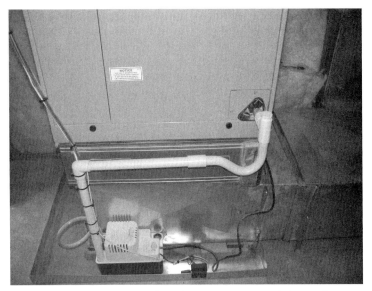

Figure 5.42 The condensate from the AC unit is pumped electrically through plastic hose to the exterior.

Well Tanks

In the past, these have been steel tanks with a Schrader valve to add a column of air as a buffer. Newer metal and fiberglass tanks with a bladder are becoming the norm.

- Check the tank for any obvious signs of damage, rust, or corrosion.
- Note leaks and/or excessive condensation.
- Recommend bubble-wrap-type nonporous insulation to reduce condensing.
- Examine gauges, fittings, and piping conditions.
- Water pressure gauges are required if the water pressure can exceed 75 psi or greater.

Water Meters

As meters are replaced, it seems more of the units contain plastic, and fewer are metal. As a result, it becomes even more important that the bonding wire be properly clamped to the piping that bridges both sides of the meter (usually a 6 gauge wire). Proper pipe grounding clamp devices must be used.

- Check all fittings, the meter, and inlet supply piping for signs of damage, corrosion, and leaks. Note materials and verify that there is at least one main water shutoff valve.

Figure 5.43 This well storage tank is a galvanized steel tank. These live a long time and need charging with air annually, as opposed to some bladder well tanks, which operate differently.

Figure 5.44 Many homes are now equipped with radio signal sending devices for water and gas meters that tell the utility your usage without the need for the meter reader to enter the home.

Sewage Ejectors

Unlike sump pumps, sewage ejectors are sealed tanks that have a submersible macerating (grinding) pump to reduce waste and paper to a slurry that can be pumped up high enough in a system to have it then gravity-feed down to the septic or sewer lines. These tanks can be metal or, more commonly are plastic. They have a discharge line and an air-venting pipe that should terminate into a proper vent, or above roof height whenever possible. The discharge pipe at the ejector ($1^1/_2$–2 inches) should have a check valve and a gate valve above that, to avoid water draining back into the tank during servicing.

- Examine visible parts of the tank and fittings for leaks, damage, or loose connections.
- Make sure all fittings and wiring are airtight and gas-tight.
- Make sure the check valve and gate valve are in place.
- Run water and listen to the discharge and check-valve operation.
- The designed life of this type of pump is approximately 8–10 years before needing service, but some can last over 20 years.
- Some units have a float-type pump alarm that can go off if the sensor feels the pump is not responding to the water level.

Figure 5.45 The sewage ejector should always have a check valve and ball valve, as well as a vent line going to a termination on the roof.

Water-Conditioning Equipment

Most inspectors exclude water treatment equipment as beyond the scope of the normal inspection. Depending on the number of homes you inspect, you may be seeing more wells and therefore more water filters, softeners, neutralizers, and specialized treatment equipment. Fortunately, the inspection process is more a matter of "Does it leak?" and "Is the equipment showing signs of damage or corrosion?" than a matter of "Is it working?" Your job is simply to eyeball this equipment and look for cosmetic needs. The actual water test result is the only definitive result that will tell if the water treatment is actually adjusted enough to be safe for the home.

Sump Pumps and Waterproofing Systems

Testing a sump pump can be very dangerous. You never want to accidentally become part of the circuit. If you are going to test the pump, make sure it looks safe to do so, and be sure to lift the float switch with an insulated tool.

Many clients tell me they are leery of homes with sumps. My opinion is that, regardless of why it was initially installed, a properly installed sump pump can deal not only with seepage and flooding from external conditions but also with a water heater burst, an accidental washing machine discharge, or a pipe leaking from an ice maker. If the water can get to the pit, the pump will help relieve the problem. Sumps also allow you to easily drain condensate lines from air conditioners and are an easy, effective means to empty a dehumidifier.

- Lift pump float switch or turn on the pump. Check for leaks or corrosion.
- Listen to the pump for odd noises or a seized motor.
- See if water is discharged and if the check valve functions properly.
- Make sure debris in the pit is not hampering the float or pump function.
- Check pipe terminations to ensure that water will not cycle back in.

Utility Sinks

Utility sinks generally are used in basement and workshop areas for cleaning and prepping items. They may be used for watering a plant, washing a paintbrush, or dumping liquids from sump pumps or dehumidifiers. Many utility sinks drain with a trap directly into the sewer line or septic system. Some restrictions may apply to certain wastes being discharged. Homes where the water is discharged out to, or pumped to, a dry well may have additional restrictions, to avoid soil and groundwater contamination.

Figure 5.46 Filtration, softening, and balancing of water can be expensive but important if the well produces problematic water. Sometimes you can smell it, other times the fixtures may be stained or the water may feel gritty. A full water test is the preliminary step toward determining what needs to be done.

- Is the faucet operation good? Is the aerator working?
- Is there functional flow and drainage?
- Check for attachment to the counter or base cabinet. Examine base cabinet for damage and stains. If there is no cabinet, check stability or attachment to the wall.
- Check drain mechanism controller.
- Look for valves and check for leaks.
- Crazing (cosmetic surface deterioration), actual cracks, or rusting would recommend replacement.
- Examine condition of trap and waste lines.
- Check pitch on drain piping. Check for pump-up systems or sewage ejectors.
- Listen for venting problems.
- Consider freeze potential.

Condensation Issues
Remember that warm moist air will drop the moisture as condensation whenever the temperatures of items around it are lower. While pipes that are showing signs of condensation may not be a deficiency, condensation can wet items and promote mold growth if the conditions are right.

Figure 5.47 Remember a sump pump needs power to operate, and the power may fail when needed most. Warn your clients to consider battery back-ups or a generator if the pump is actively pumping in wet weather.

Fire-Suppression Equipment

Fire-suppression equipment is typically beyond the scope of a home inspection, but any obvious signs of deterioration or leakage of such equipment in a home should warrant a warning of the situation to the client. Also, note in the report that this equipment is beyond the inspection scope.

If you are qualified to inspect such equipment, make sure your errors and omissions (E & O) insurance covers you and that you examine all visible sections, sprinkler heads, and piping.

Be aware that wet systems can freeze in winter, if they are vulnerable to the weather, and may require antifreeze in the plumbing. In larger applications, fire pumps may be installed and may need to be tested by the pump manufacturer's authorized service technicians.

Irrigation Systems (Lawn Sprinkler Systems)

Although irrigation equipment may be deemed beyond the scope of a home inspection in many climates, any obvious signs of deterioration or leakage of such equipment—in a home or outside, if visible—should warrant a warning of the situation to the client. Also, a note should be included in the report that this equipment is beyond the inspection scope.

Figure 5.48 Look at drains and traps. Try to determine if sinks drain to sewer or septic system, or to a dry well.

Figure 5.49 Summertime condensation will cause moisture levels to rise and mold to grow. The white insulation on the piping appears to be asbestos in friable condition.

In warmer climates, where the importance of irrigation increases, many inspectors include inspecting of irrigation equipment as an add-on to their normal home inspection.

When this equipment is inspected, the inspector should (with permission) run each zone from the control panel and look at the heads as they are operating. Any leaks, damage, or poor operation should be noted. If the heads are directing water on the building, this should be noted as needing adjustment.

The inspector should not adjust heads or valves or make repairs unless he or she is qualified to do so. Limitations of this type of inspection should be explained in your contract and covered by your insurance.

Unheated Space Concerns

In areas prone to freezing winds and temperatures, we recommend that all vulnerable plumbing, fire-suppression, and irrigation systems be properly winterized to avoid freeze-ups, including hose bibs, exterior feed lines, and outbuilding service that is not protected with heating. Garage sinks, faucets, and laundry equipment, exterior showers, fishponds, fountains, and water features carry the same warning. Pipes that must remain on and in service should be protected with heat,

Figure 5.50 In some municipalities, fire code drywall and a sprinkler head off the domestic cold water are required to be installed over oil- and gas-fired boilers and furnaces. It is really questionable whether these heads will put out a fire, especially as they get older.

heat tapes, insulation, and/or glycol antifreeze. Subterranean systems should be voided of water before winter temperatures drop.

Outdoor Pools and Spas

These may be kept in service at the whim of their owners, and as a result they may become vulnerable to freeze-up or emergency repair needs should some piece of equipment fail or temperatures drop due to weather, power outage, or mechanical failure. Pool and spa inspections are covered in Chapter 11,"Specialty Inspections,"and are another type of inspection that would typically be beyond the scope of a standard inspection.

Gas Piping

The potential for gas leaks and explosion necessitates a degree of care with both gas appliances and gas piping. All gas equipment should be bonded to allow safe discharge of any static or higher voltage away from the equipment to a good ground. Any deterioration or corrosion observed on gas piping should be noted in the report and explained to the client and the homeowner or Realtor® as a potential hazard. If there is an odor of gas, or the inspector feels there is a significant risk of danger, the equipment should be turned off and service should be very strongly recommended.

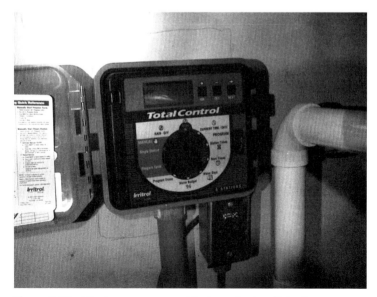

Figure 5.51   We always recommend that a professional irrigation company do the end-of-season winterizing and that operation questions be discussed with them before the closing.

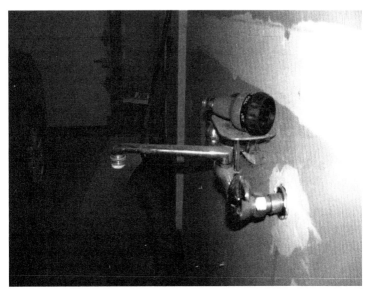

Figure 5.52 Discuss potential freeze concerns with your clients. It is very important in colder climates to avoid a potential freeze-up and damages from a burst pipe.

- Steel gas piping should be at least 6 inches from the soil and should not be strained or bent.
- Verify that there are positive shutoff valves for every gas appliance.
- Verify buried gas storage tanks' proximity to windows and entrance-ways.
- Most propane appliances are not approved to be installed in a basement or a pit.

Solar Water-Heating Equipment
Although this equipment usually exceeds the scope of the typical inspection, because it may very well be the primary heating design or the only domestic hot water system, some knowledge of operation and examination of a solar water heater may be prudent.

- Examine valves, circulators, thermostats, tanks, controls, and collectors for leaks, damage, and corrosion. Feel piping or use a thermometer to determine if functional circulation is achieved. Note temperature differentials.
- TPR valves are required for individual units, or one per ganged unit.
- Check roof fastening and supports.
- Antifreeze protection may be required in colder temperatures.

Figure 5.53 Make sure access to pools is blocked to children. Ladders should be removed or locked in the up position. You should not be able to walk across a deck or patio and fall in.

Acceptable Practices (Miscellaneous Plumbing Checks)

- Check for water hammer by opening and closing valves quickly. If a hammering noise or vibration noises are heard, air may be trapped in the lines, or additional supports may be needed. Vibrating pipes may bang against other piping or materials, making noise.
- Wet venting occurs when a fixture drain is also being used to vent another fixture. It is allowed as long as the pipe diameter is increased to the combined engineered minimum required for each fixture (with a minimum of 2 inches).
- Foot venting is allowed in islands where a direct vent line is not possible. The diameter of the foot vent would be a minimum of 2 inches on the drain and $1^1/_2$ inches on the vent.

Practices to Avoid

- Saddle fittings, drilled fittings, or tapping into and attaching into DWV piping are prohibited.

Figure 5.54 In this photo, natural gas is distributed to a boiler, a high-efficiency furnace, a gas cooktop, and a deck barbeque. Each has its own shutoff.

Figure 5.55 While the technology is not new, these types of solar panels and computerized controls are systems of the future that just make good sense.

- Fittings that require tightening or adjustments to maintain water-tightness must be accessible for servicing.
- Valves, pipes, and fittings that are designed for a directional flow must be installed according to design.
- Piping that is installed should not be installed in such a manner as to create stress or strain on the pipe or fittings.
- Strapping for support should not be so tight as to cause stress to the pipe.
- The home inspector is not required to operate any shutoff valves on any equipment.
- Testing sump pumps is at the discretion of the inspector and should be done carefully to avoid chance of shock.

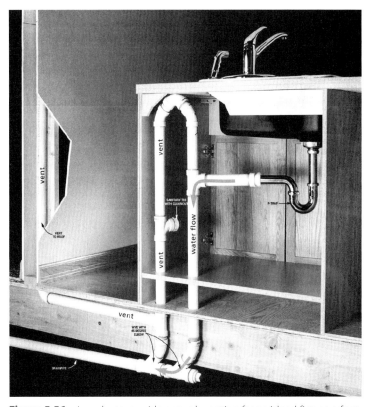

Figure 5.56 In order to provide enough venting for an island fixture, a foot vent is needed.

Resources

ALSO IN THIS BOOK:

- See Chapter 11 for saunas.

OTHER RESOURCES:

- *Home Reference Book*, Dearborn Home Inspection, 2003.
- *Residential Plumbing Inspection*, Inspection Training Associates, 4th Edition.

Chapter 6

Electrical

Electrical Service

Description

In residential situations, electric service entry normally comes from one of two sources: overhead wires from a pole on the street or in the yard or underground wires to the house. Underground service is referred to as a lateral. Most power companies prefer overhead wiring, as the heat created is easily dissipated, and finding trouble spots when a repair is needed can be easier. However, overhead wiring is exposed to weather and wind and is more vulnerable to damage to the poles or to wires being knocked down. Laterals are occasionally troubled by ground movement, excavation, and water intrusion.

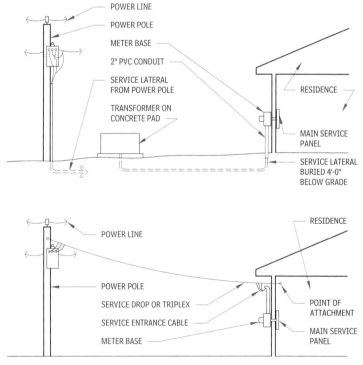

Figure 6.1   Service entrances
Source: AIA, *Architectural Graphic Standards for Residential Construction,* 2nd Edition. Copyright 2010, John Wiley & Sons, Inc.

Where the service wires are connected to the home (usually by large clamps called bugs), a drip loop is created to prevent water from following the wires into the weatherhead and getting into the panel. The point of connection is called the service drop.

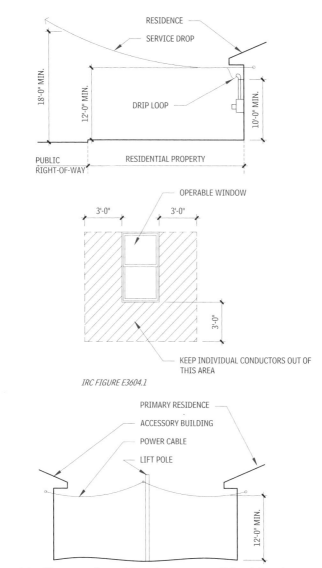

Figure 6.2 Clearances for aerial service entrances (6.2a–c); Attachment details at residence (6.2d, e)

Source: AIA, *Architectural Graphic Standards for Residential Construction,* 2nd Edition. Copyright 2010, John Wiley & Sons, Inc.

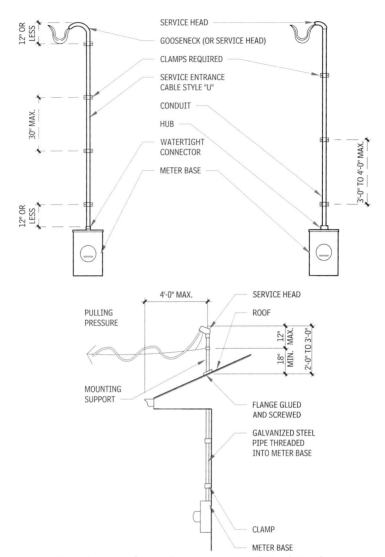

Figure 6.2 Clearances for aerial service entrances (6.2a–c); Attachment details at residence (6.2d, e) (continued)

In order to maintain proper heights and distance from the ground, a mast may be attached to the home. Whether attached to the mast or the building itself, the most common attachment is to use the neutral wire and an attaching clamp to hold the wire taut to the pole and support the two 120-volt lines around it.

When a lateral is used, an expanding collar is used to prevent settling or soil movement from ripping the meter pan off the building.

Figure 6.3 When looking at the wire connections at the weatherhead, make sure the strain relief is firmly attached to the home.

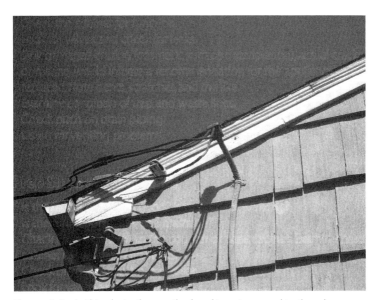

Figure 6.4 In this photo the weatherhead is not screwed to the rake molding, and needs repair.

Figure 6.5 A 200-amp service lateral. Remind your client to call the utility before digging in that area.

Assessing Existing Conditions

Service wires are normally the responsibility of the utility company to the service drop. The homeowner typically owns the service entry wire, from the bugs in, and the meter pan and panel (but not the meter).

- Check the condition of the wires from the pole to the home, if overhead. Check height, wear and tear, and support.
- Make sure the neutral is fastened properly to the home.
- Make sure any mast is installed properly and is not damaged.
- Check the weatherhead for damages.
- Look for frayed or damaged service entry wires.
- Examine the condition of the exterior rated boxes and meter.
- If there is a main on the exterior, examine the amperage.
- If trees or plantings interfere or are close to wires, recommend pruning.

Acceptable Practices

Electrical safety is critical, and a mistake in your evaluation or technique can be dangerous, if not fatal. Before placing your ladder, make sure wires are not in the way or touching metal siding, gutters, or masts.

Figure 6.6 Older 100-amp service. Note frayed or deteriorated wiring below meter.

- Are heights of wires correct? They should be a minimum of 3 feet above a peaked roof, 8 feet above a low sloped roof, 12 feet above a driveway, 10 feet above a walkway, and 22 feet above a swimming pool.
- Inspection of the service wires is visual only.
- Report rust, deterioration, or damage to the meter or meter pan, and damage of the wires, weatherhead, mast, or clamps.
- Report if the service is pulled off the home or poorly attached.
- Report if the service wire indicates less than 100 amps (now considered substandard).

Table 6.1 Service Entry Sizes

Copper	Aluminum	Service Size
10	8	30
6	6	60
4	2	100
2	1/0	125
1/0	2/0	150
2/0	4/0	200

Figure 6.7 The main breaker will be at the meter or at the main service panel.

Practices to Avoid

- Obviously, be careful. Do not touch anything that is electrified. When opening a meter pan service box containing a main, look for evidence of previous damage, burn marks, or rust. Do not open if a hazardous condition exists.
- Watch ladder placement.
- Carefully look at masts for signs of damage or leakage. Do not get too close to them when walking the roof.

Service Panels

Description

The main panel should be within 7 feet of the meter pan unless there is an exterior main disconnect. Many larger homes may have multiple panels, but the main disconnect is usually located in this box. By most standards of practice, the inspector is required to open (when safe to do so) the deadfront cover to view wiring and conditions for the safety of the home.

Dual-phase main panels consist of two 120-volt lines attached to a split bus bar. This allows single-pole breakers to allow the flow of 120 volts and a two-pole breaker to pick up the second 120 line and flow 240 volts.

Breakers or fuses are used as safety devices within the panel to stop unsafe loads from overheating the wires downline of the device. Overheated wire can melt the insulation and cause sparking, arcing, or fire.

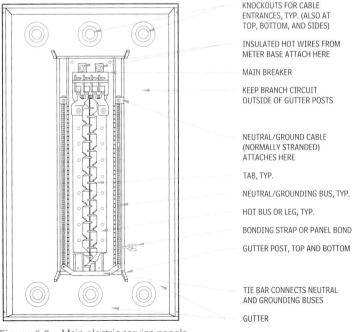

KNOCKOUTS FOR CABLE ENTRANCES, TYP. (ALSO AT TOP, BOTTOM, AND SIDES)

INSULATED HOT WIRES FROM METER BASE ATTACH HERE

MAIN BREAKER

KEEP BRANCH CIRCUIT OUTSIDE OF GUTTER POSTS

NEUTRAL/GROUND CABLE (NORMALLY STRANDED) ATTACHES HERE

TAB, TYP.

NEUTRAL/GROUNDING BUS, TYP.

HOT BUS OR LEG, TYP.

BONDING STRAP OR PANEL BOND

GUTTER POST, TOP AND BOTTOM

TIE BAR CONNECTS NEUTRAL AND GROUNDING BUSES

GUTTER

Figure 6.8   Main electric service panels
Source: AIA, *Architectural Graphic Standards for Residential Construction,* 2nd Edition. Copyright 2010, John Wiley & Sons, Inc.

Figure 6.9 Until the panel cover is actually removed, the inspector really cannot determine the quality and safety of the wiring. Standards require that the panel cover be opened when it is safe to do so.

Assessing Existing Conditions

- Using the back of your hand, feel the deadfront cover before attempting to open it.
- Look with the door open to see which, if any, breakers are off. (This is important because you can inadvertently turn a breaker off when taking the cover off.) A breaker that was already off should not be

Figure 6.10 Panels that are missing the knockouts, those with wires accessible to touch, boxes that are poorly labeled, and those missing screws should be reported and a licensed electrician recommended for needed repairs.

turned on, as this may energize something that is damaged or out of service or unsafe.

- Remove screws and place in a safe place.
- Assess wiring to each breaker for proper wire size and single connections. Look for discoloration, melted insulation, double-tapped breakers, tripped breakers, and any kind of damage, rust, or burn marks.
- Look for proper connectors bringing the wires into the box and strain relief.
- Look for a single ground going to a ground stake and/or the plumbing.
- Look for sloppy or unprofessional workmanship.
- Look for unsafe splices.
- Look for evidence of insect, rodent, or water entry.
- Look for missing deadfront knockouts.
- Clearance in front of the deadfront should be at least 30 inches wide and 36 inches from the front to allow a safe working area.

Acceptable Practices

- Most home inspection requirements and state statutes under most home inspection regulations require that the wiring in the panel be examined. That gives you the requirement by statute to open the panel deadfront cover. The argument that you are not a

Figure 6.11   Look for water stains, double-tapped breakers, corrosion, melting insulation, burn marks, etc.

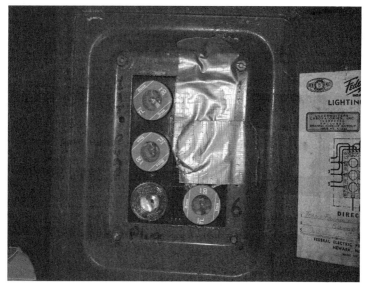

Figure 6.12   There are still plenty of homes with fuse boxes and questionable safety issues.

licensed electrician only applies if you go beyond opening the panel and examining conditions. Because this is a visual inspection, you are within the scope of your job description to open the panel.

- For testing switches and outlets, a random sample (typically at least one receptacle and one switch per room) is required. Many inspectors will test more. In the panel we are required to test all GFCI and AFCI breakers using their test buttons.

Practices to Avoid

- You are not to correct, or tighten anything, see if something is loose, or put yourself at risk. Remember that this is predominantly a visual inspection. Other than removal of the screws, your job is to look carefully and report conditions found.
- If you deem conditions are unsafe don't touch the panel. This will dictate the safety of opening the panel. Wet locations, standing water, or evidence of sparking, arcing, or hazards may come into play.

Figure 6.13 Make sure switches are at top and bottom of stairs and either side of pass-through rooms.

- Do not ignore tight spaces and poor accessibility. There should be 36 inches of clear room in front of the panel and working space 30 inches in width.
- Except for GFCI and AFCI breakers, try not to trip or turn off any regular breakers.

Figure 6.14 Testing GFCI breakers is required by most standards. Explain to your client what they do and how to reset them.

Main Panels

Description

A main panel is usually the first panel that is servicing the home. The panel will often hold the main shutoff disconnect, unless it is more than 7 feet away from the meter pan. The main breaker, when in the off position, should turn off all the power in the home beyond that breaker. This is for the safety of all concerned. Panels that have wires tapped off the hot side of the main breaker can kill or seriously hurt someone who is not aware of this situation. Mains should be so labeled. Subpanels should be downstream of the main.

Assessing Existing Conditions

- As previously discussed, we recommend removing the deadfront, if it is safe to do so, and a careful visual evaluation of the conditions found.
- Most panels have a split bus design; alternating breakers are balancing the load by taking the electricity from alternating legs of the service. The split bus helps maintain this balance and accommodates picking up two poles to accomplish 240 volts for larger appliances.

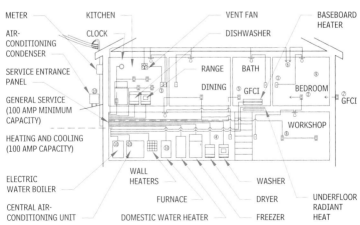

Figure 6.15 Schematic diagram of typical residential wiring and general requirements.
Source: AIA, *Architectural Graphic Standards for Residential Construction,* 2nd Edition. Copyright 2010, John Wiley & Sons, Inc

Figure 6.16 The accessibility of the wiring should not be blocked by cabinets, shelves, or other pieces of equipment.

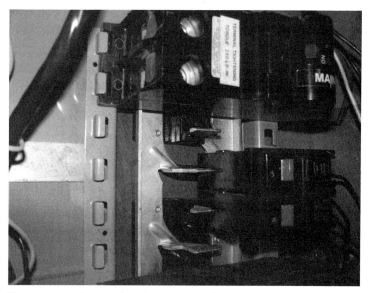

Figure 6.17 The use of a split bus allows a balancing of breaker load within the panel.

- All panels are rated for the size and number of wires allowed in that "box." If a panel looks overcrowded, you may wish to recommend that a licensed electrician service it.
- Panel manufacturers recommend that only breakers of a particular brand and rating be used in their panels. Although this may be proprietary and profit-motivated, alteration of a breaker to "make it fit" can create a dangerous condition.
- Moisture will frequently travel down a service wire and follow the wires into a panel box. Sometimes insects will follow that path as well. Make sure water or insects are not entering the panel.
- When they are surface mounted or in framed unfinished areas, you may be able to view wire entry knockouts. Make sure proper connectors/strain relief are in place.
- In the panel, make sure the neutral goes to a neutral connector and that those neutral and bare grounding/bonding wires are fastened in a manner that provides a safe path to a ground source to discharge spikes, surges, and lightning.
- If aluminum service wire is used, try to view it to ascertain if antioxidant material was used at the connectors.
- Note in your report conditions found and any deficiencies or safety items of concern.

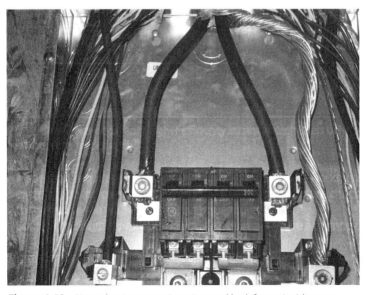

Figure 6.18 Note aluminum service wires and look for antioxidant on connectors.

Acceptable Practices

- Visually inspect wire sizes, conditions of the insulation, and breaker size appropriateness for the wire size.
- Test all GFCI and AFCI breakers in the panel.
- Visually inspect bus bars, connections, and any deficiencies.
- Examine box and ground connections to make sure the wiring is safe.
- Evaluate the size of the main and ensure that the panel is rated for that size main.
- Determine if the panel is not close enough to the meter pan (this would then require a main at the meter pan).
- Check the panel and deadfront cover knockouts for missing parts or unsafe conditions.

Practices to Avoid

- You are *not* to correct or tighten anything, see if something is loose, or put yourself at risk. Remember, this is predominantly a visual inspection. Other than removal of the screws, your job is to look carefully and report conditions found.

Figure 6.19 Pulling out the cartridge fuse would kill all the power in the home, so it is unlikely you would do this, but there are advantages to being able to see the condition of the fuses See if they are the correct amperage, and make sure there is a fuse in the slot, instead of a piece of copper tubing.

- If you deem conditions are unsafe don't touch the panel. This will dictate the safety of opening the panel. Wet locations, standing water, or evidence of sparking, arcing, or hazards may come into play.
- Do not ignore tight spaces and poor accessibility. Note accessibility. There should be 36 inches of clear room in front of the panel and working space 30 inches in width.
- Except for GFCI and AFCI breakers, try not to trip or turn off any regular breakers.

Subpanels

Description

Sometimes it makes more sense to run a larger-gauge wire to a subpanel instead of running many smaller wires a long distance. Also, it is more convenient to have a separate panel to control one section of the home near those appliances. Subpanels may also be added when the main panel has little additional room.

Assessing Conditions

- Except for bonding, mains and subs are very similar.
- Bonding makes the subpanel safer and reduces the chance for stray surges or charges to burn out electronic boards and damage sensitive equipment.
- Neutral wires (whites) should be isolated from the box and placed only on the neutral bus bar. Bare copper wires and the box itself

Figure 6.20 This panel does not have neutrals isolated as required.

Figure 6.21 A subpanel with the neutrals isolated and a ground wire path going back to the main panel will send surges back to the main instead of feeding through neutral wiring and possibly destroying computers, TVs, and sensitive printed circuit boards.

should be bonded to a separate bus bar that has an uninterrupted #6 or #8 wire going back to the main panel.
- This separation allows current a direct path back to the grounding system without the chance to flow through appliances or electrical equipment. (See Table 6.2.)

Acceptable Practices

- Visually inspect wire sizes, conditions of the insulation, and breaker size appropriateness for the wire size.
- Test all GFCI and AFCI breakers in the panel.
- Visually look at bus bars, connections, and any deficiencies.
- Examine box and ground connections to make sure the wiring is safe.
- Evaluate the size of the breakers and ensure that the panel is rated for that size subpanel.
- Determine if the bonding is isolated from the neutrals.
- Check the panel and deadfront cover knockouts for missing parts or unsafe conditions.

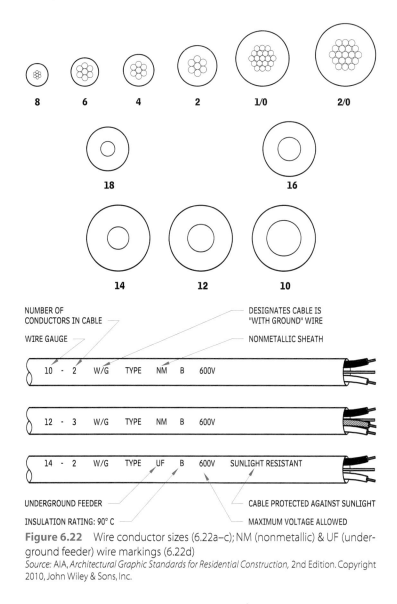

Figure 6.22   Wire conductor sizes (6.22a–c); NM (nonmetallic) & UF (underground feeder) wire markings (6.22d)
Source: AIA, Architectural Graphic Standards for Residential Construction, 2nd Edition. Copyright 2010, John Wiley & Sons, Inc.

Practices to Avoid

- You are *not* to correct or tighten anything, see if something is loose, or put yourself at risk. Remember, this is predominantly a visual inspection. Other than removal of the screws, your job is to look carefully and report conditions found.

Figure 6.23 Look at fuse boxes and the size of the fuses. Most fuse systems had 15-amp circuits run with 14-gauge wire. When the fuses blew, larger fuses may have been installed, which may allow the insulation to melt or burn before the higher-amperage fuse will blow out.

- If you deem conditions are unsafe, don't touch the panel. This will dictate the safety of opening the panel. Wet locations, standing water, or evidence of sparking, arcing, or hazards may come into play.
- Do not ignore tight spaces and poor accessibility. Note accessibility. There should be 36 inches of clear room in front of the panel and working space 30 inches in width.
- Except for GFCI and AFCI breakers, try not to trip or turn off any regular breakers.

Understanding Breakers and Fuses

Description

For many years, an Edison-based fuse was a tremendous step in the right direction to help protect the circuitry from overheating as a result of too many appliances being plugged in. Unfortunately, as those fuses blew, people figured out ways to get around the inconvenience. Some would place pennies (flat pieces of conductive material) under the fuse to save the cost of replacing it. Others would simply place a larger-amperage fuse in the socket to get that circuit back on line. Obviously, the hotter the wires get, the more vulnerable the insulation is to melting or actually catching fire. Early wiring was wrapped with cloth, later with asbestos-impregnated insulation, then later with all kinds of plastic, heat-resistant materials. If the overheating took place in a fixture or in the walls, building materials could get hot enough to ignite and start

Figure 6.24 Open fuse slots and over-fused fuses can be a hazard. Removing this cover will verify that fuses are too large.

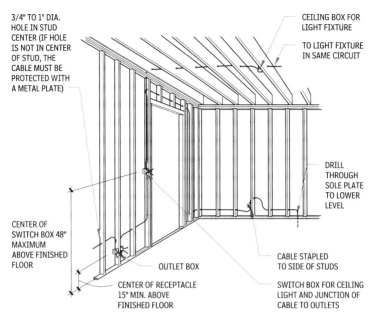

3/4" TO 1" DIA. HOLE IN STUD CENTER (IF HOLE IS NOT IN CENTER OF STUD, THE CABLE MUST BE PROTECTED WITH A METAL PLATE)

CEILING BOX FOR LIGHT FIXTURE

TO LIGHT FIXTURE IN SAME CIRCUIT

DRILL THROUGH SOLE PLATE TO LOWER LEVEL

CENTER OF SWITCH BOX 48" MAXIMUM ABOVE FINISHED FLOOR

OUTLET BOX

CENTER OF RECEPTACLE 15" MIN. ABOVE FINISHED FLOOR

CABLE STAPLED TO SIDE OF STUDS

SWITCH BOX FOR CEILING LIGHT AND JUNCTION OF CABLE TO OUTLETS

Figure 6.25 Average wattages, branch circuit protection, typical wiring in wood construction
Source: AIA, *Architectural Graphic Standards for Residential Construction,* 2nd Edition. Copyright 2010, John Wiley & Sons, Inc.

a fire. Fustat bases were created to try to make it more difficult to insert the wrong size of fuse. A base designed only for a particular amp fuse would screw in and lock permanently into the panel. Modern circuit breakers replaced this technology, first with screw-in breakers, then with Bakelite circuit breakers, then with plastic ones. Both the fuse and the breaker measure heat, but the advantage of the breaker was that it could be reset at no expense to the homeowner once installed. Also it eliminated the ease of over-fusing.

Assessing Existing Conditions

- Remember, fuses are still acceptable with a warning about over-fusing.
- There is rarely any requirement to upgrade beyond modernization.
- Look for 20-amp or higher fuses, after removing the deadfront, note the wire sizes going to the fuses.
- 14 gauge wires are designed for a 15-amp fuse. Call out over-fusing.
- Blown fuses in the panel, or a pile of blown fuses near the panel, may indicate a problem.

- Examine the panel for signs of corrosion, alteration, and arcing. This applies to circuit breaker panels as well.
- Look for proper connectors to relieve wire stress and open knockouts.
- Look for labeling of circuits for safety.
- Typical practice is one breaker per circuit. When circuits are double-tapped there may not be a safety issue, but repair should be recommended for safety.

Table 6.2 Average Wattages of Common Electrical Devices

Type	Watts
Air conditioner, central	2500s–6000
Air conditioner, room type	800–2500
Blanket, electric	150–200
Clock	2–3
Clothes dryer	4000–6000
Dishwasher	1000–1500
Fan, portable	50–200
Food blender	500–1000
Freezer	300–500
Frying pan, electric	1000–1200
Furnace blower	380–670
Garbage disposal	500–900
Hair dryer	350–1200
Heater, portable	1000–1500
Heating pad	50–75
Heat lamp (infrared)	250
Iron, hand	600–1200
Lamp, incandescent	10 upward
Lamp, fluorescent	15–16
Lights, Christmas tree	30–150
Microwave oven	1000–1500
Mixer	120–250
Power tools	Up to 1000
Projector, slide or movie	300–500
Radio	40–150
Range (all burners and oven)	8000–14000
Range top (separate)	4000–8000

Continued

Table 6.2 Average Wattages of Common Electrical Devices *continued*

Type	Watts
Range oven (separate)	4000–5000
Refrigerator	150–300
Refrigerator, frostless	400–600
Sewing machine	60–90
Stereo (solid-state)	30–100
Television	50–450
Vacuum cleaner	250–1200
Washer, automatic	500–800
Water heater	2000–5000

Source: AIA, Architectural Graphic Standards for Residential Construction. Copyright 2003, John Wiley & Sons, Inc.

Acceptable Practices

- Open deadfronts when accessible and safe to do so.
- Look at breakers and/or fuses to evaluate safe wire sizing.
- Look for evidence of "loose" breakers or sloppy workmanship.
- Look for hot-wired circuits that may not shut down when the main is off.
- Test all GFCI and AFCI circuits.

Practices to Avoid

- Do not pull mains or subpanel cartridge fuses.
- Do not turn off main breakers.
- Do not open deadfront covers on panels over 400 amps unless you are adequately trained in larger electrical panels.
- Do not open a panel if you feel there is a danger.
- Try not to take off the panel or trip a breaker if someone in the home is working on a computer. Have them back-up their data first.
- Avoid touching energized wires. This can be dangerous; you should use a voltage sniffer to verify if a circuit is alive.

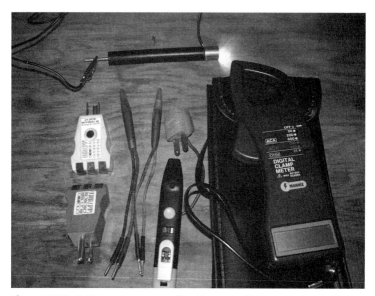

Figure 6.26 Voltage testers can tell an inspector if a wire is energized, without the need to touch it. Many unsafe situations can be safely diagnosed with one of these.

Overloaded Circuits

Description

In older homes, very few circuits were initially needed. There was minimal need for lighting and receptacles when compared with today. As we accepted more and more electrical convenience appliances, newer homes added more and more circuits, handling lighting and convenience outlets with additional "dedicated" circuits to power appliances with higher electricity demands. Typical of these would be microwaves, air conditioners, dishwashers, and waste disposals. Running a "home run" or dedicated circuit for an appliance reduces the chance that lights will dim when that appliance starts to draw electricity. Depending on what is operating at any given time, it is very possible that too many appliances may be running to maintain safe wire temperatures. When this occurs, the circuit is considered overloaded, and it may blow the fuse or pop the breaker.

Figure 6.27 As electrical usage goes up, care must be taken to avoid overheating circuits with too many items drawing electricity.

Assessing Existing Conditions

- Look for surge strips, extension cords, and outlet multipliers. Many items plugged into one circuit may result in overloading.
- Undersized service and modern usage rarely go hand in hand. Note service size and appliances in use.
- Panels with only a few circuits will limit the availability of additional outlets and lighting.
- Double breakers (twins) or double-tapped breakers indicate additional circuits added after the panel was installed.
- New work, new additions, or renovations may max out or surpass the limits of the panel.
- Additional 240-volt appliances may cause temporary dimming when motors or heavy-draw appliances are initially turned on.

Acceptable Practices

- Look at and assess panel, service, and wire size.
- Look for twin breakers, double taps, and hot-wired circuits.
- Watch for dimming when appliances are starting.

Figure 6.28 Look for unsafe wiring, especially at junction boxes in unfinished areas.

Figure 6.29 Look for open boxes, missing connectors, and damaged wires.

- Look for excessive overused circuits (note around computers, TVs and audio equipment).
- Note extension cords, wiring under carpeting, and nonprofessional work.
- Note new work going into old work from renovations and additions.

Practices to Avoid

- Do not assume that current use will match the new owner's usage.
- Do not assume or report that substandard work was "homeowner installed."
- Do not unplug or de-energize items.
- Do not "red tag." Note unsafe conditions and do point out safety concerns both to your client and the Realtor®, so they can report hazards to the owner. Follow-up with the homeowners when hazards are found that can seriously harm them.
- Even if the owner acknowledges that the items are to be fixed, still note them in your report.

Dedicated Circuits

Description

Dedicated circuits, or "home runs," are circuits designed to provide electricity to one receptacle or one appliance. Larger appliances are powered by dedicated circuits (AC units, air handlers, heat pumps, stoves, etc.), but a specific outlet for a refrigerator, sump pump, or radon mitigation system may be run simply to dedicate that line, with a single breaker to control its use.

Assessing Existing Conditions

While this is not frequently recommended, as it is difficult to ascertain, you may recommend a dedicated circuit when it is obvious that a circuit has too many items on it and a dedicated circuit would be better.

Figure 6.30 Dedicated outlets for specific appliances such as dryers, air conditioners, waste disposals, and microwaves allow what we call "home runs," whereby that specific appliance is the only one on the circuit.

Acceptable Practices

This is purely a visual assessment, without using instrumentation to test. Recommending additional circuits would depend on the future plans of the owner or buyer.

Practices to Avoid

Avoid making recommendations for upgrading the service or equipment unless the client hints that he or she will be increasing electricity usage from what the norm has been in the home previously.

For example: central air conditioning, driveway ice melters, additions, electric water heaters, electric dryers, etc.

Branch Circuits

Description

Branch circuits are defined as the individual electrical circuits downstream of the main and subpanels. They are typically lighting and receptacle circuits, but may also include specialty home runs for appliances and equipment. For the inspection, branch circuit wires should be grounded; they should in most cases not be aluminum without special attachment devices, and the polarity should be the same. Branch circuits may contain GFCI and/or AFCI protection, depending on the location and age of the installation.

Assessing Existing Conditions

Inspection of branch circuitry is normally done with a circuit tester and by visually inspecting the wires leaving the subpanel. Testers used will determine open grounds and reversed polarity. Branch circuits on older homes may have minimal grounding, and recommendations to upgrade for safety would be the norm.

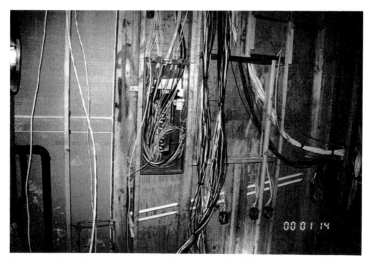

Figure 6.31 Wires have been pulled and set for different circuits off the main panel.

Figure 6.32 Multitester should be used on at least one outlet per room according to most standards.

Table 6.3 Branch Circuit Protection

Lighting (general purpose)	#14 wires	15 A
Small appliances	#12 wires	20 A
Individual appliances	#12 wires	20 A
	#10 wires	30 A
	#8 wires	40 A
	# 6 wires	50 A

Source: AIA, Architectural Graphic Standards for Residential Construction. Copyright 2003, John Wiley & Sons, Inc.

Acceptable Practices

Using a tester, random outlets in each room would be tested to confirm a solid ground, polarity, and power to the outlet.

Visually examining the subpanel would also determine that the wire size is correct, that the circuit is protected by a fuse or breaker, and that the wire has strain relief. Looking at the color and condition of the wires might indicate overheating, electrical imbalance, or arcing and sparking.

Practices to Avoid

- Before recommending repairs, make sure breakers are on and fuses are not blown.
- If the breaker is off or fuses are blown, note this, but do not re-energize them.
- Avoid calling out problems before you check to see that wall switches are in the on position, as some outlets may be switched off for convenience.
- Avoid using an unreliable testing devices.
- Do not touch or move wires in the panel.
- Do not test outlets that have appliances already plugged into them, as this may require resetting clocks and timers.

Antiquated Wiring

Description

Electrical wiring has, like most building materials, gone through countless upgrades in both materials and common practices. Most code requirements came as a result of fires in the home, loss of life and property. Material improvements and safety practices have changed the way we ground, bond, attach, and identify many products. Antiquated wiring is a reality, however, because requiring wiring in the walls and ceilings to be upgraded does impose a hardship. Many early homes will have older boxes, receptacles, and wall switches, and old wire leading to old appliances and fixtures. Old insulation becomes brittle over time, and heat and movement can cause deterioration that can lead to a shock hazard or fire. Older cloth and asbestos wiring can contribute to health concerns, and some materials such as aluminum wiring can lead to loose connections and arcing. Some older materials may give off toxic gases when they burn, and others may be simply covered with insulation and create heat traps that can shorten their designed life.

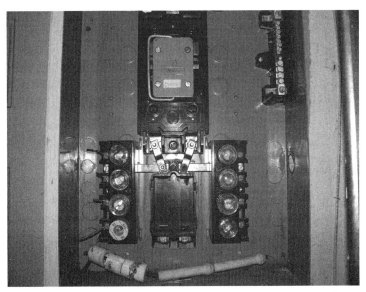

Figure 6.33   Old fuse panel and knob-and-tube material in bottom of panel

Assessing Existing Conditions

- Look for older materials.
- Look for discontinued breakers, problematic panels, and known recalls.
- Examine wire conditions, materials used, and insulation.
- Look for knob-and-tube, asbestos-covered, and lead-clad wiring.
- Look for aluminum wiring and al/cu connectors.
- Examine older wall switches for operation and arcing.
- Watch for dimming or signs of poor connections.
- Check for splices in improper locations, overfilled boxes, and missing cover plates.
- Make sure boxes are accessible, and watch clearances to combustibles and insulation.

Acceptable Practices

- Start in the panel box: Look at insulation type and wire material.
- Look at connections and splices, and see if antioxidant is on any aluminum wire connections.
- Random outlets, switches, and installed appliances should be tested and evaluated for good operation.
- Check wiring in basements, attics, crawlspaces, and eaves, because these areas may give clues to the hidden defects or safety concerns in the wall and ceiling areas.
- Note all deficiencies in your report.

Practices to Avoid

- Do not energize circuits that have been disconnected, that have blown out fuses, or that have the breaker off.
- Do not assume a line is dead. Test with a voltage sniffer before handling.
- Don't forget to re-set GFCI outlets after testing.
- Remember to report insulation installed around or on knob-and-tube wiring, as this can hold the heat and cause the insulation to deteriorate faster.
- Note polarity issues, because these can devastate newer solid-state and component circuit boards in case of a surge or lightning strike.
Remember to check for appropriate grounding on all appliances.

Ceiling Fans

Description

Fans are generally for cooling in warmer months, but they can also effectively move warm air around a home during cooler periods by stirring the air and maintaining more circulation. Modern ceiling fans tend to be quieter and less apt to wobble and vibrate, but much depends on the quality of the unit and proper installation.

Most fans have dimmer or multispeed switching and a reversing switch as well. Critical also are the weight of the unit and the installation of the unit to the ceiling. Attachment to the box may be fine, but the box itself may need additional support due to vibration and weight.

Combination fan and light units may add circuit boards or additional wires to regulate the lighting as well, either remotely or with pull chains.

Figure 6.34 These fans can help save hundreds by recirculating already heated or cooled air.

Assessing Existing Conditions

- Look at the unit for signs of problems or unprofessional installation.
- Listen to the unit for motor noises, wobble, or imbalances.
- Use the wall controls and/or pull chains to test all operations.
- With circuit board units, you may need to know test codes to run in diagnostic modes (for example, Casablanca fans).
- Damaged, drooping, or missing paddles are an indicator of damage or moisture.
- Units installed in damp locations may deteriorate and may require GFCI protection.
- Check height and voice headroom concerns if the unit is too low.

Acceptable Practices

- Turn on fans and lights, and test all operations if energized.
- Report any corrosion, wobble, or deficiency.
- If the unit is poorly or questionably installed, try to determine if the box is anchored to the ceiling, if visible.
- Test reversing switch.

Practices to Avoid

- Do not pull, manually stop, or bump into the fan when operating.
- If the fan begins vibrating or wobbling wildly, turn it off and suggest service; do not try to adjust it.
- If there is arcing/sparking or dimming during operation, turn the fan off and suggest service. Do not try to "fix" it.

Receptacle Outlets

Description

Convenience outlets, wall outlets, and receptacles are simply an easy way to bring electricity in a safe manner to the room or device that offers an easy manual disconnect. As the codes changed and electrical usage increased, we saw changes in the requirement for more outlets and locations specifically demanded in heavy usage areas. To avoid the problems caused by extension cords and potential trip hazards, lamps and corded appliances were required to have either a 3-foot or 6-foot cord. Then the requirement for wall outlet spacing could be every 12 feet, and countertop appliances and lamps would reach the outlets without the need for additional, potentially unsafe wiring.

Assessing Existing Conditions

- Using your tester, check random outlets for power, polarity, and grounding.
- Report any sparking, loose boxes, and burn marks.

Figure 6.35 Old wet location outlets in baths, kitchens, garages, and outside, should be upgraded to GFCI safety outlets.

Acceptable Practices

- Random testing of at least one outlet per room is a minimal test. The more the better.
- Test GFCI and AFCI outlets with an appropriate test device.

Practices to Avoid

- Do not unplug devices plugged in (or you may have to reset them).
- There is no requirement to open these boxes.
- Watch out for switched outlets, as they may give you a false reading.
- Damp locations and wet locations will require GFCI-type outlets; these must be tested with a GFCI tester.

Figure 6.36   Wet location GFCI outlets have greatly reduced electrocutions.

Split Receptacles

Description

A split receptacle is one in which the connective link between the top outlet and the bottom has been disconnected, and each may be electrically fed individually; one may be switched while the other is constantly on, or both may be switched independently. This may be found where night-table lamps may be operated by a wall switch while the alarm clock remains on, as an example. Another common spot is a double receptacle fed under the kitchen sink by a three-wire feed—one outlet for a disposal and one for the dishwasher. This may or may not have a bar on the breaker in the panel to blow both if there is a problem. Split receptacles can be confusing when tested and a hazard when double-fed, unless the person is aware of the feed and switching wiring.

Figure 6.37   Powering one outlet with two separate feeds can supply a waste disposal and a dishwasher with two home runs, but can surprise someone who does not expect a second circuit to be hot when the first is off.

Assessing Existing Conditions

Be alert to the existence of double feeds. If an outlet has the link broken in the box, the upper and lower receptacles are working independently. Test each with that in mind. Look for additional switching.

Acceptable Practices

Use a regular voltage tester, and be tuned in to typical locations where split receptacles might be the norm.

Practices to Avoid

Try to make clients aware of such conditions so they understand that turning off one breaker may not eliminate the chance of a shock.

Polarity

Description

Black and white wires typically carry the electricity from the panel to the outlets or to appliances that are "hard wired." When wired properly, the black wire is fused or circuit-breaker-protected. If we maintain polarity—that is, all the blacks going to the gold side of the receptacle and all the whites to the silver—safety circuits in some appliances, electronics, and fixtures can handle spikes and surges without the problems these can otherwise cause. In subpanels, isolating the neutral wires from the bond wires keeps a clear path for stray charges to follow the path of least resistance to the main panel, instead of traveling through the more sensitive circuits where they can do damage.

Figure 6.38 Newer equipment comes with polarized plugs. Polarizing will keep the hot side from damaging some lighting and more sophisticated electronic devices such as stereos and computers.

Assessing Existing Conditions

- A simple voltage tester can determine polarity issues, and this should be used when doing random testing.
- Report any polarity issues and subpanels that do not have neutrals isolated.

Acceptable Practices

- Use a voltage tester that shows polarity deficiencies.
- Report on outlets and locations that are reversed.

Practices to Avoid

- Make sure the client is aware that simply reversing polarity on one outlet may create polarity issues on outlets downline of that outlet. The whole system should be checked by a licensed electrician.

Ungrounded Outlets

Description

Older wiring simply delivered electricity to a room. Grounding (or creating a safe route for spikes, surges, static electricity, or faults) became an increasingly important concept as the code writers tried to reduce house fires. Adding a ground path in metal-encased wires (BX cable, for example) was achieved by linking the external metal sheathing to the main panel with a conductive connector and to the receptacle with a conductive metal box and connector, with the "ears" of the receptacle touching the box. This grounding was dependent on many small contacts being done properly. With the advent of Bakelite and plastic boxes, plastic connectors, and plastic-clad wiring, the addition of a comparably sized bare copper ground wire made it easier and more reliable to create the ground wire path all the way back to the main panel box.

Ungrounded receptacles that experience a problem may use other paths to discharge voltage to ground, such as the metal cabinet or a person with damp shoes who touches a faulty appliance. This can present an annoying shock or become deadly, depending on the intensity of the problem.

Assessing Existing Conditions

- A simple electrical tester with the capability of detecting a ground should be used by the inspector when testing outlets.
- Checking for proper grounding in the panels will indicate if there is a problem to the outlets.
- Check for grounded wire and proper terminations.

Acceptable Practices

- Check the panels for ground paths. Main panels should have the panel, all neutrals, and all bare copper wires bussed to a ground wire leading to the ground stake and to the main plumbing line with a proper clamp and bridging any meter.
- There should also be a ground wire without splicing or interruption to at least one, preferably two, driven ground rods.

Figure 6.39 A driven rod or ground stake helps to discharge undesired electricity into the earth.

- The neutral wire providing service to the home should be directly wired at the pole on the street to a ground wire and driven rod as well.
- Antioxidant should be placed on all aluminum wires.
- Check that wires going to branch circuits contain a third wire that is specifically a ground. If not, check that the two wire systems maintain a ground by using the metal exterior of the sheathing with firmly attached conductive connectors, and that grounding of the device is made right to the outlet.
- Recommend that two-prong nongrounded outlets be upgraded to three-prong, and that larger appliance outlets for dryers and stoves be upgraded to newer grounded cords and outlets.

Practices to Avoid

- Do not touch the washer and dryer at the same time, because most dryers are not grounded. You could become the ground path.
- Do not touch disconnected or damaged metal conduit.
- Reaffirm the importance of grounding to your client.
- Don't forget to look for bonding wires on wet-location equipment such as hot tubs and pools. Check for GFCI protective circuits. Do test these and remember to reset them.

Switches

Description

Switching mechanisms add convenience and safety for many appliances. Switches at stairways allow the user to turn on a light from whatever direction they are going, using three- or four-way switching. Being able to kill the power with a switch allows convenient counter operation of appliances and remote lighting. Thermostat-controlled, motion-, light-, or heat-sensing switches can protect us, and humidistat controls can make us more comfortable. Switches for fans, speakers, and thermostats add to our comfort.

Assessing Existing Conditions

Testing a random number of switch units around the home will indicate deficiencies and safety levels. Your inspection is required by most standards to test at least one outlet and one switch in each room. In most cases, simply flipping the switch will be all that is required.

Figure 6.40 Wall switches allow us to locate controls where it is convenient. For the home inspector, it is not always obvious what controls what. Remember to reset all switches to the original setting when you are done.

Acceptable Practices

- Test wall switches, appliance switches, and countertop switches for use, noting deficiencies, lack of cover plates, and looseness of devices.
- Report broken and non-operational switches.
- Three-way and four-way switches can be tested by turning on switches at different locations, to make sure they operate properly.
- Dimmers should be tested and noted when noisy, hot, or not functioning. Dimmers not wired for three- or four-way locations will not allow the fixture to work properly in certain positions.

Practices to Avoid

- If any unsafe conditions result in the process of testing, turn the unit off and report it.
- Do not move switches that are taped or have notes attached that say not to turn them on.

Open, Overfilled, and Improper Boxes

Description

Electric boxes, wall and ceiling boxes, panels, and even the meter pan are all listed for specific use and can only contain so many energized wires.

Manufacturers rate the boxes and have them tested by UL. The restrictions or allowable loads, number of breakers, number of wires, and so on, are typically marked on the boxes. Junction boxes that contain too many wires can get too hot and melt the insulation. Dimmers and switches also can generate enough heat to melt or burn the wires. Boxes must be rated, have enough room, and have proper rated covers to protect the home and the homeowner.

Figure 6.41   Rated boxes are designed for a specific number of wires, specific gauges of wire, and a rated cover. Too many wires, or more than are rated for, will cause overheating. Overheating can cause insulation to deteriorate or burn.

Assessing Existing Conditions

- Look at junction, switch, and outlet boxes around the home.
- Note less accessible areas such as basements, attics, crawlspaces, and eaves.
- Note overfilled boxes. Note multiple wires entering boxes. Note open uncovered boxes as a hazard.

Acceptable Practices

- Report all deficiencies noted.
- Explain potential hazards.
- Recommend that a licensed electrician repair deficiencies.

Practices to Avoid

- The inspector is not required to open junction and connection boxes, switches, or outlets.
- These are visual inspections, with the exception of removing the deadfront panel.
- Do not do repairs; identify hazards and suggest that they be taken care of by a licensed electrician.

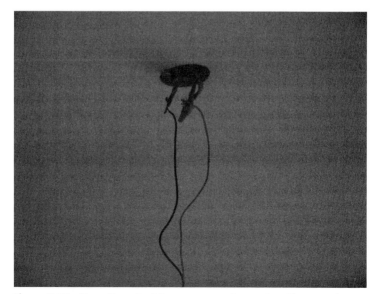

Figure 6.42 You will see foolishness on many inspections. Note unsafe conditions, and explain to your clients that practices like this can burn a home down.

Chapter 7

Heating and Air-Conditioning Systems

Hydronic (Hot Water) Heating

Description

A hydronic heating system includes a heat source, a fuel being used to raise the temperature of the water, a circulator to move the heated water to each area of the home to be heated, a radiator or system to transfer the heat from the water to the air, and safety equipment (auto-feed valves, check valves, expansion tanks, tridicator gauges, pressure relief valves, flow valves, and bleeder vents).

Hydronic heat simplified: The boiler heats the water to a preset temperature at the request of a heat call by the thermostat. Water can be heated by natural gas, propane, or oil. When the water is hot enough, the circulator turns on and moves the hot water to the radiator, the heat is transferred to the air currents in the room, and the cooler water returns to the boiler to be reheated. When the thermostat is satisfied,

Figure 7.1 Boilers create heat by burning a fuel in a chamber that transfers that heat to water, which is circulated to a radiator or a coil.

Figure 7.2 A group of four circulators, each controlling a "zone," is controlled by turning up a thermostat. The pump pushes the water around the loop.

the circulator/boiler turns off. Circulators typically move the water. Additional circulators or electronic zone valves can be added to increase the number of zones and give the homeowner greater control of the heating.

Hydro-air heat: The boiler heats the water to a preset temperature, in response to a heat call (thermostat controlled). When the water is hot enough, the circulator turns on and moves the water to a coil in an air handler, where a blower (large fan) forces air across a warm coil to send heat to the room from a register. The blower turns off when the coil has cooled and the thermostat is satisfied. While natural gas, propane, and oil are the more typical fuels, electric heat pump and electric resistance heating coils can be used.

Assessing Existing Conditions

The following conditions signal areas that may require further inspection:

- Leaks, signs of corrosion, burn marks, and missing or plugged equipment.
- Radiators that are missing (every habitable room requires a heat source).

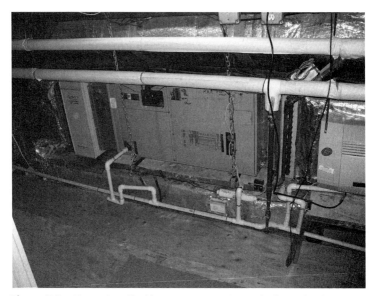

Figure 7.3 The air handler blower moves air across the heated coil, transferring the heat to the air and warming the air.

- Radiators that are too small in size or linear footage, or those with valves turned off.
- Auxiliary heating modes noted (extra electric plug-in heaters, kerosene heaters, etc.).
- Oil and gas smells, noisy operation, signs of soot, and intermittent cycling.

Types of Equipment

A properly set up hydronic heating system should have the following components:

- Circulators (usually one per zone; however, in some instances, several zones can be serviced by one circulator using thermostat-controlled zone valves)
- Flow control valves
- Purge/vent controls
- Electric zone valves
- Pressure relief valve
- Auto-feed and backflow preventer

Figure 7.4   This unit has had leakage issues as well as flame roll-out problems. Note burn markings and signs of corrosion.

Figure 7.5   This type of circulator pump requires annual lubrication to avoid bearings going bad.

Figure 7.6 These valves prevent water from circulating unless the thermostat is calling for heat.

Figure 7.7 A purge valve allows air to be removed (bled) from the piping.

Figure 7.8   Zone valves open and close when the thermostat calls for heat.

- Boiler with gas- or oil-burner pack
- Burn chamber and target board
- Stackpipe, draft hood, and/or barometric damper

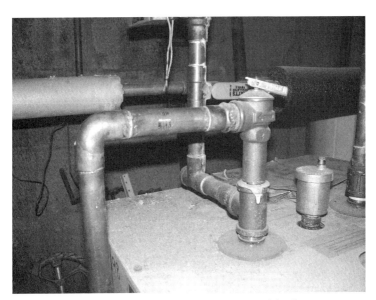

Figure 7.9   This safety device should be routed toward the floor.

Figure 7.10   The burner pack injects oil and air in a fine spray and ignites the mixture with a high-voltage spark.

Figure 7.11   Dilution or make-up air is drawn into the draft hood on gas fired systems to help the exhaust go up the chimney. Oil fired units use a barometric damper.

Acceptable Practices

Heating equipment is typically sized for the coldest day of the year. Registers for heating are best placed on the floor and on the outside walls.

Cooling registers work best on the ceiling.

Effective heat may be compromised by poor distribution, drafts, and moisture.

Thermostats

Older equipment—Mercury-containing controls: The thermostat is manually controlled using liquid mercury switches. If intact, these pose little danger. Local restrictions and recycling requirements may apply.

Newer equipment—Electronic controls may be battery operated or receive electricity from boiler or furnace controls. Most offer set-back and scheduling capability for energy conservation. Computerized sensors can turn zones on or turn off with some specialized equipment. Some thermostats simply open dampers or valves to allow heat to a different zone.

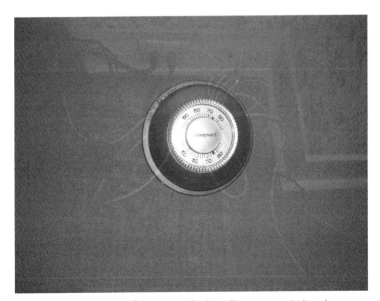

Figure 7.12 This type of thermostat had small mercury switches that would make electrical contact when turned.

Visual Inspection

- Is unit damaged? If so, recommend replacement/repair.
- Is unit level? If not, recommend repair.
- If unit is operating but showing signs of wear and tear, recommend service contract.
- If unit is beyond its life design, recommend replacement.

Test

1. Turn up 10 degrees F, and let run.

2. At boiler, continue inspection.

Hydronic Equipment

Visual Inspection

- Look for stains, corrosion, burn marks, and any leakage.
- Assess age and designed life; look for problematic equipment.
- Visually check for safety equipment:
  - Expansion tank
  - Pressure relief valve
  - Proper extension piping
  - Multiple zones and controls

Figure 7.13 This type of thermostat is programmable and allows the user to set comfort levels for different hours and days.

Figure 7.14 Hydronic systems, whether heated by gas or oil, can effectively heat even the largest home. Look closely for signs of damage or poor maintenance.

Figure 7.15 Carbon monoxide can make a family sick, or worse. Look closely for poorly installed hoods and smoke pipe. Make sure relief valves are piped correctly and that they terminate by the floor. Burn marks and soot can indicate poor combustion.

- Tridicator gauge
- Stackpipes, draft hoods, and connections
- Insulation on piping

Test

1. Run unit.

2. View combustion.

3. Look for soot, spillage, and poor drafting.

4. Listen to combustion noises and mechanical issues.

5. Feel pipes; when circulator is on, pipes should get warm.

Reporting

- For boiler units older than 15 years:
  - Recommend annual service contracts and maintenance checks. The projected life expectancy of most boilers is 15–25 years.
  - Oil pump pressure, if there is a gauge, should be about 100 pounds.

Figure 7.16 Unprotected oil lines can be damaged or crimped. Look for protective wrap or concrete around the piping that can easily become damaged.

- For furnace units older than 15 years:

  - Recommend annual service contracts, monthly filter changes, and annual service contracts. The projected life expectancy of most furnaces is 15–20 years.
  - Always recommend that the integrity of the heat exchanger be checked—by professionals—to avoid damage that can allow carbon monoxide to enter the home.
  - Always recommend carbon monoxide alarms, smoke detectors, and heat alarms.
  - Any stain, burn mark, or sign of corrosion should indicate need for a service call or a record of a recent service check.
  - Filters: 1-inch media, replace monthly; 6-inch media, every 3–6 months, depending on conditions; charcoal media, depending on manufacturer; electronic filters, monthly cleaning.
  - Oil-burning equipment needs annual cleaning, oil filter changes, and safety checks.
  - The smoke pipe should be pitched up toward the chimney thimble, and each section should be screwed together. The thimble section should be cemented in with high-temperature furnace cement.
  - Both oil and gas draft measurements should be checked annually.

Oil Tanks and Lines

- Indoor oil tanks are usually 275, 330, or 550 gallons in size. The tank for safety should be no closer to the boiler (or furnace) than 10 feet.
- Fuel lines for oil are usually $\frac{1}{2}$-inch copper and, because they can easily be crimped, they need to be protected from foot traffic.

Gas-Fired Equipment

Description

Probably one of the more popular types of home heating, gas-fired heating equipment uses natural gas or propane. Furnaces are also referred to as "forced air" heat. The fire produced by the gas warms a metallic heat exchanger, and air blown across the hot metal is heated and distributed as warm air through ducting. Gas is also popular for hydronic heat.

Gas flows through the regulator to a manifold to individual burner inlets.

A draft hood allows dilution air to help cool and drive hot exhaust up the chimney.

Figure 7.17 Blowing hot air around a home acts as a homogenizer. Air is constantly being recirculated, and dust, dirt, gases, and contaminants may not be adequately filtered out.

Figure 7.18　As the pressurized gas mixes with air, it heats the heat exchanger, and when the sensor gets hot enough, the blower circulates the warmed air.

Assessing Existing Conditions

Most gas has an odorant added so you can smell leaks.
For every cubic foot of gas, 1 cubic foot of dilution air and 1 cubic foot of combustion air are needed.
Most boiler/furnace rooms require 1 sq. inch of opening for air per 5,000 BTU.
When there are high and low vents, 1 sq. inch per 1,000 BTUs is required.
The lower vent is usually 6–8 inches off the floor.

Types of Equipment

A properly set up gas-fired forced-air heat system should have the following components:

- Blowers (air handlers)
- Limit switches
- Ducting, registers, and returns
- Electric damper-zone controls
- Burn chamber and target board
- Stackpipe and draft hoods

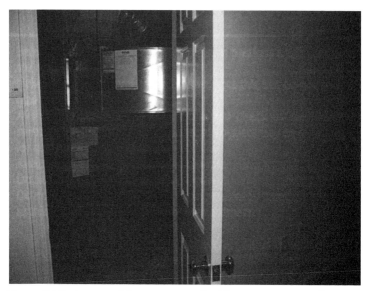

Figure 7.19 In parts of the country, gas-fired furnaces are a cost-effective and dependable means of heating a home. They have a designed life of 15–20 years.

Acceptable Practices

Three types of draft: (1) Atmospheric (usually open burn chamber, very hot exhaust); metal flue is typical. (2) Induced (typically more controlled burn chamber, with more complicated heat exchanger removing more of the heat from the exhaust, requiring a small fan to help induce the cooler exhaust up the chimney); smaller diameter but metal exhaust is typical. (3) Forced draft (higher efficiency units take even more heat out of the exhaust, requiring a very controlled enclosed burn chamber and primary and secondary heat exchangers); air intake and discharge are controlled with plastic piping and inducer fans. Additional sensors are typical, as are issues of voiding the condensate produced in these units.

Pans are required below the condensers and float switches on units installed on upper floors.

Units in an attic should have access hatches (minimally 20 × 30).

There should be a 24-inch-wide walkway and an area by the unit with a 30 × 24-inch working space with a service outlet, an emergency switch, and a light. The unit should not be more than 20 feet from the access hatch.

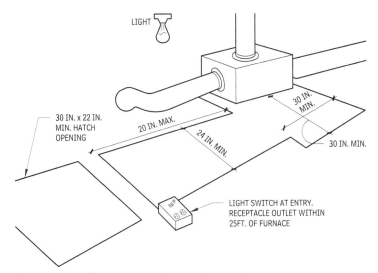

Figure 7.20 When a furnace is located in an attic space certain requirements must be met.

Thermostats

Older equipment—Mercury-containing controls. The thermostat is manually controlled to use liquid mercury switches to make contact. If intact, these pose little danger.

Newer equipment—Electronic controls may be battery-operated or receive electricity from the boiler or furnace controls. Most offer set-back and scheduling capability for energy conservation. Computerized sensors can turn zones on or turn off with some specialized equipment. Some thermostats simply open dampers or valves to allow heat to a different zone.

Visual Inspection

- If unit is damaged, recommend replacement/repair.
- If unit is not level, recommend repair.
- If unit is showing wear and tear, recommend maintaining with a service contract.
- If unit is beyond its life design, recommend replacement.

Test

1. Turn up 10 degrees F, and let run.

2. At furnace/air handler, continue inspection.

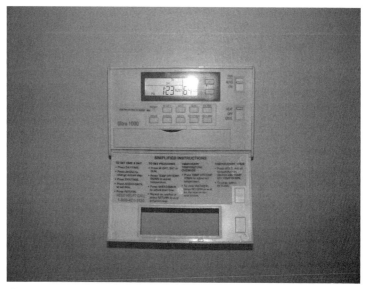

Figure 7.21   In order to make things easy, we always turn up the heat or turn down the cooling by 10 degrees. That way, we always know what to return it to.

Figure 7.22   Make sure filters are correctly sized, actually installed, and sealed with a cover so crawlspace or attic contaminants cannot enter.

Furnace

Visual Inspection

- Look for stains, corrosion, burn marks, and leakage.
- Assess age and designed life.
- Visually check for safety equipment.
- Look at blower—direct drive or belt.
- Inspect AC coils if accessible.
- Inspect auxiliary heating.
- Inspect limit switches.
- Inspect inducer fans.
- Inspect vacuum sensors.
- Inspect temperature sensors.
- Inspect emergency switches.

Test

1. Run unit.

2. View combustion area.

3. Look for soot, spillage, poor drafting, loose belts, and bad bearings.

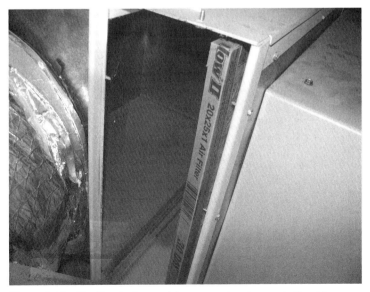

Figure 7.23 The filter is dirty and the access door is open in the attic missing a proper cover. Seasonally hot or cold air from the attic will take away from the unit's efficiency.

4. Watch flame for flicker and color.

5. Listen to combustion noises, mechanical issues, and short cycling.

6. Take temperature readings at register and return.

7. Check all safety equipment.

Reporting

- For furnace units older than 15 years, recommend annual service contracts and maintenance checks. The projected life expectancy of most furnaces is 15–20 years.
- Recommend monthly filter changes and annual service contracts.
- Always recommend that the integrity of the heat exchanger be checked to avoid damage that can allow carbon monoxide to enter the home. (This is usually outside the scope of a home inspection.)
- Deteriorated boxes, ducts, or flex ducting and disconnected pieces can take away from the efficiency and the safety of the unit.
- Always recommend carbon monoxide alarms and smoke and heat alarms.
- Any stain, burn mark, or sign of corrosion should indicate need for a service call or a record of a recent service check.
- Filters: 1-inch media, replace monthly; 6-inch media, every 3–6 months, depending on conditions; charcoal media, depending on manufacturer; electronic filters, monthly cleaning.

Steam Heat

Description

This is an older-technology heating system using one or two pipes to deliver steam to radiators. In many areas of the Northeast, this system is still prevalent.

One-pipe systems—The boiler makes steam, which travels up a riser to the radiator; air is released from the radiator until the valve senses the steam vapor and closes. Heat is given to the radiator, then to the air around it; as the steam in the radiator condenses, it changes back to hot water, and the condensate flows back down the same piping to be reboiled.

Two-pipe systems—The boiler makes steam, which travels up a riser to the radiator; air is released from the radiator until the valve senses the steam vapor and closes. Heat is given to the radiator, then to the air around it; as the steam in the radiator condenses, it changes back to hot water, and the condensate flows back to the return pipe, to the Hartford loop, and back to the boiler to be reboiled. Steam traps are used to avoid vapor returning to the boiler.

Assessing Existing Conditions

Steam boilers will have the following components:

- A sight glass, used to determine the height of the water in the boiler.
- A blow-off valve, in case of excessive pressure; set at 15 psi.
- A low water cut-off, as a safety in case the water level is too low.
- An automatic fill valve to raise the water level.
- A pressuretrol to gauge the pressure.
- A Hartford loop, a piping design to avoid a leak downstream of the boiler draining the water out of the unit.
- A blow-down valve to allow the owner to flush out sediment from the low-water cut-off.
- Steam is a low-pressure system; 0.5 to 5 psi is normal (typically 1–2 lbs).
- The gauge reads so low you might think it is broken.
- Automatic feeders were invented to avoid "boiling away" of the necessary level of water.
- Low-water cut-offs prevent boiler operation with too little water, known as a "dryfire."

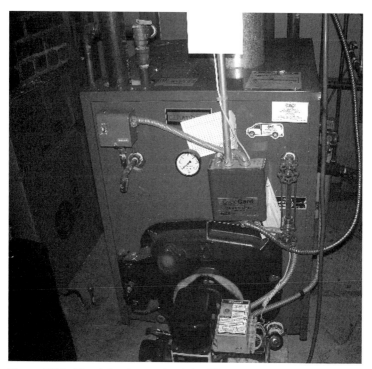

Figure 7.24 The sight glass on the right differentiates steam equipment from hot water.

Figure 7.25 Steam gauges often look broken because the reading is usually below 1 psi (which is normal).

- In the early days of steam, "firemen" were required to monitor fuel, water, and safety in larger buildings.
- The blow-off valve (pressure) is typically set at 15 psi (home inspectors do not test these).

▶ **BTU (British thermal unit):** Unit of energy needed to raise the temperature of one pound of water one degree Fahrenheit.

The following conditions signal areas that may require further inspection:

- Any leaks, drips, or stains.
- Lack of blow-off valve, auto-feed, low-water shutoff, or Hartford loop.
- Presence of asbestos insulation.
- Lack of insulation on the steam pipes.
- Valves in the off position.
- Cracks or damages.
- Spillage, damages to chimneys or stackpipes.
- Combustibles too close to unit.
- Noisy operation, cracking or banging noises.
- Gurgling or spitting.
- Radiators that do not heat up.
- Systems that are water-bound.
- Lots of rust and sediment in the water and sight glass.

Figure 7.26 A low-water cut-off has a float that operates when there is not enough water in the vessel; it automatically shuts down the heat till the water level is restored.

Acceptable Practices

Run steam systems early in the inspection because they take quite a bit of time to heat up the radiators.

Noisy operation may indicate service needs or required maintenance flushing.

Hissing of the air valves is appropriate.

Recycling on and off or surging is an indication that the unit needs service.

Retrofitted units may have both steam and hot water loops.

Steam Heaters

Visual Inspection

- If unit is damaged, recommend replacement/repair.
- If unit is not level, recommend repair.
- If there are signs of wear and tear, recommend an annual service contract.
- If unit is beyond its life design, recommend replacement.

Figure 7.27 This radiator is for steam. It is a one-pipe system with a steam vapor valve.

Test

1. Turn up 10 degrees F, and let run.

2. At boiler, continue inspection.

Steam Equipment

Visual Inspection

- Look for stains, corrosion, burn marks, and leakage.
- Assess age and designed life.
- Visually check for safety equipment.
- Look at relief valve (set for 15 lbs).
- Check for and examine condition of pressuretrol.
- Check for and examine conditions of sight glass.
- Check for radiator leaks, corrosion, and stains.
- Check for asbestos insulation.
- Inspect conditions of the Hartford loop. Look for corrosion, leaks, and damaged piping.
- Inspect condensate pump, if installed.

Test (at Boiler)

1. Run unit.

2. View combustion area.

3. Look for soot, spillage, poor drafting, and damages.

Figure 7.28 Steam units always have a sight glass. Most will have low-water cutoffs, a Hartford loop, and a pressuretrol.

4. Watch flame for flicker and color.

5. Listen to combustion noises, mechanical issues, and short cycling.

6. Take temperature readings at gauges and see if pipes get hot.

7. Check all safety equipment.

Reporting

- For steam units older than 15 years, recommend annual service contracts and maintenance checks. The projected life expectancy of most boilers is 15–25 years.
- Always recommend that the firebox area be checked to avoid damage that can allow the fire to damage the outer box. Look for burn-through and scorching.
- Deteriorated boxes, plumbing, and radiators and lack of insulation can take away from the efficiency and the safety of the unit.
- Always recommend carbon monoxide alarms, smoke detectors, and heat alarms.
- Any stain, burn mark, or sign of corrosion should indicate need for a service call or a record of a recent service check.

Figure 7.29 This simple set of fittings will prevent the boiler from losing all its water in case of a leak on the return side. This is what we call a Hartford Loop.

Electric Resistance Heat

Description

While not as desirable in many areas because of increased costs, electric baseboard heat is easy to care for and rarely breaks. Other than paying the electric bill and performing minimal maintenance, electric heat is almost maintenance-free.

Assessing Existing Conditions

Electric baseboard components:

- Radiators and covers
- A thermostat
- A circuit breaker

Acceptable Practices

Electric Heat

Visual Inspection

- If interior unit is damaged, recommend replacement/repair.
- Damaged fins can be repaired or replaced.
- Because the units get very hot, it is recommended that combustibles, bedding, and window treatments be kept away from electric heat.
- Convenience outlets should not be installed above these units because the insulation on cords can melt.

Test

1. Turn up 10 degrees F, and let them heat up.

2. Does the unit turn on when the thermostat is turned up?

Electric wall heaters: Test the same way. Look for proximity to combustibles and burn or scorch marks.

Electric Furnaces

Description

While not as desirable in many areas because of increased costs, electric furnaces can be effective when fossil fuels are not available. An electric furnace works with several banks of high-resistance heating coils that warm air blown across the elements. The heat is then circulated, just as with any fossil-fueled forced-air system.

Assessing Existing Conditions

Electric furnaces will have the following components:

- An air handler with a blower and filter.
- A bank of several electrically controlled heater elements.
- A circuit breaker.
- A high-limit switch and safety sensors.
- Newer units may have a safety interlock switch on the blower compartment.
- Registers and at least one return.

Figure 7.30 Testing the electric resistance heat requires an ammeter.

Acceptable Practices

Electric Furnaces

Visual Inspection

- If interior unit is damaged, recommend replacement/repair.
- If exterior air conditioning unit is not level, recommend repair.
- If there are signs of wear and tear on either unit, recommend an annual service contract. Note any damages.
- If either unit is beyond its life design, recommend replacement.

Test

1. Turn up 10 degrees F, and let run.

2. At furnace, continue inspection.

3. Does the blower kick on appropriately?

4. Is the filter installed? Is the filter sized properly, and is there an adequate cover for the filter area? Is the filter dirty? Dirty filters can slow air movement and damage the equipment.

5. Does the blower sound okay? It should turn smoothly with either a direct drive motor or fan belt. Excessive noise or squeaking or banging may indicate service needs.

6. Do the heater elements turn on? Is heat generated? Amps can be tested at the coils, or higher temperatures can be measured at the register.

Heat Pumps

Description

Heat pumps use refrigerant as the medium for the transfer of heat. When using the air outside to heat the refrigerant, the outside unit draws warm air over a coil, using a fan, and the coil (of cold refrigerant) absorbs the heat. The compressor pressurizes the gas and makes it even hotter. That hot refrigerant is sent inside to a second coil. As air from inside the home is drawn across the hot coil, it is heated and blown around the home. The now cooler refrigerant is sent back outside to absorb more heat.

A heat pump has a reversing switch and actually operates like an air conditioner in reverse in winter, and as an air conditioner in summer. Because it is not burning a fuel but rather transferring heat or cooling, significant savings can be made if the climate is moderate. Heat pumps

Figure 7.31 In many states where the climate does not achieve big temperature swings, using a heat pump can be very economical. In colder states, back-up heat must be used to ensure that comfortable temperatures are met. Back-up heat can be provided by high-resistance electric coils in the ducts or a gas- or oil-fired burn chamber.

are able to raise temperatures slowly. And it is often recommended that set-back-type thermostats not be used, but rather to pick a moderate temperature and not keep changing the settings.

Assessing Existing Conditions

Heat pump furnaces will have the following components:

- An air handler with a blower and filter.
- A bank of several electrically controlled heater elements (if the unit has back-up electric heat).
- A circuit breaker (for powering the electric heat).
- A high-limit switch and safety sensors.
- Newer units may have a safety interlock switch on the blower compartment.
- Registers and at least one return.
- Units using other types of back-up heat may have additional equipment.
- A thermostat with controls for heat and cool, fan auto and on, auxiliary heat (regular heat pump mode), and emergency heat (back-up heat).

▶ Note: In many condo complexes, the heat pump is the responsibility of the owner. As the life expectancy of these units is often only 7–13 years, look for evidence of multiple brands and differing equipment, if you wander the complex.

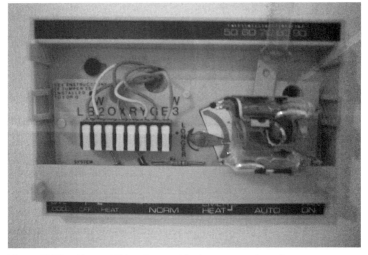

Figure 7.32   Note additional control for "emergency heat."

Acceptable Practices

Heat Pumps

Visual Inspection

- If interior unit is damaged, recommend replacement/repair.
- If exterior unit is not level, recommend repair.
- If there are signs of wear and tear on either unit, recommend an annual service contract. Note any damages.
- If either unit is beyond its life design, recommend replacement.

Test

1. Turn up 10 degrees F, and let run.

2. At furnace, continue inspection.

3. Run unit, and listen for blower fan issues.

4. Take differential readings; 15–25 degree differential is typical.

5. Heat pumps generally give off temperatures of about 95 degrees F. So the air may feel cool to someone testing the heat at the register by hand.

6. Take amperage readings on one leg of the electric element to determine if it is working.

Reporting

- For heat pumps units older than 15 years, recommend annual service contracts and maintenance checks. The projected life expectancy of most units is 7–13 years.
- Recommend monthly filter changes and annual service contracts, if available.
- Look for scorching around breakers and coils.
- Dirty filters and lack of insulation can take away from the efficiency and the safety of the unit.

Geothermal Heat Pumps

Description

As described in the preceding section, heat pumps use refrigerant as the medium for the transfer of heat. When they use the temperature of the soil and water stored below ground in a well, large tank, or pond, we call this process geothermal. The water in the earth is a constant at 55 degrees; running the water around the refrigerant coil will transfer its heat to the refrigerant and warm it. The compressor pressurizes the gas and makes it even hotter. That hot refrigerant is sent inside to a second coil. As air from inside the home is drawn across the hot coil, it is heated and blown around the home. The now cooler refrigerant is sent back outside to absorb more heat. Geothermal is felt

Figure 7.33   Often regarded as the fuel of the future, geothermal heating may, with tax incentives, encourage more people to make the higher initial investment to achieve long-term low-cost heating. Shown is a "slinky loop" of poly pipe that would be buried about 6 feet deep into the soil.

to be the heating system of the future because it does not use fossil fuel, except the electricity that runs the blower. The problem with geothermal heat is that installing tanks, drilling wells, or laying piping in ponds can be expensive.

A geothermal heat pump has a reversing switch and actually operates like an air conditioner in reverse in winter and as an air conditioner in summer. Because it is not burning a fuel but rather transferring heat or cooling, significant savings can result. Because it is using the heat of the earth, the long-term investment can achieve very economical heating and cooling costs. Geothermal heat pumps, like other heat pumps, are able to raise temperatures slowly. And it is often recommended that set-back-type thermostats not be used.

Assessing Existing Conditions

A geothermal heat pump furnace will have the following components:

- An air handler with a blower and filter.
- A heat exchanger and a circulator pump.
- A bank of several electrically controlled heater elements, if it has back-up electric heat. Units using other types of back-up heat may have additional equipment.
- A circuit breaker (for powering the electric heat, if it is installed).
- A high-limit switch and safety sensors.
- Newer units may have a safety interlock switch on the blower compartment.
- Registers and at least one return.
- A thermostat with controls for heat and cool, fan auto and on, auxiliary heat (regular heat pump mode), and emergency heat (back-up heat).

Acceptable Practices

Geothermal Heat Pump

Visual Inspection

- If interior unit is damaged, recommend replacement/repair.
- If there are signs of wear and tear, recommend an annual service contract. Note any damages.
- Are there any signs of leakage on plumbing, circulators, or equipment?
- Is unit beyond life design? If so, recommend replacement.

Test

1. Turn up 10 degrees F, and let run.

2. At furnace, continue inspection.

3. Run unit, and listen for blower fan issues.

4. Take differential readings, 15–25 degree differential is typical.

5. Heat pumps generally give off temperatures of about 95 degrees F. So the air may feel cool to someone testing the heat at the register by hand.

6. Take amperage readings on one leg of the electric element to determine if it is working.

Reporting

- For geothermal heat pump units older than 15–20 years, recommend annual service contracts and maintenance checks. The projected life expectancy of most units is 15–20 years.
- Recommend monthly filter changes and annual service contracts, if available.
- Look for scorching around breakers and coils, if the unit has electric back-up heat.
- Dirty filters and lack of insulation can take away from the efficiency and the safety of the unit.

Radiant Heating

Description

Radiant heating over the years has taken different forms. Levitt Homes on Long Island, in the 1950s, had slab-constructed homes with a centrally located hot water boiler. A circulator pushed hot water through the copper tubing in the slab. The slab home was warm and pleasant to live in. In the 1960s and 1970s, we saw both high-resistance electrical and circulated plumbing grids. For many years, silicone tubing and polybutylene piping were installed in ceilings, floors, and wall panels. Leaks, deterioration, and suspicion that leaks were inevitable created mistrust of the system. With the advent of cross-linked polyethylene, radiant heating is once again creating a new category of heating technique. Electric grid heating is being used under tile in bathrooms as well.

Assessing Existing Conditions

Radiant heat is controlled by a thermostat. It is usually located in the same room where the radiant heat has been installed. Equipment includes:

- A grid of electric resistance heating coils or a loop of hydronic tubing connected to a circulator and heated by a boiler.
- A circuit breaker (for powering the electric heat, if it is installed).
- A thermostatic zone valve and/or a circulator pump.
- A thermostat with controls for heat only.

Acceptable Practices

Radiant Heating

Visual Inspection

- Is there any visible sign of damage?
- Are there any signs of leakage on plumbing, circulators, or equipment?
- Is the thermostat working?

Test

1. Turn up 10 degrees F, and let run.

2. Using a laser thermometer, take wall, floor, and ceiling temperatures.

3. Be careful not to damage any equipment.

Reporting

- Check breaker if electric.
- Either the system reacts to the thermostat or it doesn't. Take temperature readings.
- If it's a water system, check for leaks and vulnerability to freeze-ups.

Wood and Coal Stoves

Description

Wood and coal stoves became very popular as an alternative to fossil fuels during the oil embargo of 1973–1974. People went out and bought wood furnaces, wood stoves, and coal stoves, and installed these units in their homes. Many were installed improperly and unsafely. As you inspect, look carefully for unsafe clearances and installations that can be hazardous.

Assessing Existing Conditions

Examine the stove for damage and signs of cracks, stains, and deteriorated gaskets; check for proper venting.

- Manufacturers of these stoves were required to determine the safe clearances from combustible walls, ceilings, and floors.
- Most units required a noncombustible floor below and minimum wall distances. Some units came with heat reflectors that could lessen the clearances when installed properly.
- Distance from the front door of the stove to the combustible floor was usually at least 18 inches.
- Flue piping could not be reduced in size.
- Firebreak collars were required between floors, and clearances from combustibles were specified, depending on the flue pipe used.

Acceptable Practices

Wood and Coal Stoves

Visual Inspection

- Is there any visible sign of damage?
- Are there any signs of leakage on flue piping?
- Is there a proper termination cap and an ash screen?

Test

- We do not test wood stoves.

Figure 7.34 Look carefully at clearances and potential safety issues. Your clients may need to report that they have a wood stove to their insurance company.

Reporting

- Check conditions.
- Look for damages and proper clearances.
- Suggest fire extinguishers, smoke detectors, and carbon monoxide alarms.
- Make sure the room has a secondary heating system.

Antiquated Systems

Description

The chances are good that, as you do your inspections, you will come upon some systems that should have been put out of their misery long ago, or sent to a museum—boilers covered with asbestos fibers, old gravity systems, and boilers that are still feeding one-pipe steam systems.

Know that the proper response should never be, "It's still got some life to it." Instead, advise that the unit has exceeded its designed life and should be replaced.

Assessing Existing Conditions

Examine the equipment for damages, signs of cracks, stains, deteriorated gaskets, unsafe materials, and improper venting.

- Look for asbestos material.
- Look for corrosion and damages from water.
- Look at distances from combustibles; look for scorching on metal surfaces.

Figure 7.35 Look carefully at clearances and potential safety issues. Your client may have trouble getting rid of these old systems.

- Look for unsafe or untested technology.
- Flue piping should be intact and in good shape; it should not be reduced in size.
- Look for poor circulation or pipes that are deteriorated.

Acceptable Practices

Antiquated Systems

Visual Inspection

- Is there any visible sign of damage?
- Are there any signs of leakage or soot?
- Is there a proper termination cap and an ash screen?

Test

1. Follow all safety guidelines.

2. If the system is off, do not turn it on.

3. Remember, most heating systems had a designed life of 15 to 30 years. Even if it is working, it may not have safety upgrades or be heating efficiently.

Figure 7.36   Old wall furnaces may not have safe pilot lights. They may have years of debris in them and may be too close to doors and combustibles.

Figure 7.37 Unsafe for kids and pets. There's really no way to make this safe.

Reporting

- Check conditions.
- Look for damages and proper clearances.
- Suggest fire extinguishers, smoke detectors, and carbon monoxide alarms.
- Make sure the client understands the implications of buying old technology.

New-Technology Systems

Description

There's always something new coming down the road that will require some analysis and some suspicion, but hopefully it will be backed with some intelligent building science.

Assessing Existing Conditions

Regardless of the technology, you will need to look at its external condition. In almost every instance, with home-oriented equipment, we start by looking for signs of deterioration, leaks, cracks, and poor maintenance. Upon closer examination, we look at function and safety. Is it doing what it was designed to do, and does it look as if it will continue to do so?

Once you have examined the exterior, the function, and the potential for operating as designed, you may need to get on the Internet quickly to determine what it is, and what it is supposed to do. There is no shame in telling your client that you have never seen this device before, and that you will get back to him or her ASAP with more information. Don't fudge or make something up. You cannot possibly know everything, especially about new technology.

- Some new items quickly catching on in homes are instant water heaters, both gas-fired and electric units. These seem to provide not only great energy savings but also a quick answer to getting hot water to a bathroom that's a long way from the water heater tank.
- Another item that is selling well is electric heaters in the configuration of a wood stove. It looks as if there is a fire, but it is actually a faux fire that looks great while electric resistance heat is being blown out from the unit.
- Another popular item is the ventless gas fireplace. These do not require a chimney. I am nervous about these, as I worry about bad sensors or some dynamic failing. With any failure homeowners can get sick—or worse. For years, we were told that kerosene heaters were safe indoors, and now we have found out that they do indeed give off lots of carbon monoxide, which can kill you.

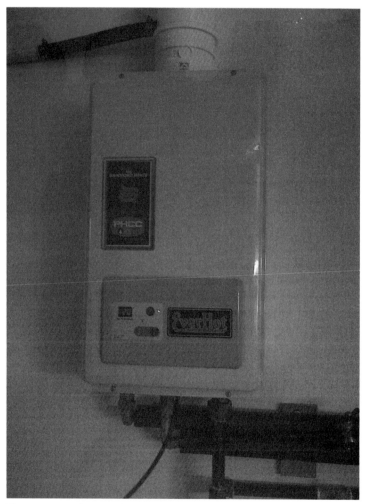

Figure 7.38 These tankless water heaters have become very popular, especially if a bathroom is distant from the water tank.

- New-generation programmable thermostats give the homeowner more flexibility to save by turning temperatures down around the clock.
- New adjustable-speed hydronic furnaces speed up or slow down depending on detectable speeds and restrictions of the ducting.
- One company has a microwave-heated instant water heater coming out this year.

Figure 7.39 Look carefully at clearances and potential safety issues.

Acceptable Practices

New Technologies

Visual Inspection

- Is there any visible sign of damage?
- Are there any signs of leakage or unsafe operation?
- Look at specifications and safety warnings.
- Be skeptical.

Test

- I do not recommend testing an items that is a mystery. Read up on it and approach it as new technology.
- Your search engine can be your best friend.

Reporting

- Check conditions.
- Look for damages and proper clearances.
- Suggest safety concerns.
- Make sure the room has a secondary heating system.

Air-Conditioning Split Systems

Description

Split systems have a condensing unit outside and a cooling coil or evaporator/air handler inside.

Through-the-wall split units are typically wall-mounted, with the condenser unit directly outside. They are usually zoned for small areas.

A package unit is usually a rooftop-mounted heat and cooling unit. They are often found on condos and used on most commercial applications.

Assessing Existing Conditions

Split Systems

- Remember that visual inspections are not technically exhaustive and require the inspector to look for signs of deterioration and deficiencies; they do not evaluate the equipment's capacity or reflect accurate balance around the home. Individual use of the home, and personal requirements of the new homeowner will affect their comfort needs. This is not an area the home inspector can project an opinion on. The inspector will use normal operating controls to test function but cannot establish how long the unit will operate (projected life expectancy).
- Check the condition of the interior air handler.
- Check for cosmetic damage that may be from wear and tear, lack of support, or vehicular damage (if the unit is in the garage).
- Look at the blower cover, duct seams, and the condition of the filter. Dirty filters can slow airflow, causing icing and affect the efficiency of the unit.
- Listen to the blower when it is operating. Some blowers are direct drive motors, and others run with a fan belt. Listen for bearing noises, imbalances, and obstructions.
- If the state of cleanliness of the unit is bad, it may suggest the need for service.
- Look at wiring for signs of melting, arcing, or rodent damage.

Figure 7.40 Split systems require an exterior unit and an interior unit, with suction and pressure lines connecting them.

Figure 7.41 Here are the outside units. Obviously, in this home there are two air handlers, so there are two exterior units. Unfortunately, the units are being crowded by the overgrown shrubbery, so trimming is critical to efficient use.

- Look at the condensate areas for signs of leakage. Is there a drain, a condensate pump? Is it plugged in? Generally does it look as if it functions?
- If there is a humidifier, is it clean and operational?
- With the blower on, search for signs of air leakage at seams around the plenum.
- At each register, feel for cooler air coming out. Using a laser thermometer can be helpful to speed up this process.
- Check the thermostat for proper operation, and test emergency switches to ensure that the unit turns off when switched.
- At the exterior unit, listen to the fan for odd noises. Bent blades, damaged grills, and cabinets that are deteriorating may indicate falling tree limbs, auto damages, or poor installation location.
- Look for the box to be level on a pad or slab, and not buried in mulch.
- Look for service disconnects within eyesight, preferably near—but not blocked by—the equipment. Make sure wires are neatly installed and not lying on the soil.
- Look for impingement caused by shrubs or decks, and determine that the unit is not too close to the home, or other units. Good airflow is critical around the condensing units.
- Make sure dryer vents are not too close to the inlet vents to the cabinet, because the moisture and lint will clog the unit.

Figure 7.42 Although they are noisier, high-velocity ducts and nozzles can get air conditioning to many rooms thought impossible to cool in the past.

High-Velocity Split Systems

- Using smaller-diameter ducting and faster fans, high-velocity systems make it easier to retrofit older homes and places where ducting is difficult.

Through-the-Wall Split Units

- Look at conditions on the inside unit. Look for signs of damage, leakage, and wear and tear.
- Examine all visible refrigerant lines and wiring. Look for gaps where lines enter the home.
- Examine the exterior unit. Look for damages, a level base, and signs of deterioration.
- Make sure there is a disconnect within eyesight, preferably near—but not blocked by—the equipment.
- Look for impingement caused by shrubs or decks, and determine that the unit is not too close to the home, or other units. Good airflow is critical around the condensing units.
- Make sure dryer vents are not too close to the inlet vents to the cabinet, because the moisture and lint will clog the unit.

Figure 7.43 Smaller in size than regular registers, there may be several ducts entering a medium-size room.

Figure 7.44 These units are designed for single-room applications. The inside part is generally hung on the wall.

Package Units

- Though rarely found on residential single-family units, package units are commonly found on low sloped rooftop applications and may be found on condo complexes where room in the condo unit is not dedicated to heating and cooling.
- Examine the unit carefully for deterioration and wear and tear.
- As these units are exposed to the weather year-round, your visual inspection may detect water, sun, and wind damages.
- Look at clearances from intake and exhaust and from surrounding equipment.
- Check filters and accessible ducting.
- Look for safety shutoff switches or breaker disconnects.
- If the unit has a heating system, this should be tested as well, weather permitting.

Air-Conditioning Heat Pumps

Description

Common in many warm climates and very typical on small homes and condos, electric heat pumps can provide both cooling and heating, using refrigerant and back-up emergency heating during the colder months.

- These are split systems with added equipment that includes a reversing valve to redirect the refrigerant during change of operation from heating to cooling, to take heat from outside and release it inside.

Figure 7.45   Since the heat pump will be working throughout the winter, we need to raise units in snow areas, or provide feet for them to keep them out of the snow.

- Heat pumps are usually installed with feet to raise the exterior box out of potential snow and ice.
- Heat pumps in colder climates will have a back-up, or "emergency or auxiliary heating mode" that can be controlled at the thermostat.
- While electric resistance coils are common, gas or oil could be used as the back-up heating system. Electricity used for heating is usually expensive to run.
- Check as you would for a regular air-conditioning split system.
- Test functions on thermostat to make sure back-up heat and air conditioning work properly.
- Check for exterior disconnects and emergency switches inside.
- Examine the boxes for wear and tear.
- With an ammeter, heating elements can be tested in back-up if that is part of your inspection. A 220 unit, when operational, will draw approximately 20–22 amps.

Figure 7.46 Through-the-wall units are installed in a sleeve and give the same benefit as a window unit, without using a window for the hole.

Figure 7.47 Individual room units are often outside the standards, because they are considered portable units. However, looking at the safety of the installation may save a life or avoid a bad situation. Make sure it cannot easily fall out of the window.

Single-Room Through-the-Wall Units

- These units are self-contained and should be examined for signs of damage, wear and tear, and leakage.
- They should fit the built-in sleeve to avoid leakage of air or water around the unit.
- Filters on the unit should be checked for cleanliness.
- Use normal controls to test operation of all features. (Some will have multiple speeds, fan only, high and low cooling, and some may incorporate heating modes as well.)
- Life expectancy of these units can be 10–15 years, depending on use.

Window Portable Units

- Although not required by most standards, portable window units can be evaluated by the inspector when they are installed in a window.
- Look for signs of deterioration and wear and tear.
- Look to make sure the unit is fastened in a safe manner to the window sash, frame, and any other parts, so that it will not unexpectedly drop if the window position is shifted.
- Look at the cord, plug end, and receptacle for signs of deterioration, melting, or burns.
- Check the filter for cleanliness.
- Operate normal controls to determine if the unit is working.
- Life expectancy of these units can be 10–15 years, depending on use.

Acceptable Practices

- Air conditioning can be critical in hotter climates, and the life expectancy of the units may be dramatically shortened by longer seasonal use. Weather and localized damages can also shorten the life of the equipment.
- A typical AC exterior unit has a designed life of 15–20 years. Some units are stamped with the date of manufacture; many dates are coded into the data plate. Although a unit may last longer, there is no way to predict how long a unit will last before it should be replaced. Older units using Freon® as a refrigerant are still legal, but more environmentally friendly refrigerants are replacing these units.
- Checking temperature differentials is the best way to determine the effective cooling operation. To find the differential, measure the temperature at the register and the return on split units; for wall units, take a reading at the discharge point and a reading in another point in the room. Usually a temperature spread of at least 15–20 degrees is a normal expectation. Filter cleanliness, blocked air vents, and loose fan belts may all have an effect.

Figure 7.48 Look for rust and cabinet deterioration; these tend to last less than 15 years.

- Recommending annual service contracts is always a good idea, and immediate service is recommended if deficiencies are noted. Filter changes should be recommended on a 4–6 week basis with thin filters, and every 6 months with media filters; monthly cleaning should be recommended with electronic units.

Practices to Avoid

- Obviously, be careful. Do not touch anything that is electrified. When checking any of these units, only operate them with normal operating controls, and do not turn on breakers or disconnects if they have been turned off by others. Turning on a breaker on a unit that is being serviced by others or one that has been purposely turned off can cause additional damage, electrocution, or fire.
- When doing your exterior perimeter inspection, look at the equipment for physical damage or signs of service needs before you run it.

Figure 7.49 Dryer vents too close to air-conditioning units will cause lint to clog the coils.

- Note levelness and the condition of the disconnect. If a unit is held in place on a wall or window, look for adequate support.
- When running units, do not stand directly in front of wall and window units when you turn them on for the first time, because dust, debris, and moldy air may come right at you.

Reporting

General Information

- A normal-sized house (approx. 1600–2000 sq. feet) will require approx 2.5 to 3 tons of cooling: 30K–36K BTU in New England, more down south.

Figure 7.50 Route water away from the unit to avoid wet pans and damaged ceilings.

- Refrigerant lines: The larger tube is the "suction" line, which is typically insulated and is cold. The thinner line is the liquid line and is warm to the touch (about 90 degrees F). In most cases, on the bottom of the box for the AC coil will be a PVC tube (usually ¾-inch in diameter), which is the condensate drain.
- Cooling coils can be A-shaped or flat coils.
- Condensate pumps can be used to pump water away from the unit to a spot where it can be safely discharged. Condensate is considered clean water, and it should not be directly discharged into a waste pipe without an air gap.

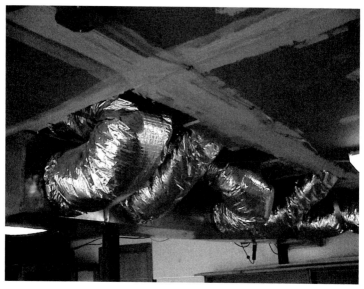

Figure 7.51 Ducts in a garage should be steel ducting or flex ducts boxed in drywall to prevent carbon monoxide from entering the home.

Chapter 8

Interiors

Interior Doors

Description

Interior doors and windows offer ventilation, security, and access. Obviously, proper operation indicates good installation, but poor operation may raise questions about structural shifting, expansion or contraction from moisture, or poor workmanship. The inspector is required to operate random doors and windows throughout the home as a matter of standards. Random testing may miss a problem, so we urge checking the operation of all accessible units.

Interior doors should close properly and latch for privacy. Doors that rub may indicate swelling and higher moisture conditions within the home. Gaps at the top that taper may indicate structural movement. Gaps at the bottom may indicate that the door is allowing return air to circulate or that the door was undercut too high.

Closet doors may have friction closers or magnetic latches. Typical locksets may need striker plate adjustments and/or just need tightening of the hardware over time.

The interior features of exterior doors need to be examined as well. The inspector should look especially carefully for security hardware, latching issues, weather-stripping details, and energy efficiency on exterior doors. Insects are more prone to attack wood doors in climates where termites are in abundance.

Assessing Existing Conditions

Interior Doors

- Check the physical condition of the door. Are panels broken, surfaces cracked, broken, or patched? Is the lockset loose, damaged, or missing?
- Look at hinges. Are there enough for the weight of the door? Are there screws loose or missing?
- Does the door hit obstructions, or does it close properly?
- Does it rub, stick, or hang up on trim or jamb?
- Is there too much gap on top, bottom, or sides?
- Does it latch properly and lock, if it is a bedroom or bathroom?

Figure 8.1   Properly weather-stripped, solid entry doors can really make a big difference to both energy efficiency and security. Check gaskets and latching effectiveness.

- Does it make noise when opening or closing?
- Interior doors should not swing in over a stairwell drop without a landing.

Figure 8.2   Look at gaskets and weather-stripping for damages or missing sections.

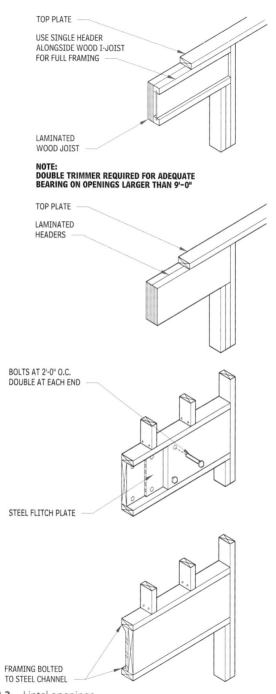

TOP PLATE

USE SINGLE HEADER
ALONGSIDE WOOD I-JOIST
FOR FULL FRAMING

LAMINATED
WOOD JOIST

NOTE:
DOUBLE TRIMMER REQUIRED FOR ADEQUATE
BEARING ON OPENINGS LARGER THAN 9'-0"

TOP PLATE

LAMINATED
HEADERS

BOLTS AT 2'-0" O.C.
DOUBLE AT EACH END

STEEL FLITCH PLATE

FRAMING BOLTED
TO STEEL CHANNEL

Figure 8.3 Lintel openings.
Source: AIA, *Architectural Graphic Standards*, Eleventh Edition. Copyright 2007, John Wiley & Sons, Inc.

Figure 8.4 When one side of a jamb settles, it can change the position of the door and effect how it closes and latches.

Pocket Doors

- Pocket doors are often problematic in operation and flimsy in construction. Examine tracks, wheels, and hardware.
- People may hang photos or artwork that can protrude into the door damaging the surface or stopping it from opening or closing.
- Latches may be tricky to engage or lock.

Closet Doors

- Check latching mechanisms and/or locksets.
- Slider doors need floor guides.
- Rollers on bypass doors may be damaged, missing, or in need of adjustments.
- On louvered doors, check for damaged or missing louvers.
- Some mechanical and magnetic doors require pushing to unlatch.
- Glass doors should be tempered.

Doors to a Garage

- Many municipalities require a fire-rated door.
- Operable windows or screens are usually prohibited.

Figure 8.5 Pocket doors offer a functional degree of privacy when door-swing room is limited. Unfortunately, these doors tend to be problematic and fragile. Check operation, look for damages, and check latching mechanisms.

Figure 8.6 Sliding closet doors can easily fall out of their upper track if the lower guides are loose, broken, or missing. This can be a real danger to children pulling on a slider door.

Figure 8.7 Sometimes it is very difficult to tell if glass is tempered. Warn clients that nontempered glass can shatter and leave large shards that can be dangerous.

- Weather-stripping to keep fumes in garage from entering the home is a safety suggestion.
- A step down to the garage floor is recommended to keep flammable liquids from flowing into the home.

Acceptable Practices

Test as many interior doors as possible, because each may have differing problems or damages. Opening random doors is a setup for problems.

- Be aware of differing door sizes and heights. Report custom sized (small) as they may be problematic with access for wheelchairs and furniture.
- Check door swing and see if doors hit toilets, shower doors, cabinets, and the like. Look for doorstops.
- While it is common practice to undercut doors for air movement, cutting the doors too short can be a problem, and adding high pile carpet might block air movement.
- Look for settlement, rubbing, or sticking; all indicate problems.

Figure 8.8   Some municipalities require metal or solid rated doors to the garage. None should have windows that open. Some require self-closing door spring hinges or a closer.

Figure 8.9   Test operation of doors. Many will rub, which may indicate settling or movement. Make sure locksets latch and hardware is working.

Figure 8.10 In this photo you can see lead caning and broken glass. Both potential concerns should be reported.

Practices to Avoid

- Do not force or pry open a door. Write it up. If access was blocked, note that in your report. Unlocking areas may expose you to unexpected hazards or require you to protect or take responsibility for what has been locked up.
- Be careful with locksets. Keys may not be available.
- Watch ladder placement near doors.
- Pocket doors and sliders may fall off their track. Be gentle with them.

Windows

Description

Window technology has gone through many advances over the last 30 years, and today's windows may be single glazed, dual glazed, or even triple glazed. Some may have external or interior storm windows, and others have reflective materials or special gases held between the panes for improved reflectivity, privacy, and/or energy efficiency.

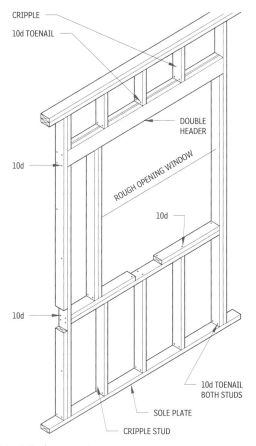

Figure 8.11   Window opening.
Source: AIA, *Architectural Graphic Standards*, Eleventh Edition. Copyright 2007, John Wiley & Sons, Inc.

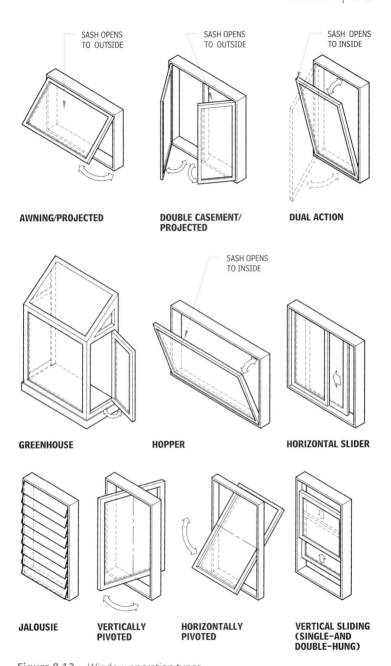

Figure 8.12 Window operation types.
Source: AIA, *Architectural Graphic Standards for Residential Construction.* Copyright 2003, John Wiley & Sons, Inc.

Figure 8.13 Newer-technology wood and vinyl replacement windows greatly reduce the potential concern for lead dust generated by the window surfaces rubbing.

Differing styles of windows require slightly different testing technique to open and close, but it is critical to open and close them to determine conditions. Bad operators, missing hardware, and rotted sections all become obvious when the window is tested.

Missing locksets, indications of alarm sensors, torn screens, and lack of weep drain holes all should be reported.

Bad glazing, damaged gaskets, broken glass, and missing screens can all lead to additional costs for the homebuyer.

Definitions

Panes or *lites*—Glass pieces inserted in the window.

Sashes—These hold the panes. Some sashes move up and down; others tilt or are hinged.

Stiles—The sides of the sash.

Rails—The top and bottom of the sash.

Muntins—Small pieces (usually wood) that separate multiple panes in a sash.

Jambs—The trim on the sides of the window frame.

Sill—The bottom of the window frame.

Dual pane— A sealed window consisting of two panes of glass and a seal between them.

Triple-glazed—A window is triple-glazed when an additional pane is added to the Thermopane.

Fogging—This occurs when moisture gets into the void between the glass and fogs the visibility.

Assessing Existing Conditions

- Look for damages. Broken or cracked glass or missing layers of glass may or may not be obvious.
- Look for seal damages. Moisture trapped between glass surfaces may etch the glass and fog it, making it undesirable. These may require replacement.
- Operate the opener, unlatching latches, if they have tilt-in features or security latches. Test all features to ensure good operation.
- Look at the hardware to see if it is dirty, rusty, or damaged.
- Look at wood and trim details for signs of air or water intrusion.
- Look for square and plumb. (Although this is not part of the standards, a poorly installed window may be an indicator of additional deficiencies that may not have been seen by a building official.)

Figure 8.14 When moisture is drawn into the center of a Thermopane window, the moisture can cause fogging and etching of the glass.

Figure 8.15   It is not always cost-effective to replace cracked glass unless it is deemed to be a hazard.

Acceptable Practices

- Most home inspection requirements and state statutes under most home inspector regulations require that random windows be tested, often at least one per room. We recommend that you test as many as possible during your inspection.

Practices to Avoid

- Remember, skipping a window may allow you to meet the standards but miss a problem. Try to operate as many as possible.
- Skylights often look as if they leak because of condensation. Don't misinterpret the signs of water entry.
- Don't ignore damaged or missing window locks, loose sashes, and/or bad glazing (loose or missing putty).
- Although fogged glass is more a cosmetic than a weatherization issue, replacing the glass will be expensive. Note fogged windows.
- Locations that require tempered glass should have it, or you should recommend upgrading for safety.
- Don't force or use tools to open windows that are painted closed.

Figure 8.16 Remember that windows that open outward may restrict walking areas or become a hazard. Some upper-floor windows may be low to the floor, requiring tempered glass and child fall protection.

Figure 8.17 As warm air rises it can condense on the cold skylight lens and drip. This is not a leak, but dripping and water stains might lead the unaware to that conclusion.

Wall Surfaces

Description

Interior wall surfaces may be drywall that has been painted, or plaster if the home is older. Paneling, wainscoting, and wallpapered surfaces, though cosmetic in nature, all impact the value of the home. As a result, reporting conditions may surpass required standards, but it will be appreciated by your client. Tile, veneers, and unusual surface coverings such as fabric or wall-mounted carpet may make visibility difficult. When this occurs, try to limit your liability (if any exists) by reporting the wall surface and the resulting inaccessibility. Paint conditions often indicate housekeeping conditions, lack of maintenance, and potential leaks at stained areas. Plaster can decay and exhibit cracks and calcification problems. Tile can crack or need grout and sealant. Many of these signs are symptoms of other issues.

Figure 8.18 Check hidden areas behind furniture and draperies. While many cracks are merely cosmetic, they do give you information about changes taking place within the home.

Assessing Existing Conditions

- Look carefully at doors, windows, and areas where loading of the structure may show signs of settling or cracks. While many cracks found in a home are superficial, some cracks may indicate undersized support, shifting, or settling and may require intervention by an engineer. In some cases, drywall will shift from moisture content changes, and the outer paper may tear diagonally. As your experience level increases, you will be more comfortable with these judgment calls.

Acceptable Practices

- Look at wall surfaces for any signs of distress, paint or tile damage, and stains. Photograph and/or report findings in your report.
- Any cracks of substance may be the result of shrinkage or settling. Movement may indicate structural issues and require an engineer's opinion.

Figure 8.19 Cracks caused by expansion and contraction often will rip the paper on the drywall. Many times these are superficial.

Practices to Avoid

- Level and plumb are desirable in a home but rarely found after a few years, as a result of normal settling, shrinkage, and movement. If the conditions found are compromised, that may not mean there is a chronic problem.
- The inspector should remember and remind the client that the inspection is a snapshot in time and that conditions will change.
- Excessive movement should always be reported and an engineer consulted.

Interior Finishes

Description

Interior finishes include painted drywall, plaster, tile, paneling, wallpaper, wainscoting, veneers, and textured materials. Fabrics and other materials can create interesting variations.

While typically cosmetic in nature, interior finishes can offer clues to conditions within the home from a whole gamut of conditions. These include, but are not limited to, water intrusion, contaminants, movement or settling, or building components simply deteriorating over time.

Assessing Existing Conditions

- Look carefully for signs of moisture, leakage, condensation, or stains.
- Remember that the previous cause of the deterioration may no longer exist, and the condition may now be simply cosmetic. Conversely, you may be looking at old stains and find new damage from a new source.

Figure 8.20   Look for movement, poor workmanship, and previous damages.

- Holes may be the result of physical damage (from the inhabitants) or may be the result of intrusive forensic repairs. Getting histories from tenants or owners may give you needed information.
- The inspector should formulate questions to ask that help him or her to understand any damages or previous repair history.
- Cracked tile may indicate movement, poor surface preparation, or bad substrates. Bouncy floors and floor systems that are too thin are apt to crack tile and stone.

Acceptable Practices

- Scan each room's wall surface with a good light, looking for damage and deterioration. Note drywall seams and cosmetic variations.
- Note cracks, splits, and stains. Be suspicious of paint touch ups and fresh paint.
- Note peeling paint, plaster fractures, cracks, and deteriorating materials.

Figure 8.21 Indicators of exterior leakage. Moisture meters can further help to determine if the water is actively entering.

Figure 8.22   More indications of temperature and moisture swings.

Practices to Avoid

- Don't move so quickly that you miss the clues to conditions you must find in each room. Check doors, windows, ceilings, walls and floors carefully.
- Don't forget to look inside and up at the ceiling areas in closets for signs of previous damage that may not have been fixed.
- Don't move furniture or wall hangings, but do look at areas of concern. Sometimes just getting closer to the wall or near the furniture will alert you to additional problems.

Ceilings

Description

Ceiling surfaces deteriorate rapidly as moisture leaks through. Plaster will fracture and discolor, metals will rust, and paneling will sag. Often the ceiling is the spot you will find the damage, and a problem is hard to ignore when the ceiling is dripping, sagging, or falling around the inhabitants. Most homes will have some staining over time, which may indicate a more chronic leak or a previous situation. New materials may represent new potential problems—for example, drywall imported from China (known to have high levels of sulphides) or some latex paints that may not meet longevity expectations.

Assessing Existing Conditions

- Look for water stains, plaster fractures and cracks, delaminating materials, and warping or sagging.
- Use of a bright flashlight and closely evaluating the perimeter edges may define subtle stains or damage.

Figure 8.23 Coffered ceilings may or may not be structural. Look for sagging, cracks, and stains.

Figure 8.24 Plaster fractures are difficult to hide cosmetically. They may indicate that the keys behind have broken and that the ceiling could crack further and fall.

- Drop or suspended ceilings will have to be checked by lifting random tiles, if possible.
- Metal ceilings may have rust, corrosion, or paint deterioration indicating a problem.

Acceptable Practices

- This is purely a visual assessment, and in most cases the inspector will not be using instrumentation to test.
- If there are any active leaks, or concern that there may be an active leak, the inspector may choose to use a moisture meter or thermal infrared camera. These go beyond the standards.
- Use a voltage sniffer on metal ceilings before coming into contact with them, to avoid a shock potential.

Practices to Avoid

- Use care with suspended ceiling tiles. Debris may fall from tile or above it. Some rodent fecal material may be on the tile as well.
- Avoid damaging the tiles.

Figure 8.25 Bathroom ceilings may get wet from the shower, from steam, from outside, or from above. Ask the owners for the story.

- Avoid making recommendations for upgrading the electrical service or older equipment, unless the client hints that he or she will be increasing the usage from what the norm has been in the home previously.

Flooring

Description

The perceived value of many homes is tied directly to the installation of hardwood floors. But in recent years, woods of many species, as well as a wide range of veneers, vinyls, and "floating floors," have been used to improve the look and comfort of our homes. Ceramic tile, glazed and unglazed flooring, and all kinds of natural stone have also become very popular. Wall-to-wall carpeting and area rugs are very common and make inspecting somewhat more difficult, as the conditions below are not visible.

Assessing Existing Conditions

Inspection of floor surfaces really deals with identifying the flooring, establishing the stability of it, looking at physical conditions, and looking for damages.

Figure 8.26 Look for scratches, gouges, patching, loose tiles, and cracks. Sometimes just by walking on a floor, you'll know there's a problem. Lift carpets and rug edges to be sure.

Figure 8.27 Watch transitions between rooms for trip hazards.

Acceptable Practices

- Walking the floor while listening for creaks and squeaks, noting loose floorboards, and observing any physical damage such as stains, burns, or scratches is part of a regular home inspection.
- Determine if the materials were poorly installed or if they are deteriorating in such a manner as to require an expensive replacement, and mention this in your report.
- Levelness and molding gaps are frequent concerns with older homes. Your inspection should note damages, poor workmanship, and irregularities.
- Some clues to determining if there is hardwood flooring beneath carpeting are to look at registers in the floor for heat and air conditioning. Another is to lift a corner of carpet in the closet to see what is below it. A less destructive way is to ask the owner.
- Be sure to lift corners of area rugs to check floor conditions.

Figure 8.28 Tapping on the tiles lightly may give you a hollow sound if they are loose.

Figure 8.29 Cracks below ceramic tile are often caused by floor shifting. Thickening the floor with additional plywood is often the best fix when tile is removed.

Practices to Avoid

- Do not drag tools or furniture across the wood floors.
- When there are wall-to-wall carpets, do not forget to explain the visibility limitations.
- Don't move too fast … Look at tiles carefully. Look for finish damage, cracks, loose adhesives, and sloppy installations.

Figure 8.30   New carpeting may be hiding old stains, burns, scratches, and different species of wood flooring. If there is no visibility, report this.

Staircases, Handrails, and Guardrails

Description

Staircases allow us to travel safely from floor to floor, when they are built in a standardized manner and allow for minimal variation in riser height and tread width. When there are more dramatic variations, the stairs become more difficult to traverse and less safe. Handrails are typically required on stairs that have three or more treads, but safety inspectors may feel more comfortable recommending handrails whenever they feel that a handrail will upgrade the safety of the stair.

Basic components of a staircase include risers, treads, stringers, and handrails. Stringers are the diagonal supports that tie the stairs to the landings. These can be wood, metal, or composite materials. Additional stringers are added as the width of the stair increases.

Figure 8.31 Check balusters, looking for loose handrails, uneven risers, and proper support below.

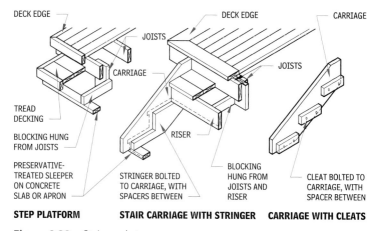

Figure 8.32 Stairs and steps.
Source: AIA, *Architectural Graphic Standards*, Eleventh Edition. Copyright 2007, John Wiley & Sons, Inc.

Spacing between guardrail spindles or balusters should not allow a 4-inch sphere to pass through. Older requirements allowed larger gaps that were found to allow a child's head to become stuck, and potentially dangerous situations could occur.

Guardrails should be between 36 and 42 inches high, and no openings should allow the four-inch ball to pass through.

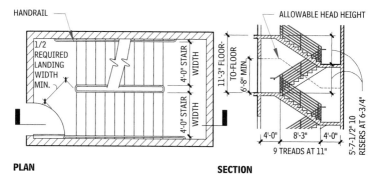

Figure 8.33 Residential stair design.
Source: AIA, *Architectural Graphic Standards for Residential Construction*. Copyright 2003, John Wiley & Sons, Inc.

Figure 8.34 Handrails are required when there are more than three treads. For safety, any step benefits from a handrail.

Assessing Existing Conditions

- Examine the stairs for stability and construction.
- Railings should be fastened and not loose.
- Balusters should be secured and not loose.
- Risers should be consistent and not vary more than ³/₈ of an inch.
- Maximum riser height should not exceed 8 inches.
- Minimum tread depth (also called run) should be 8¼–9 inches.
- Minimum tread width should be ½ inches.
- Minimum stairway width should be 34–36 inches.
- Minimum ceiling height in a stairwell is 6 feet, 5 inches to 7 feet—the higher the better for comfort and moving furniture.
- Doors should only swing in when there is a landing, not over a stairway. If there is no landing, the door should swing out, opening away from the stairs.
- Winder stairs (with pie-piece–shaped treads) are found in many older homes, though rarely on the "main" staircase. Winders can be dangerous if there are treads that reduce in size to less than 6 inches on the inside edge. Stairs like these to basements or attics may limit access for storing larger items.

Figure 8.35 Newer requirements deem that there should be at least 6 inches of tread at the narrowest point, but many older stairs fade to a point. Winders can be very dangerous, as a slip can bring you right to the bottom.

- Spiral staircases are really winders as well, and should only be used as a secondary access, because of fire safety concerns. However they have been very popular as the primary access to lofts and attic living spaces.
- Railings are usually required on stairs where there are more than two treads. They are required to be installed 34–38 inches measured from the bullnose.
- Handrails should be rounded or oval, and should be mounted at least 36–42 inches high. Most codes require railings to return to the wall to avoid catching purse straps or leashes.
- Bullnose projections shall be a minimum of 1½ inches.
- Stairs with more than six treads will have a light switch at the top and bottom on the wall near the handrail, at a convenient height.

Acceptable Practices

- Look at staircase components that are visible and accessible to determine conditions.
- Note shaky, squeaky, and bouncy conditions.
- Note variation in the rise and run, and any trip or stumble hazards.

Figure 8.36 As I climb the steps, I tap on each spindle and try to move the rail. Openings larger than 4 inches are unsafe for small children.

- Note cracked treads, loose handrails, openings in guardrails, loose guardrails, and so forth. Photograph and/or report findings in your report.

Figure 8.37 Bulkhead steps often leak water, and seepage and efflorescence are frequently found.

Practices to Avoid

- Do not use excessive force against handrails or guardrails as this may damage them.
- Some clues to determining if there is hardwood flooring beneath carpeting are to look at registers in the floor for heat and air conditioning. Another is to lift a corner of carpet in the closet to see what is below it. A less destructive way is to ask the owner.
- Be sure to lift corners of area rugs to check floor conditions.
- Don't forget access to finished attic and basement bedrooms may require additional egress windows, doors, or staircases.
- Do not damage spiral staircases with your tools when climbing.

Living Spaces

Description

Inspecting "living spaces" in a home—that is, living rooms, bedrooms, dens, and dining rooms—requires the same skills, with a focus on the priorities and some specialized equipment that may be typical in these rooms.

Breaking down the significant items necessary to inspect in all these rooms: The inspector would look at ceilings, floors, random windows and doors, outlets and switches for lighting and appliances, and any heating and cooling equipment.

Specialized equipment might also include: ceiling fans, humidifiers, dehumidifiers, fire-suppression systems, fireplaces, home theater equipment, motorized and manually operated skylights, wet bars, and so on.

Figure 8.38 Try to "see" everything you need to report on when you are in each room. Having to go back eats up time.

Figure 8.39 Never place your equipment or your report on antique furniture, and never sit on chairs in formal dining rooms—unless you wish to buy them.

Assessing Existing Conditions

- Check ceilings for cracks, peeling, plaster fractures, and water stains.
- Check floors for damage, scratches, and stains. Look for unusual bounciness and unlevel areas.
- Test windows and doors looking for damages, cracks, and racking and hardware damages. Broken windowpanes and settled doors may be a sign of structural issues.
- Look for energy leakage, bad hardware, and security needs.
- Make sure outlets are properly wired, and switches are working. Check three-way and four-way operation.
- Look for radiators, thermostats, and heat/cooling registers. Make sure each habitable room has heating and/or cooling, depending on climate.
- Run fans and other appliances to ensure good operation.
- Understandably, some items may be beyond the scope of an inspection unless you have training in them, but inspection of these may be offered for additional fees.

Figure 8.40 Make sure there is a heat register, a radiator, or some form of reasonable heat in each habitable room.

Acceptable Practices

- This is purely a visual assessment, and in most cases the inspector will not be using instrumentation to test.
- When checking ceilings and wall surfaces, a very bright flashlight can scan the surfaces and pick out uneven areas, painter's holidays, and water stains.
- Lifting edges of floor coverings may reveal unexpected damages or stains.
- If there are any active leaks, or concern that there may be an active leak, the inspector may choose to use a moisture meter or thermal infrared camera. These go beyond the standards.
- Any insect activity or damages from insects should be reported.
- Just as in the plumbing chapter, if you run a sink, look at the faucet, all fittings, the integrity of the sink, the vanity, and venting issues and electrical safety.

Figure 8.41   Watch for chronic signs of water entry, especially in parts of a home that are seasonally used (such as apartments and pool houses).

Practices to Avoid

- Don't place fingers close to upper sashes when opening windows; damaged operators may allow upper sashes to fall, injuring fingers.
- Remember that sticky door hardware can trap an unsuspecting inspector in a room.
- Do not practice engineering unless you are one. Serious cracking may indicate structural issues, requiring an engineer.
- Don't forget to turn off appliances you turn on, and reset thermostats and controls after testing.
- If you unlock something, reset the lock after testing.
- Use caution with suspended ceiling tiles. Debris may fall from tile or above it. Some rodent fecal material may be on the tile as well.
- Avoid damaging the tiles.
- Avoid make recommendations for upgrading the electrical service or equipment, unless the client hints that he or she will be increasing the usage from what the norm has been in the home previously.

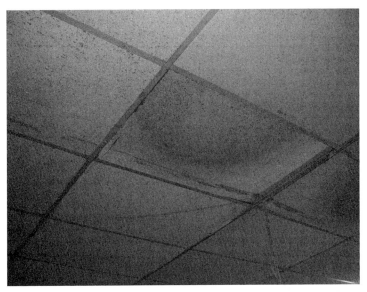

Figure 8.42 Water stains are pretty obvious on ceiling tiles. They may be from leakage or condensation.

Bathrooms

Description

Over the last 50 years, the importance of the bathroom has been elevated from a single full bath in the average home to convenience bathrooms tied to each bedroom, powder rooms, and even baths serving service areas or a pool. The perceived value of many homes may be reflected by the size and number of bathrooms, as well as the equipment in each. Over the years, styles with different tiles, stones, and synthetic materials being manufactured for use in bathrooms have increased the interest, beauty, and value of these areas. Fixtures such as bidets, shower walls with multiple heads, radiant flooring, and jetted bathtubs/bubblers, steamers, saunas, and heating and venting have made these bathrooms much more than a luxury fitted room.

Figure 8.43   A careful evaluation of all water fixtures is imperative when evaluating bathrooms. Functional flow of several fixtures at the same time and functional drainage should be checked.

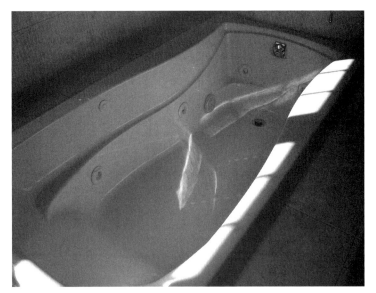

Figure 8.44   Filling the tub and testing it reduce the chance of leakage or problems later. Take your time to go over operation and safety with your client. Make sure there is an access panel for servicing the equipment.

Assessing Existing Conditions

Inspection of bathrooms includes running and checking of plumbing, heating, cooling, and electrical systems; and looking for material damages, stains, deterioration, and accessibility to hidden equipment such as pumps, steam generators, and heat vent and fan lights. Understanding the proper operation and conditions may become more difficult with a larger number of items present. The inspector will have to devote more attention, as well, to health conditions, proper ventilation, and areas where germs and bacteria, molds, and hazards may exist.

Acceptable Practices

- A general look around for moisture signs, water stains, leaks, and deterioration should begin your bathroom inspection.
- Toilets—both low water use and older toilets—should be checked for proper operation, proper installation, and inner workings.

Figure 8.45   Many inspectors have been known to exclude the bidet from their inspection. A bidet should be treated like a sink with potential cross-connection hazards.

Figure 8.46   Older homes may still have "s" traps. These can be problematic and should be noted in your report.

- Newer-technology toilets may require additional knowledge about manufacturers' recalls and systems that are problematic.
- Proper spacing for comfort and the stability of the unit should both be examined. Loose toilets often create an opportunity for leaks and floor deterioration.
- Multiple flushes may be required to test adequately.
- Bathtubs should be filled and examined for obvious cross-connections, tile and edge seal, function of fill and drain, and proper and adequate valve supply. Hot water should always be plumbed on the left and cold on the right. In newer bathtubs, the controls should not require the bather to get wet while setting the water temperature.
- Jetted bathtubs and bubblers will require accessibility to the serviceable equipment without having to damage tile or cut the wall surfaces. Those without such access may indicate nonprofessional installation or installation without the permitting process or municipal code inspection.
- Look at glass surfaces in the vicinity of the tub, windows, shower enclosures, and doors for evidence of tempered glass.
- Thermostat controls may indicate under-tile radiant floor heating or steamers. Test with normal controls.

Figure 8.47 Older sinks like these had individual nonmixing faucets. It was very easy to be burned or scalded by hot water that could only be mixed with the cold in the basin.

Figure 8.48 Running multiple fixtures will test normal family usage and give you an indication of available water pressure and volume.

- Damaged tiles, hollow soundings, deteriorated tile grout, and sealant may lead you to chronic leaks behind surfaces.
- Check around shower and tub windows for deteriorated grout and sealant, and voids below that could allow water to end up in areas below.
- Operate shower doors, looking for friction, misalignment, and damage. Note gasket and sealant deficiencies.
- Light fixtures, heat lights, night-lights, and vent fans all should be clean and operating properly.
- Damp locations should have GFCI protected circuits that are protected from splashing.
- Jetted bathtubs should be GFCI safety outlet protected.
- Listen for bearing deterioration and excessive noise on vent fans, improper venting, and terminations. Suggest upgrading plastic corrugated vent hose lines to smooth pipe.
- Bidets should be evaluated for potential cross-connections, proper installation, and drain operation.
- Sinks should be checked for leaks and examined for proper installation, feed and drains, venting, and trapping. Appliances should have angle stops for safety.
- Medicine cabinets, shower rods, towel bars, and grab bars should be firmly anchored to the walls for safety.

Figure 8.49 Make sure toilet clearances are met. There are many bathrooms that are converted from spaces that are too small for comfort. Make sure central powder rooms and bathrooms are properly vented to the outside by a fan, window, or skylight.

Practices to Avoid

- Do not move toilets that are loose so far as to create damage.
- Do not let water run unattended, especially in bathtubs and showers.
- Make sure toilets do not continue to run.
- Check drain lines before running water.
- Asking the owner if there are any appliances that are broken, before the inspection, may prevent testing a malfunctioning appliance that could leak or flood.
- Don't forget to make sure timers, thermostats, and controls are returned to the off position.
- Make sure shower valves are left on tub fill setting, not shower head or body washers.
- Do not put too much weight on towel holders.
- Make sure bath venting pipes are terminated properly to the outside, and not directed where the hot, moist air can do damage or grow mold.

Figure 8.50   Watch for older unsafe bath heaters.

Figure 8.51   A very popular new addition to bathrooms specifically designed for seniors is a walk-in bathtub.

Kitchens

Description

Kitchens are where most people spend time preparing for meals, entertaining, and gathering with the family. They are also an area where many different appliances are apt to be working in tandem to help with the preparation and storage of food. As a result, kitchen inspections are complicated and can be time-consuming.

Many inspectors feel that inspecting kitchens does not require the testing of appliances. While I do not share this opinion, the kitchen inspection presents many challenges, regardless of whether a more detailed inspection of individual appliances is performed.

Modern kitchens are much more utilitarian than traditional ones, and as a result, we see more kitchens with office work areas and country kitchens where the family is entertained; larger pantries and even laundry functions may be nearby. More than ever, kitchens have become the center of many household activities.

Figure 8.52 Modern kitchens will often contain appliances worth more than $15,000 and cabinetry and countertops worth two to four times that. Careful evaluation of a kitchen should include all these items.

Figure 8.53   When inspecting glass-top cooking appliances, take care to inform your client if burners heat glass quickly and are slower to cool. These can be burn concerns.

Assessing Existing Conditions

When inspecting kitchens, it is generally a good idea to try to work systematically, looking at cabinets, counters, and equipment; opening doors and drawers; and looking for loose countertops. Test outlets with a combination GFCI outlet tester; test switches for lighting, dishwasher, and waste disposal disconnects; and test any special equipment outlets. Islands should be examined carefully to make sure they are fastened to the floor and not apt to tip.

Building and safety codes have played a large role in kitchen upgrades over the years, and familiarization with safety requirements will help with your inspection process.

Acceptable Practices

- Open and close all cabinet drawers and doors, and examine hinges, door hardware, and construction. Look for proper fasteners, loosely hung cabinetry, and any signs of stress. Examine base cabinets in the same manner, also paying attention to water stains, signs of rodent or insect activity, or poor housekeeping.

Figure 8.54 You must have an ongoing understanding of newer features and how the appliances work.

- Check counter surfaces for damages to the material or veneer, and check to see that they are well fastened. Look at backsplash surfaces and proper sealant at seams.

Figure 8.55 The microwave has become an important cooking appliance, especially for defrosting and quick heating.

Figure 8.56 Safety issues with islands include concerns about children turning on easily accessible burners, pulling appliance cords plugged into low receptacles, and the like.

- Check island base cabinets, and ascertain that the island is secure.
- Look at all sinks, making sure faucets are operating properly and not leaking at the counter or in the base cabinet below. Examine traps and fittings for leakage and corrosion. Look for valves to shut off the water.
- Examine electrical safety under the cabinets, and test all outlets at counter height and on any islands for GFCI safety outlets. Make sure they are wired properly, and test to ensure that they are working.
- Check sinks for proper flow and drainage.
- Test lighting, and look for any deterioration or problems with overhead lighting and switching, under-cabinet lighting, specialized lighting at work stations, and outlets specifically for appliances such as microwaves and disposals.
- Open refrigerator doors, dishwashers, and ovens to make sure proper clearances are met for safe operation.
- If testing appliances, see the special chapter on appliances (Chapter 11).
- Make sure anti-tipping devices are installed on ovens, and that dishwashers are secured to the countertop or side cabinets with fasteners.
- Examine hoods and downdraft exhaust units to ensure that they are ducting outside and not terminating unsafely or ducting into attics or crawlspaces.
- Check clearances above stoves and cooktops, and look for safety concerns where heat might cause a fire. Recommend upgrades for safety whenever you find deficiencies.

Figure 8.57 Look for safety upgrades that can be added, such as ducting to the outside, GFCI safety outlets, windows that open, backsplash fire protection, and so forth.

- Make sure ducting for hoods uses smooth pipe, not corrugated, which can catch grease and clog or cause a fire.
- Look at floor surfaces for damages, trip hazards, or signs of water.
- Check for gas valves for gas-fed appliances, and make sure the valves are accessible.
- Look for heating and cooling. Many kitchens do not have adequate radiator sizing or enough registers to keep the room warm, or cool in summer.
- Watch traffic patterns, and look for hazards (sharp corner edges, wires dangling, poor venting, unsafe windows, etc.).

Practices to Avoid

- Do not turn on appliances or fixtures without looking at them carefully first, to determine if they are in service and functioning safely.
- Look for signs of poor housekeeping and unprofessional work before operating appliances or putting yourself in harm's way.
- Avoid wet floors, wet countertops, and hot cook tops and stoves. Place your report and materials in a safe, dry place.
- Remember to check to make sure ovens, cooktops, and tested appliances are off, and that popped GFCIs are reset.
- Look inside appliances before turning them on. A rarely used appliance may make a perfect storage cabinet, but when turned on, an oven or dishwasher may ruin what was being stored in it.

Garages

Description

Both detached and attached garages have in recent years become the norm. Many larger homes can now accommodate more vehicles than previously, and storing them inside creates new challenges for home safety.

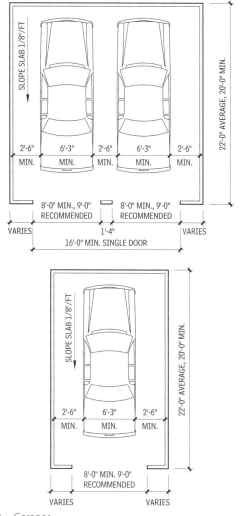

Figure 8.58 Garages.
Source: AIA, *Architectural Graphic Standards for Residential Construction.* Copyright 2003, John Wiley & Sons, Inc.

Figure 8.59 Check for photoelectric sensors and auto-reverse features on the opener. Make sure they work.

Driving a vehicle into an enclosed space has always been a concern, because of exhaust gases, stored fuel, the weight of the vehicle, and poor driving skills.

Figure 8.60 Look for loose tracks that can bind; check springs and cable retainers. Pictured is wood and gasket deterioration.

Garage inspection, though simple in scope, requires an understanding of some rather important safety considerations.

Assessing Existing Conditions

- Inspect floor surfaces, and look at the pitch of the slab or paved surface. Make sure liquids will flow away from the home, and not into basement areas.
- Some cracking may not be significant, but extensive movement and settling may be reason to suspect settling and possible structural concerns necessitating an engineer.
- Examine walls and ceilings for water stains, cracking, deterioration, and fire blocking. Most requirements demand $5/8$-inch fire-code rated sheetrock between the living space and the garage and a rated door in between.
- Watch out for openings in the ceiling, heat ducts or registers open to the garage, or plumbing leaks.
- Garage doors should have counterbalancing springs or torsion bar springs to assist the lifting of the door. These doors are large, heavy,

Figure 8.61   Great care must be taken to avoid bringing products of combustion and carbon monoxide into the living spaces.

Figure 8.62 Spring protector cables allow the spring to open and close, but protect against the potential for the spring to break and fly off.

and potentially dangerous. If they are powered by an opener, the opener should have an auto-reverse on impact and photoelectric sensor protection as well.

- Springs should have cables running through them to prevent the spring from breaking and flying into an object or person. Opener mechanisms should be securely fastened to the ceiling, tracks secure, and roller hardware in good shape.
- Look for damaged door trim on the sides of the door from vehicular damage, and examine the gasket on the bottom of the door. These help keep rodents out.
- If there is an automatic opener, safety placards and a trolley release to remove the door from auto-operation should be in place.
- If there is no exterior door to enter a garage, a trolley disconnect should be mounted by cable into the door so the door can be opened during power outages.
- Check outlets in the garage for GFCI protection.
- If there is heating, cooling, or oil tank equipment in the garage, make sure there is vehicular protection.
- If the heating and/or water heating is located in the garage, the ignition point must be at least 18 inches off the floor.

Figure 8.63 Depending on where this drain flows to, this could be an environmental nightmare.

Acceptable Practices

- Test garage doors for safe operation.
- Examine cracks, gaps, and openings.
- Make sure doors to the home are solid, and preferably fire rated (no operable windows or screens).
- Evaluate whether any interior supports have been removed from the garage central supporting beam or girder.
- Test outlets for proper wiring and GFCI.
- Look for exposed unprotected plumbing pipes and fittings.

Practices to Avoid

- Do not test garage doors when cars are below them. Watch garage door windows and the mounting hardware when testing the door operation.
- Do not leave garages open if you opened the door. The owner may not want others to see in the garage.

Figure 8.64 Photoelectric sensors protect kids and pets. They should ideally be mounted at 4–6 inches from the floor.

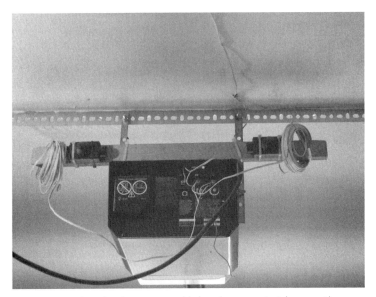

Figure 8.65 It only takes a reasonably handy person to take away the safety mechanisms and make a piece of significant equipment deadly. Here the photo eyes have been aimed at themselves on the ceiling, removing the safety devices from their original purpose.

Chapter 9

Insulation and Ventilation

Insulation

Description

In order to keep a home more energy efficient, we use many forms and types of insulation to slow the loss of heat or cooling from the home, depending on its location. Most configurations of insulation work by trapping air in pockets or layers of material. We measure the resistance of heat transfer in R-values. The higher the R-value, the more effective the insulation is. Although many state and national standards do not require the inspector to disturb the insulation to determine conditions and depth, most clients will have an expectation that the inspector will be looking for this information. Also, regionally (especially in the Northeast), concerns about possible asbestos content may become an issue.

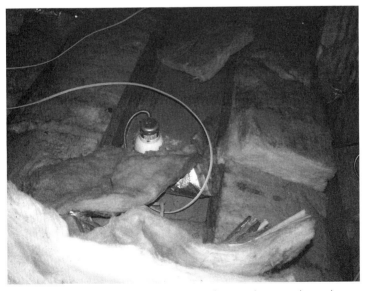

Figure 9.1   As the cost of energy rises, it makes good sense to have plenty of insulation in your home to keep heating and cooling from escaping. Just as importantly, we must keep good airflow above the insulation to draw away attic moisture to reduce condensation. Make sure recessed lights are not covered with insulation. The open voids in the picture will allow heat loss and result in greater energy cost if not correct.

Fiberglass Insulation

- Batts—Precut pieces of spun fiberglass of various thicknesses, which may or may not have a vapor barrier of kraft paper or foil.
- Rolls—Specific linear foot rolls of spun fiberglass of various thicknesses, which may or may not have a vapor barrier of kraft paper.
- Blown fiberglass—Pieces of loose-fill spun fiberglass that can be blown into cavities.
- Sealed fiberglass—Fiberglass that has a sealed package to contain loose fibers, to limit airborne material.

Cellulose Insulation

- Made from recycled paper and treated with borates to reduce its flammability, cellulose can be sprayed in cavities using a dry or moist mix.
- A vapor barrier can be applied first. Then the cellulose is blown, the excess is cleaned off, and the drywall is applied.

Figure 9.2 Spun-glass fibers trap air and provide an excellent and very stable material for insulation.

Figure 9.3   Cellulose is made from recycled paper with flame retardant additives. It is an excellent insulation material and can be easily blown into voids and attic spaces.

Foam Insulation

- Foams have become very popular. They are typically a mixture of two chemicals that cause a reaction when they are sprayed out of a mixing nozzle. The foam expands, creating small trapped air bubbles, which slow heat exchange.
- Foam can be bought in sheet goods and cut to size, or it can be manufactured on site and sprayed into the cavity as it expands, to fill a void. Any excess would then be trimmed, and the drywall would then be installed.
- Foam is usually more expensive than cellulose and fiberglass to produce because it is petroleum-based.

Balsam-Wool Insulation

- This was an older, now extinct, type of insulation made by Weyerhaeuser. It is still found in older homes.
- It consisted of an asphalt-coated paper vapor barrier with loose balsam-wool fibers inside.
- If the paper is cut, the insulation will fall out. It has a rather low insulation R-value.

Asbestos Insulation

- While rare now, there was a time when asbestos fibers in a binder were sprayed in some attics.
- This can be a health concern and should be removed professionally.
- It was often a white powdery mix like clumped cottage cheese.

Figure 9.4 Suggesting to clients that they add a foam box over the pull-down stairs will save them lots of money over time. Teaching good energy sense is always appreciated.

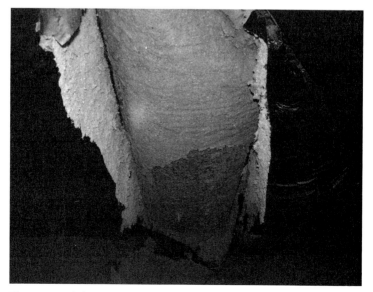

Figure 9.5 Balsam was an older form of insulation that can be damaged easily and deteriorates with age. If it gets wet, it should be replaced.

Vermiculite and Pourable Bag Mix Insulation

- Used predominantly to retrofit older homes, loose bags of materials were poured into the joist bays to reduce heat loss.
- In recent years, some asbestos content has been found in some installations and brands.

Hard Foam, Foam Sheathing, and High-R Board Insulation

- Used in crawlspaces, basements, and damp locations, polystyrene bead board and other formulations are used for their denseness and small cells of trapped air. Some are covered with foil vapor barriers and may be reflective as well.

Pipe Insulation

- Pipes are commonly wrapped with fiberglass, preformed foam, and combined wraps with a plastic covering.
- Older homes may have asbestos-impregnated paper and asbestos insulation in an adhesive binder. This type may be wrapped with tape, plastic, or foil. Asbestos insulation was typically held in place with metal clasps or bands.

Figure 9.6 Hard foam can insulate foundation walls and be used to make insulating boxes above pull-down hatches.

Figure 9.7   Newer closed cell foam insulation. There is a slit that is opened, and the tube slides over the pipe.

Assessing Existing Conditions

Properly installed insulation leaves no voids or gaps and significantly slows air movement and temperature migration. While most inspections take place with finished drywall and limited access, there are several locations in a home—such as attics, unfinished basements and crawlspaces, and closet/storage areas—where a glimpse of framing, vapor barrier placement, and insulation installation may be examined and evaluated. When these opportunities are available, we recommend that you look and report type, thickness or R-value, and the presence or lack of vapor barrier. Report any voids, missed areas, and poor workmanship. In climates where energy consumption will be costly, recommending insulation where none exists, or more if there isn't enough, is prudent. If older, less-effective types are in place, recommending replacement with new may be wise advice. With asbestos materials, in most cases careful removal by a mitigation company using EPA-mandated mitigation techniques will be required.

Figure 9.8 If this material is disturbed, fibers can become airborne, creating a hazard. It is beyond your scope, and it may be illegal to cut samples for lab analysis without certifications.

Figure 9.9 Make sure insulation covers evenly and does not impinge airflow from soffits at the ends of the rafter bays, nor come within 3 inches of recessed lighting cans (where labeled).

Acceptable Practices

- When in areas that are accessible, note type of insulation, thickness, R-value, and conditions.
- If there is not enough insulation for the local climate, recommend more.
- If vapor barriers face the wrong direction or are missing, recommend repair.
- If there is evidence of nesting, droppings, or unhealthy conditions, recommend clean-up or removal and replacement.
- Lifting a few random sections will help determine conditions, but will also allow the inspector to note drywall ceiling conditions.
- Asbestos-containing materials in the insulation may create unsafe conditions for the owners and the inspector.
- Wearing a respirator and eye and hand protection is prudent.
- Pipe wrap that is loose, wet, or made of asbestos may require replacement.
- Recommend insulation above pull-down stairs and above attic hatches.

Figure 9.10 Expanding foam can fill narrow voids that can become drafty if not insulated before the drywall goes up.

Practices to Avoid

- Try not to disturb the insulation or cause materials in, or on, the insulation to become airborne.
- Wearing a good respirator can keep all those fibers and fine dusts out of your lungs.
- Do not do sampling unless you are qualified to do so.
- Avoid crawlspaces where there is obvious friable asbestos on the pipes in bad shape, or where it is in friable condition on the ground.
- Be careful not to rip or damage installed vapor barriers.
- Do not walk on or traverse raw insulation. There may be no support or large voids below it. Falling through could be painful and destructive.
- Do not assume that thicknesses and R-values are consistent.
- Never allow your clients to wander the attic without warning them they could fall through.

Ventilation

Description

Proper ventilation, or air movement around the home, is crucial to comfort and health. We look at air movement in attics, crawlspaces, and areas around the home in order to determine if fresh air is entering the home. Natural air exchange can keep the air healthier; it helps move contaminated air out of the home or dilutes it to reduce ill effects. Ventilation occurs mechanically when bath vents, oven hoods, dryer vents, and/or attic fans are operated. Static ventilation occurs when heat causes warm house air to rise, or drafts influence household air circulation to move out of the home. Good ventilation can reduce moisture and allow fresh air to enter the home. Unfortunately, fresh air may carry dust, pollen, or other fine particulates such as bacteria, fungi, germs, unsafe gases, and lots of moisture. Building scientists have in recent years rethought their position on how to achieve good ventilation. These changes do not always follow local and international codes. They include preventing moist summer air that is

Figure 9.11   Thermostatically controlled attic fans can draw excessive heat out of an attic and lower cooling costs in summer. In this photo, the bath vent is dangling in front of the fan. Bath fans should be ducted to the outside as efficiently as possible, to void moisture and odors.

Figure 9.12 Although venting may be required by building codes, building scientists are recommending closing vents to crawlspaces, because this will keep hot moist air from condensing in the cool crawlspace and growing mold.

heavily laden with water from entering subgrade areas. Because the building materials in these areas are cooler, condensation will result, and damp odors, moisture issues, and mold will be the end result. Because the emphasis on tightening up the energy aspects of a home is a recent development, some of the new thinking may go against traditional building technique, but with energy-efficient homes it certainly makes more sense to increase attic ventilation and avoid crawlspace and basement ventilation to the outside.

Assessing Existing Conditions

- When in areas that are accessible, the inspector should note the means of ventilation, and recommend increasing the ventilation in the attic when necessary. This may require adding fans, additional air venting, or mechanical systems.
- For crawlspaces in climates that tend to be highly humid in summer, it may be prudent to recommend not allowing wet air to circulate in those areas. Closing off those vents, adding insulation, and maintaining

good circulation of the dry air is recommended. Dehumidification may be another way to solve higher moisture levels.

- Running bath fans, oven and cooktop hoods, as well as dryer vents can cause a negative pressure, drawing in the same amount of exterior air that is being pushed out. This may enter through gaps in the insulation and/or openings in the envelope, or be drawn from chimneys and vents.
- When air is exhausted out of the home, the air that is drawn back into the home may be contaminated. The air may be an unwanted temperature, more humid than the home air, or contaminated with soil gases.
- Appliances that require make-up air or dilution air may not receive enough to function safely or properly, causing backdrafting and spillage at draft hoods.
- Attics without proper air exchange will have the opposite effect. Heat will rise, and condensation in the attic will cause wet conditions conducive to rot and mold on the framing and sheathing.

Figure 9.13 Whole-house fans were used to cool the home in hot summer weather. Moving lots of air through the home creates a negative pressure that can cool the home but also draw dirt, pollen, radon gas, and carbon monoxide throughout the home. Pilot lights can be blown out, and raw gases can be drawn into the home.

- Static and mechanical means (fans with a thermostat or humidistat control) will help to void unwanted heat and moisture in attics and unfinished spaces. If there is not enough air movement, however, unhealthy conditions may be created.
- Trapped heat below roof surfaces needs to be removed to avoid overheating framing, sheathing, and roofing. This could reduce their life expectancy.
- Look for blocked vents, ridge vents that are not open to the exterior, and small, ineffective gable vents.
- Bathroom venting and dryer venting both exhaust tremendous amounts of moisture that should not be vented into the home, the garage, or unfinished spaces. This includes soffit and rafter bays.
- Windows in the attic typically leak if left open, and allow almost no ventilation if kept closed. Windows allow light to enter, which can be nice, but they don't provide year-round venting unless left open. Look for stains around windows and vents. Suggest louvers where venting is needed; these are more resistant to water entry.

Figure 9.14 Most gable vents are too small for necessary venting of an attic, and in many instances the screening is dirty and filled with bees' nests and nesting materials for birds. This should be cleaned and rescreened if airflow is reduced.

Reporting

- Closed or blocked vents in attics and in crawlspace areas should be noted in your reports.
- Use care around attic fans. Check for power supply switching, and see if the fans are mounted unsafely. Bad fan installations or a damaged unit may be noisy or transfer vibrations throughout the home.
- Small circles on the surfaces of an attic floor, on insulation wrap or on the vapor barrier, are indications that condensation is dripping from the cold nails.
- Any sign or smell of mustiness or mold should be reported.
- Fans blowing directly into the attic or crawlspaces should vent to the exterior in as short a duct as possible, to reduce the opportunity of condensation.
- Switches may be accidentally left in the off position and as a result eliminate the venting process.
- Radon venting from under the slab should only be exhausted at roof height to avoid recontaminating the home.

Figure 9.15   Moisture-laden warm air migrates up to the attic. The moisture condenses on the cold nails and frosts them. The second waft of warm, moisture-laden air melts the frost and creates the dripping onto the floor (interior rain) that causes the circular water stains.

- Whole-house fans can create tremendous depressurization, pulling exterior air, pollen, radon gas, exhaust, and products of combustion (carbon monoxide) into the home. These should be evaluated for safety and function.
- Dual-speed circulation fans may be used on ducted air handlers to circulate air within the home, and some newer-technology heat recovery units will take fresh air from outside and mix it with home air.
- Dirty filters will slow air movement. Recommend cleaning or replacing old filters.

Acceptable Practices

- Moldy areas that are small can be carefully cleaned by the homeowners. Larger areas should be evaluated by professionals.
- Cleaning cooling and heating ducts can stir up allergens and may add additional odors in the ducting. Freshly "cleaned" ducts may be dirtier than you think. Some of the chemicals and techniques used may increase noxious odors and stir up more allergens.
- Damp odors are a symptom of moldy conditions; use your nose, but beware that you may be exposing yourself to unsafe conditions.

Figure 9.16 This fan is too big to use just for voiding heat in the attic. Upgrade to a smaller thermostat-controlled fan.

Practices to Avoid

- Do not open installed humidifiers without protecting yourself with a respirator as these are rarely adequately cleaned and can be very dirty and unhealthy. Opening them may expose the inspector to dangerous levels of germs, bacteria, and mold.
- Do not enter crawlspaces unless you are wearing a respirator and protective clothing to avoid airborne dusts, fecal material, and mold.
- Leaks, drips, and surface standing water in crawlspace and basement areas should be noted, and vapor barriers recommended.

Types of Mechanical Venting

Description

"Spot ventilation" is defined as venting used for a specific area—for example, bathroom fans, dryer vents, and oven hoods.

Acceptable Practices

Bath Fans

- Usually required if there is no window or skylight, vent fans are necessary to void moisture and odors from bathrooms, darkrooms, saunas, and areas with multiple bath fixtures. Turn on bath fans and listen to the unit. If there is a light, test that as well. Some units have heat bulbs, heat coils, and night-lights, as well. These may also have timer switches.

Figure 9.17 Note that there are fans in bathrooms. Run them to see if flapper dampers open and if the fans make vibration or bearing noises.

Figure 9.18 Recommend that dryer venting be "efficiently" run to the outside, using smooth metallic pipe and as little metal flex line as possible. Plastic corrugated pipe is no longer allowed in many municipalities.

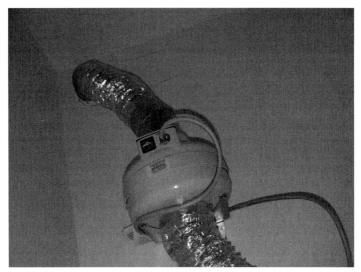

Figure 9.19 A newer trend is to install remote fans to reduce fan noise in the bathroom. Smooth rather than corrugated vent piping will improve the efficiency.

Figure 9.20 Trying to tie all the venting together to use fewer fans probably won't work, especially with all the corrugated connections.

- Look for the exhaust, and make sure the cover or louvers are intact and that the vent is working.
- Look at the venting material, and make sure it is efficient, safe, and connected properly.
- Corrugated materials and elbows take away from function and should be minimally used.
- Long runs often will be ineffective.
- Dirty fans and those with damaged impellers and broken bearings will be noisy.
- Long runs through unconditioned spaces may be water-stained or wet from condensation.

Dryer Vents

- Many house fires and dryer fires have been caused by plastic corrugated vent pipe. As a result, most municipalities will not allow flex plastic vent piping anymore. When you see this pipe, you should recommend upgrades to smooth metal dryer pipe with as little flex pipe and as few angled sections as possible.
- The last 20 years has seen a cheapening of the exterior "flap"-type vent termination that typically gets dirty and/or deformed and stays open,

Figure 9.21 These flap units may warp over time and stick in the open position. Birds and bees may find these desirable for nesting.

allowing insects and birds into the opening to nest. Recommending a better-quality magnetic type vent flap will avoid the problem in the future.

- Dryer vents should not terminate close to other equipment, especially air-conditioning units, where the lint and moisture can be drawn into the coils.
- Look behind the dryer to determine if the line has been accidentally disconnected or crushed.
- Look for evidence of mold behind washers and dryers.
- Run the dryer for a few moments to see if the drum and elements get warm, and to ensure that the exterior flap opens when in use and closes when not.

Oven and Range Hoods

- While not required by code in most situations, a good range hood can prevent fires and keep cooking areas cleaner by sending smoke, heat, grease, moisture, and odors outside.
- This type of vent should not be piped with plastic, nor should flex lines or corrugated plastic or metal pipe be used. High temperatures and grease can accumulate, causing fires to occur.

- Some hoods are not vented to the outside and instead work with a filtered recirculating system. This is usually a compromise based on a tricky location or difficult type of installation. The filters must be keep extremely clean and degreased regularly to maintain some degree of effectiveness.
- Professional hoods are usually recommended when larger cooktops or stoves are installed. These often have heavy-duty multispeed blower fans, multiple-filtration filters, and higher capacity to move air. Cleaning them regularly is required.
- There must be at least 24 inches of clearance to the stove from the base of the hood, and if there is no hood or fire protection, clearance of 30 inches is required.
- Older-style through-the-wall vents are usually less desirable, because the exhaust must be drawn to the wall or ceiling location. These are harder to keep clean and less effective. Some are controlled by switch controls, others by a pull-chain switch. These are often drafty and allow cold air into the kitchen in winter.
- Downdraft hoods—should not use corrugated venting material and should have as few angles as possible. Long lengths are apt to be less effective at removing the heat, smoke, grease, moisture, and

Figure 9.22 A good hood will draw moisture, odors, heat, steam, smoke, and grease to the exterior. Filters should be checked for cleanliness and, if visible, ducting should never be flex corrugated type.

Figure 9.23 Make sure duct goes to the outside—not to the attic, garage, or an enclosed porch!

odors. These may have a column that rises mechanically at the counter or just a high-velocity fan that draws the exhaust downward to a termination outside. These must not terminate into basements, crawlspaces, or living spaces.

Attic Vent Fans

- Usually controlled by a thermostat or humidistat with a toggle or kill switch, the attic fan is usually about 8–12 inches in diameter and functions to remove built-up heat in the attic space. These may have timer switches as well.
- Attic vent fans may not work as well if used in conjunction with ridge and soffit venting or can vents, as the fan may draw in outside air instead of exhausting attic-heated air.
- Listen for noise levels, bearing noises, and poor functioning. Some attic vent fans may be roof-mounted "mushroom" types, motorized turbines, or gable-mounted fans.

Whole-House Fans

- These were large 30–36-inch attic-floor or gable-mounted fans on a switch or on a timer that were used to cool the home.
- While these are certainly capable of increasing home ventilation, they were originally used in warmer climates to create a negative

Figure 9.24 This type of "mushroom" fan is typically on a thermostat in the attic.

pressure in the home to help provide natural drafts by cracking open certain windows and drawing cooler air into the home.

- Watch clearances on these units, and watch accessibility to children when fans are operating. Some homes will have screening around fans for protection.
- Do not run these without looking in the attic to make sure there are no stored items close to the unit or insulation above it.
- These fans are often noisy and stir up quite a bit of air. They move so much air that they can radically change the house dynamics, causing doors to slam, drawing radon and other soil gases and dirt into the home, and causing backdrafting of chimneys and draft hoods, which can be very dangerous—even fatal—to those living in the home.

Power Exhaust Vents

- Some heating systems and water heaters may have power vents to help move the products of combustion up the chimney or out of the home more efficiently. These are vents, but they are more tied to the better functioning of the equipment than to venting the home.
- Radon air mitigation systems often have power venting systems to draw air and soil glasses from below the foundation and crawlspaces and exhaust it at roof height.

Figure 9.25   Old technology with potential safety issues.

Figure 9.26   Inducer blowers help blow products of combustion up the chimney.

Figure 9.27 Make sure that screening is intact and that the roofing has been cut below the cupola so heat can escape.

Figure 9.28 Check flashing and screening on these, as they may let windblown water and insects in.

- Can vents, ridge and soffit venting, gable end vents, and nonpowered turbine vents are considered static vent systems. This type of system relies on heated air being buoyant and naturally rising. When they are installed properly, hot air is allowed to void naturally, and this can be very inexpensive and efficient.
- Opening windows, doors, and skylights can provide additional static venting, relying on the same principle and natural airflow from wind.

Reporting

- Note in your report the type and methods of venting found in the home.
- Note deficiencies and recommend actions needed.
- Combinations of various venting systems on a home may add to the venting or may compete negatively with each other. If you observe these conditions, put them in your recommendations.
- Beware of any situation where products of combustion or carbon monoxide can be drawn into the home.
- Be aware that soil gases and radon can also be drawn into the home.

Figure 9.29 Many turbine vents are still around. They often need lubrication, and turn with the slightest wind.

- Recognize mold smells and conditions conducive to moisture entry that can lead to rot, mold, and insects.
- Recommend vapor barriers over raw soil in crawlspaces and dirt-floored basements.
- Recommend covers over sump pump pits and waterproofing equipment.
- Recommend caps or traps on all drainage piping.
- Make sure terminations of vents go outside and will not blow back into the home or other equipment.

Resources

OTHER RESOURCES:

- New York State Energy Research and Development Authority, 1-866-nyserda, www.nyserda.org
- US Environmental Protection Agency, Indoor Air Quality Information Clearinghouse, 1-800-438-4318, 1-800-sos-radon, www.EPA.gov.

Chapter 10

Fireplaces and Solid-Fuel-Burning Appliances

Fireplaces

Solid-Fuel-Burning Appliances

Fireplaces

Description

While fireplaces are highly desirable for many buyers, they create an interesting challenge for inspectors, similar to that of inspecting heat exchangers in a heating system. Because so much of the unit is inaccessible, and therefore NOT visible during the inspection, the temptation is to comment that it looks fine—when in reality the inspector is commenting on only a small piece of the actual unit. Because fireplaces can leak heat, smoke, and dangerous fumes, it may be wiser to explain to your clients the limitations of your evaluation ahead of time, and remind them of this in your contract and in the written report. Cracks in a chimney liner, or a chimney that is not fully lined, may not only result in costly repairs but can set fire to the home if the chimney gets too hot. The inspector is warned to know his or her limitations and to explain them to the client.

Examining the visible and accessible sections will give the inspector clues to previous maintenance (or lack of maintenance); previous repairs; conditions of the firebox, crown, and top layers, flashings,

Figure 10.1 Most fireplaces will perform poorly if the rear reflecting wall is removed. While adding an extra dimension to the aesthetics of the room, a two-sided or open designed fireplace will heat the rooms less efficiently.

counterflashings, and crickets; and the amount of use the fireplace and chimneys have experienced.

Definitions

Draw or *draft*—The ability for the heat, smoke, and products of combustion to rise and escape the chimney into the atmosphere.

Hearth—The platform in front of the fireplace (often integral to the foundation) that helps to create a fire-resistant area in front of the fire. Hearths are usually 18 inches in distance from the firebox and 8 inches wider than the mouth of the firebox, for safety. They are usually constructed of 4–6 inches of stone, concrete, tile, or other noncombustible material.

Firebox—The area of the fireplace where the fire is contained. Usually constructed of brick, concrete block, or stone.

Damper—A metal door that is opened when the fireplace is in use, to allow products of combustion out into the chimney, and closed when not in use to slow drafts and warm air loss up the chimney. The damper control handle can be in the fireplace or can come through, inside the front of the fireplace face. Dampers should be located approximately 6 inches from the top toward the front of the firebox, but also can be cable and spring loaded units mounted on the crown of the chimney.

Figure 10.2 Chimneys that are not cleaned regularly can build up with creosote and cause a chimney fire.

Figure 10.3 Plant life growing on the siding or brick will hide damages and hold moisture. It will not allow the sun to properly dry the home.

Smoke shelf—By design, the smoke shelf is above or to the side of the damper and helps to create a natural air movement that sends the smoke rolling up, and helps to deflect snow, water, and downward air currents.

Mantle—A wood shelf usually for decoration. Should be no closer than 6 inches above the firebox, and farther if it projects more than 1 1/2 inches.

Ash dump—A small chamber designed so that ash can be swept from the fireplace to a safe cooling area, which can be cleaned out later from the chimney cleanout.

Chimney liner—A metal or terra cotta central lining to prevent heat getting out of a regular unlined chimney and setting the home on fire.

Assessing Existing Conditions

Fireplace and Firebox Inspection

- Carefully examine the exterior of the firebox area. Look for soot, burn marks, and proximity to combustibles.
- In most cases, if there is a wood mantle, certain set-backs are required from the sides and top, and the thickness of the wood

must be taken into consideration as well. See Figure 10.5 for specific measurements.

- Cracked tile, damaged screens, and damaged hearths should be examined to determine if there is a need for repairs or maintenance.
- Loose fireplace doors, broken hinges, cosmetic damages, and poorly clamped installations should be noted.
- With the popularity of flat-screen TVs, there are more TVs being mounted above fireplaces. This could be a problem if the heat accumulates above the mantle area. You may wish to warn your client.
- In the firebox area, look for signs of usage—usually soot stains, water stains, rust, or soot on the damper and handle. Ashes in the base may indicate that the fireplace has been used often. Deposits of heavy black crust (creosote) may indicate not only heavier usage but also the burning of fuels that give off more ash (softwoods and paper).
- If the damper or the damper handle is disconnected, damaged, or missing, report that.
- Some fireplaces have a spring-loaded damper mounted on the crown of the chimney (up top). A spring-loaded chain is pulled to close the cover on this mechanism. Unhook this and then close it again, to test operation.
- Any signs of mortar voids, interior cracks, or damages would indicate the need for a chimney expert to quote a repair.

Figure 10.4 Getting your head in far enough to see up the flue is important, but also remember that floating debris can get in your eyes.

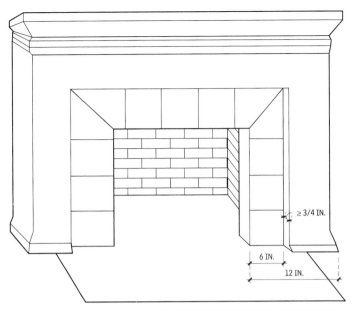

NO COMBUSTIBLE MATERIAL IS ALLOWED WITHIN 6 IN. OF THE FIREPLACE OPENING. 1 IN. CLEARANCE IS NEEDED FOR EACH 1/8 IN. OF PROJECTION OF COMBUSTIBLE MATERIAL WITHIN 12 IN. OF THE FIREPLACE OPENING. FOR EXAMPLE, A 3/4 IN. PROJECTION NEEDS 6 IN. OF CLEARANCE.

Figure 10.5   Masonry–Fireplace Clearances

Figure 10.6   Spring-loaded top damper covers keep water and debris out when the fireplace is not in use, and keep the flue warmer when there is no fire.

Figure 10.7 This chimney may look okay from the ground, but a closer examination shows that the crown and many top courses are cracked.

Note: In many parts of the Northeast, there have been frequent reports of scam artists visiting homes that have been recently purchased. The scammers offer inexpensive chimney inspections and report that the homes have "damaged" unsafe flues needing replacement liners. Homeowners often pay upwards of $1,600 to have them install a chimney liner. Even if done well, there is rarely a need for the liner, and often a follow-up call to the inspector alleges that he or she should have found the deficiency at the inspection—lawyer's letter to follow. Warning your clients of known scams can protect them—and you—from this type of fraud.

Exterior Chimney Inspection

- Examine all brick and masonry surfaces. Look for cracks, surface damages (spalling), and unnecessary plant life that may be growing on the surfaces.
- Whenever possible, recommend removal of climbing ivy or other plants that attach themselves to the masonry and hold moisture.
- If accessible, check flashings and counterflashings for damage and signs of poor installation.

Figure 10.8 The screen will keep sparks and ash in the firebox. Glass doors should be open during larger, hotter fires to avoid shattering.

- Proper flashing and counterflashing will not allow water to enter, but movement, climate changes, and poor workmanship will change conditions.
- The crown of the chimney and the upper courses must not exhibit cracks or damage.

Insert Fireboxes and Modular Prefabricated Units

- Prefabricated inserts must be installed according to the manufacturer's requirements. Unfortunately, these are rarely available to you on site. Examining for obvious visible defects and damages would be the priority. A closer examination for voids, burn marks or water stains should follow. Glass doors and screens should always be recommended.
- These may also be called zero clearance fireplaces. Because they are metal and not masonry, they are much lighter and do not require a foundation to support them. As a result, they can be installed in more locations around the home.

- Zero clearance units must be installed following the manufacturer's required installation manual.
- When glass doors and screens are installed, specific requirements of the manufacturer must be met. Aftermarket doors must be approved by the manufacturer of the unit before they are installed.

Figure 10.9 One way to cut the cost of masonry for a fireplace is to install a vented prefabricated fireplace.

Solid-Fuel-Burning Appliances

Assessing Existing Conditions

Wood, Coal, and Pellet Stoves

- Wood stoves became very popular during the years of the oil embargo and the next 20 years after that, because wood scraps and trees were plentiful. Unfortunately, many of the woods burned were not aged heartwood, so they were more prone to adding soot and contaminants to the air.
- Coal stoves offered another added dimension to home heating, allowing a homeowner to burn coal as an alternative to gas or oil.
- Wood and coal stoves can get very hot, and clearance from combustibles can be a big safety issue. If the manufacturer is known and/or the stove is UL listed, the clearances should be published. See Figure 10.10.

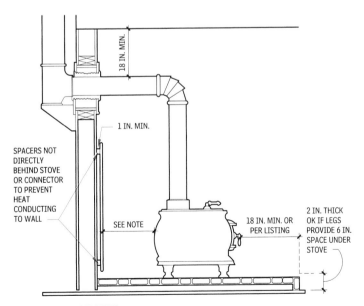

18 IN. MIN.

1 IN. MIN.

SPACERS NOT DIRECTLY BEHIND STOVE OR CONNECTOR TO PREVENT HEAT CONDUCTING TO WALL

SEE NOTE

18 IN. MIN. OR PER LISTING

2 IN. THICK OK IF LEGS PROVIDE 6 IN. SPACE UNDER STOVE

WOOD STOVE CLEARANCES

Figure 10.10 Wood stoves require set-backs and clearances, to avoid fires. Recommend that the client ask for manuals and manufacturer's requirements.

Figure 10.11 Make sure (if accessible) that clearances to combustibles are met. Also look for stains or deterioration on the flashing and cap.

- Pellet stoves have become very popular in the Northeast over the last 10 years. They burn pelletized wood and can burn very efficiently. Many of the stoves are mechanical and self-feed the pellets into the burn chamber.

Exterior Metal and Wood Chase Chimneys

- Metal flue pipes can be single-wall, dual-wall and triple-wall pipe. Each has a use, and each has requirements for clearance from combustibles. Most single wall requires you keep combustibles back at least 9 inches with gas appliances and 18 inches with oil burning equipment. For most dual wall applications, 1–2 inches would be required with proper through-the-wall and through-the-ceiling fire stops.
- Wood chases must follow these interior clearance restrictions and be properly flashed and capped. Spark arrestor caps and screening are usually required.
- Wood stoves need to be cleaned more frequently than fireplaces for safety.

Caps, Screens, and Crickets

- Chimney caps and screens can be simply installed and can easily improve chimney conditions and safety. Screens prevent wildlife from entering and large pieces of ash from landing on the roof. The cap will also help to keep rain and snow from entering the

Figure 10.12 Weather and wildlife can enter a chimney lacking in caps and screening. This crown also needs sealant repair to avoid further damages.

Figure 10.13 Crickets are required to divert water away from the back of the chimney. This chimney needs sealant on the counterflashing to keep water out.

chimney and wetting the liner and damper, which can cause odors and rusting of the damper mechanism.

- On older chimneys wider than 30 inches, a cricket flashing was required. On newer units, many municipalities require crickets regardless of width. The cricket prevents debris and water from accumulating behind the chimney and creating potential water entry issues.
- Chimneys should protrude at least 36 inches out of the roofing and should be 2 feet taller than any surface within 10 feet.
- Look first at the equipment. If you see damage, rust, corrosion, or suspicious installations, recommending a fireplace expert will be required to determine if safe operation is possible.
- Look next at distances from combustibles and determine if reflective walls or noncombustible surfaces look as if they will protect the home.
- Look for stored items too close to stove that could melt or catch fire.
- Look for protection from wood or coal rolling out, and check whether children and pets can be hurt easily.
- Check chimneys for clearances, caps, and screens. Make sure they are relatively clean and not filled with creosote.
- Check ducting for mechanical connections, integrity, and fire blocking.
- Look at chimney tops, and caps and screens. Examine the cricket and pointing.

Figure 10.14 If chimney is overgrown with ivy, cracks and damages may go undetected.

Figure 10.15   All the convenience of a fire without the need to feed it wood. A flick of a remote and the room gets toasty! You may wish to recommend going over proper operations with the owner; asking for the original owner's manual is a good idea for safe operation tips.

- Check dampers, hardware, and door enclosures.
- Hearths should project out from the fireplace at least 18 inches and 8 inches beyond either side of the opening.
- Check ash dumps and cleanout doors. If filled with ash, they should be cleaned. Missing doors or grates and damaged hardware should be reported.
- If visible, make sure chimney sections are mechanically fastened together.
- Shared flues should be reported.

Acceptable Practices

- Inspectors are not expected to light or extinguish fires in fireplaces or stoves. Nor should they have to move firewood, ash, or kindling.
- Limited flue visibility in inaccessible areas, and areas where soot or ash blocks the view, naturally limits the inspection scope.

Figure 10.16 Make sure you look carefully at conditions both outside at the roof and inside in the attic.

Practices to Avoid

- Try not to damage doors when opening or knock over personal possessions around the fireplace.
- Wood stoves should not be within five feet of an oil tank, and should be at least 4 feet from any combustible wall. The ceiling should not be less than 50 inches above the stove.
- Reflectors made of metal or masonry material can be added to reduce the clearance, as long as they are mounted properly, spaced out at least an inch.
- Floors should be protected.
- Be wary of hot and/or dirty surfaces.
- Animals, dirt, and debris may be in the smoke-shelf area. Use care when inspecting.
- Lighting a gas-fired log unit is beyond the standards and scope of an inspection. Gas logs in almost all cases are not to be used for burning wood.

Figure 10.17 Small damages will need immediate repairs to avoid bigger damages that will otherwise result over time.

Resources

OTHER RESOURCES:

- *Home Reference Book*, Dearborn Home Inspection, 2003.
- *Mechanical Inspection*, Inspection Training Associates, 2004.

Chapter 11

Specialty Inspections

Overview of Specialty Inspections

Description

Specialty inspections never really existed in the early years of home inspection. The focus of the inspection began to include educating the purchaser, that is, not only explaining how a heating system works (or how to maintain it), but also discussing what options might be available to increase efficiencies and safety. The inspection toolbox now includes more than a flashlight and a clipboard. Infrared technology, blower doors, moisture meters, boroscopes, and new listening devices are creating an atmosphere of heightened sophistication. Inspections today are more forensic in approach, and often the detective work is exciting to watch. Some of these technologies go way beyond the standards of practice and the expected level of care we have grown used to. The standards are being rewritten to include some of the new testing and inspecting procedures that just make sense to use on a regular basis. Clients buying homes now are much more focused on energy usage and the health of their families than ever before. We will discuss some of these issues with the understanding that this chapter is apt to change with the times and demands of an ever-changing future. This chapter should be looked at as an explanation of some newer ancillary services you may wish to consider, that may increase your own menu of services.

Manufactured and Modular Home Inspections

Description

Popular for many years, the house trailer of the 1940s and 1950s has become one of the most popular means of purchasing a ready-made home across the country. Delivered to a site and hooked up to existing utilities, these units meant fast, easy comfort that could be quite economical. In fact, over the last 60 years, they have become very sophisticated and often very luxurious homes that have been placed on both semi and permanent foundations.

Figure 11.1 Manufactured homes are singlewide and double wide "trailer" homes that are still very popular. They are built completely and sold with wheels, axles, and a hitch to drive them to their new location. They generally have a skirt around their base to hide the frame and axles. These homes have very specific criteria to look at, and inspecting them requires knowledge of both HUD regulations and the safety requirements they must meet. They may be installed in parks for temporary hook-ups or placed on a more permanent foundation on privately owned land.

A manufactured home is a singlewide or double wide trailer that is manufactured in a factory and delivered as a one- or two-piece finished home.

A modular home consists of compartmentalized special-order boxes that, when assembled, become a home. Unlike most manufactured homes, these homes can be customized both in the factory and in the field. They offer the inspector much more to examine and to comment on, as a consultant, when they are being put together. Care should be taken to understand the basics of modular home construction and to acquire a good comfort level with the process of manufacturing the components and the requirements that dictate how you would inspect them.

Assessing Existing Conditions

Manufactured Homes

Manufactured homes require quite a bit of knowledge to properly inspect. We recommend you take a course on manufactured homes, or at least do more to educate yourself about them, as they fall under

Figure 11.2 It's not your father's trailer home. Modular homes are custom designed from soup to nuts and can be everything from simple to ultra luxurious.

rules of both the Department of Transportation and Housing and Urban Development programs. Construction techniques, basic requirements, and inspection challenges may vary depending on where the home is located and how permanently it has been installed. Because of their design there are accessibility and visibility limitations that make manufactured homes trickier to inspect than traditional houses.

Acceptable Practices

- As most manufactured or mobile homes come from the factory complete and ready to live in as a single component or at best a few pieces, inspectors need to recognize the interrelationship of the systems and the basic requirements that have been established by government and industry standards.
- Checking under these homes often requires coveralls and kneepads and a willingness to crawl below the skirting that covers the axles and undercarriage that allow these units to be portable. In most instances, wheels will have been removed once the unit is set on blocking or a foundation.
- Strapping to hold the home in place with some type of anchoring is important, especially in wind-prone and severe weather locations.
- Any ductwork under the unit should be at least 4 feet off the ground.
- Heating and water heating equipment should be labeled as approved for mobile homes with proper safety devices and appropriate terminations.
- All these homes have a registration "insignia" located on each section.
- Proper setbacks must be met for proximity to other units and permanent structures.
- Check connections for water, gas, and waste. Look for leaks. Electrical connections should be rated for 50 amps and be a rated cord.
- Look for grounding of metal components and a ground lug so the unit can be grounded with a ground system or ground bar.
- All bath, kitchen, and exterior outlets require GFCI outlets.
- Check for smoke and carbon monoxide alarms.
- Staircases no less than 4 inches or greater than 8-inch risers all must be the same height, plus or minus ¼ inch.
- Additional tools required will be coveralls or disposable clothing, knee pads, nut drivers to get into enclosures, and a guidebook on mobile home inspections.

Practices to Avoid

- Do not perform these inspections without proper experience and knowledge of these homes.
- Avoid crawling under the skirt without proper personal protection equipment and a good light. These areas may be home to wildlife that can hurt you when threatened (raccoons, possums, skunks, rats, and snakes are all typical).
- Avoid sharp edges and projections. Avoid getting hurt below the units.
- Avoid climbing onto roofing, as roofs may dent.
- Do not run water for long periods, as charges or fees may incur.

Modular Homes

No longer a new phenomenon, modular homes are becoming more popular and a more sensible decision for builders, to cut the time of construction and deliver a home that is stronger, drier and often easier to deliver than an on-site stick-built home. For the home inspector, there are differences and concerns that should be looked at carefully, but many issues with new construction homes are avoided if the home is well built in the factory.

Acceptable Practices

- As you look at the home you may wish to explain the difference between on-site and stick-built homes, as opposed to modular and prefabrication. There are many misconceptions about quality and value of these homes.
- Carefully examine the exterior of the home. There should be no evidence that the modules were delivered as separate entities. Seams should blend, alignment should be straight, and there should be no evidence of stress damage or out-of-alignment issues.
- Look for gaps, damages, and indications that something had to be adjusted because the foundation was not level or correct.
- Check staircases on exterior and interior for proper riser heights and trip/stumble hazards, because staircases are typically done on site once the boxes are stacked and assembled.
- In the attic, look for strapping and proper alignment and proper fastening of the hinged rafters and roof assembly.
- From the outside, make sure that shingles have been properly finished off, and that trim details are finished without alignment issues or gaps.

Figure 11.3 One telltale sign of modular construction is attic roof framing that uses stamped hinges. Another might be the height of outlets and receptacles. A third might be the sign-off paperwork typically in a kitchen cabinet.

Figure 11.4 Finished home with siding, tile, and windows all installed at the factory.

- End gables should be properly fastened and secured.
- Penetrations through the roofing and siding should be sealed, and conduits bringing power, venting, refrigerant, plumbing, and heating should have fire stops and proper insulation between floors.
- Obviously, some requirements will differ from state to state. Be familiar with your state's requirements, which may supersede others.
- Look for interior cracking, damages, and signs of on-site repairs caused by transport and installation.
- Try all doors and windows to make sure there is no racking or movement distortion.
- Examine connections, especially heating, chimneys, and the like.
- Look at information sheets, placards, and sign-off paperwork.
- Treat foundations as you would those of any home. Look carefully for signs of moisture, cracks, or damage.
- Not all modular homes are the same, nor is their quality the same. Look carefully at the details.

Practices to Avoid

- Avoid scaring the buyer when you identify a modular built home. Many of these are first rate and may be better than an on-site, stick-built home. However, most homebuyer's will not be told a home is modular by the Realtors® or the seller and may feel "fooled" or "tricked" as there is no requirement to identify the building construction technique to them in the disclosure.
- Avoid missing the signs of a modular home. Look for hinged rafters, straps for lifting the roofing, bolt patterns, odd height outlets and switching, wider main girders and labeling under the sink or in kitchen cabinets.
- Do not assume the construction was finished by the modular factory. Some will put the home together with their own crews while others will allow the builder to finish the home themselves.
- Do not assume there is a certificate of occupancy nor that the home is totally completed. Look for evidence of movement, cracks, settlement, and problems that could have occurred during construction, transport, or set-up.

New Home Inspections (Phase Inspections)

Description

These inspections are typically funded by the builder or by the lender, or, in the situation where the home is being custom built, by the buyer. Phase inspections allow the inspector to actually watch various stages of the construction in order to participate by giving input before and during the construction. Often, the inspector can be the eye of the client, making sure each step of the building process achieves the level of quality and professionalism required. What differentiates this type of inspection from a regular inspection is that the inspector will see the insulation, rough plumbing, and electrical and can better advise the client that the workmanship is hitting the mark, or not.

Figure 11.5 Phase inspections give the inspector insight into the quality and completeness of the workmanship.

Assessing Existing Conditions

- Depending on the number of visits, the inspector should be checking all attachments and following the plans, looking for deviation and poor workmanship.
- Many times, the general contractor may not see that there is a deficiency.
- Having another set of eyes on site can catch issues before they are covered over and cost more to fix.
- While this is not typically a code compliance inspection, code infractions may indeed be found.

Acceptable Practices

However the phase inspections are set up, the inspector is carefully evaluating per the plans and building requirements to make sure that what is specified is properly completed and that recommendations are made if any deficiencies are found.

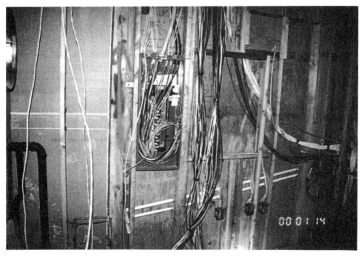

Figure 11.6 Making sure things are done before the drywall goes up is critical.

Foundation Phase Checks

- In the footing and foundation phase, the inspector will check distances from grade to the footing, width of footing, footing drains, and waterproofing.
- Look for cracks, settling, and signs of damage.
- Make sure there is foundation insulation, that sills are treated lumber and properly bolted, that all J-bolts have washers and nuts, and, if straps are used, that they are properly nailed.
- Check foundation wall framing for fasteners and insulation.
- Look for any necessary bracing.
- Safety items will include egress windows and access doors.

Walls and Ceiling Checks

- Inspectors should be looking at framing, drilling, notching, and alterations made to accommodate plumbing, electrical, low voltage, and HVACs.
- Look for proper fastening, bracing, and nailing details.
- Look to make sure bearing is carried from floor to floor, and check headers, girders, and posts.

Figure 11.7 Wires, insulation, laundry sinks, lighting, and other optional features can all be added when you are giving consultations in mid-construction.

- Check fire stopping, insulation, sheathing, and exterior siding.
- Inspect roofing and flashing.
- Check window and door installation.

Rough Mechanical Checks

- The inspector will look at rough wiring, terminations, and connections for high and low voltage.
- Check plumbing feed, drains, and venting.
- Check heating, insulation, and venting.
- Look for pans below air handlers and water heaters on second floors, or higher.
- Check fireplace installation and safety.
- Inspect any gas and/or fuel piping, central vacuum systems, and miscellaneous installations.

Finish Inspections

- Inspect moldings, tile, drywall, and wainscoting.
- Check installation of vanities and cabinets.

Figure 11.8 After the phase inspections and the typical warranty, the buyer should be feeling pretty comfortable about the home.

- Check installation of plugs, switches, and fixtures.
- Look at trim details and finishings.
- Inspect decks, patios, and balconies.
- Look at appliances, garage doors, screening, and accessories.
- Inspect bath fans, safety items, and miscellaneous installations.

Practices to Avoid

- Phase inspections can contribute to a better building and add quality control, or they can create tension and animosity. Make sure you fully understand what is recommended and what is required. When items are properly installed, don't forget to note the positives as well as deficiencies that may be uncovered. The end result should be a safer home.
- Take photos of existing conditions, and do not assume fault.
- Do not list items as unworkmanlike or unprofessional; just list deficiencies, and do not make judgments.

Swimming Pool Inspections

Description

Many homes will have pools for the recreation of the family. Inspectors will often be asked if a pool inspection can be added onto the regular home inspection. This additional service can certainly be offered, with the proper training.

Safety Issues

Many towns, cities, and states have very specific ordinances or codes for safety in regard to both above-ground and built-in pools. A pool inspector should be aware of local issues and requirements.

- For example, all pools in Connecticut are subject to the following regulations: to be surrounded by a fence that is at least 4 feet tall, and access gates must be self-closing and self-latching. Pool gates

Figure 11.9 Pools require additional training not just about operation, but about liability, state laws, and maintenance.

must swing open away from the pool area. And doors from a home that enter the pool area must have an audible alarm that notifies the homeowner that someone has entered the pool area.

- To avoid the fencing requirements, above-ground pools must have side walls 4 feet or higher, and a fold-up ladder that can be latched and locked in the up position. There may be a requirement to simply fence around the ladder.
- Fencing cannot have openings that will allow children to climb it or crawl under it.
- Diving boards and diving rocks can only be installed if the pool depth meets the requirements for such installations. Diving boards and slides do increase a homeowner's liability for accidents.
- The depth of the pool should be clearly marked whenever possible but always when there is a diving board or rock.

Assessing Existing Conditions

- Check pool fencing. Make sure that it is intact, that it is at least 4 feet tall, and that there are no unprotected areas.
- Check gates and doors entering the pool area. Gates must self-close and self-latch.
- Doors entering the pool area must have an alarm notification loud enough to alert occupants that someone has entered the pool area.
- Check deck for cracks and tripping hazards.
- Make sure the decking surface pitches away from the pool, for drainage.
- Check coping connection and tile for loose or missing pieces.
- Check liner, base, or gunite for damages.
- Check flow from discharge inlets and suction at weirs and skimmers.
- Check main drain and base for cleanliness, equalizing drain covers and additional safety equipment to reduce the chance of entrapment.
- Note lighting and verify GFCI protection, note low voltage and proper boxes; check for splash concerns in the pool area and any overhead wiring.
- Examine slides, diving boards, and diving rocks and ladders for defects or unsafe conditions.

Acceptable Practices

- Check pool equipment for proper installation and operation.
- Look for plumbing leaks when operating and when static.
- Higher psi may mean the filter needs backwashing or cleaning.

Figure 11.10 The age and safety of the pool equipment can greatly affect cost of operation.

- Air bubbles may indicate pipe or fitting leaks.
- Look at controls and timers for proper installation and operation.
- Look for cracks, leaks, weathering, damages, and deficiencies.
- Feel water flow at the inlets to establish good circulation.
- Check pump for air and bubbles at inlet.
- Note low water levels.
- Note equalizing drains and anti-entrapment equipment.
- Try to get pool service company information and any previous service history.

Practices to Avoid

- Do not turn on equipment that has been turned off at the breaker or disconnected for winterizing.
- Do not turn valves.
- Do not walk away from equipment without returning it to its original setting.

Figure 11.11 Make sure that access is locked in a way that will keep kids safe.

Spas, Swim Spas, Jetted Bathtubs

Description

While these are outside the standard of practice, the inspector may be willing to give an opinion on conditions found and safety concerns. In most cases, the inspector should be familiar enough with the equipment to know what should be checked and be able to provide a meaningful service without incurring liability.

Assessing Existing Conditions

- In all instances, you are looking for deterioration of surfaces, damages, and/or safety issues.
- Check for electrical outlets too close to the unit or within splash zones.

Figure 11.12 Spas can be fun but also a hassle because of liability, cost of operation, and chemical maintenance. Many clients will have mixed emotions about equipment that requires ongoing maintenance.

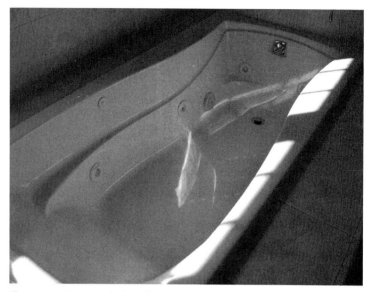

Figure 11.13 Knowledge of the operations, health concerns, and sanitation issues is critical to a new owner.

- Look for ladders and steps for easy exiting, and protective safety covers if the spa is outdoors. Spa covers that are damaged will absorb water and become very heavy. These will need replacing.
- Spa water should be chemically treated for best sanitation, and water sampling is the only way to determine if the unit is chemically safe. Therefore, to avoid skin rashes, clean your hands after handling pools, spas, and jetted tubs, and recommend that clients practice proper sanitation and respiratory problems.
- Spas and hot tubs should never exceed 104 degrees F.
- Look for leaks, stains, damaged wood if skirted, and signs of mold or insects.
- Jetted bathtubs are usually surrounded by plywood-framed boxes that may have been tiled. To avoid leakage, grout and sealant on tiles and edges must be maintained. Make sure there is an access panel to service pumps, heaters, and any other equipment. It should be readily accessible and not require removal of tile or drywall.

Acceptable Practices: Tubs

- Make sure equipment is filled to proper water heights before testing (generally above jets and water sensors).
- Run equipment using normal controls.

- Check jets, aerators, bubblers, and lights.
- Look at equipment when operating for leaks or any deficiencies.
- If the tub is heated, look for temperature rise or amperage draw (220V electric heaters usually draw about 22 amps when heating).
- Check for physical damage to skirts, surrounds, and surfaces.
- Encourage installation of grab bars, handrails, and safety fencing.
- Check for ground fault circuit interrupters and make sure electrical outlets are out of splash zones (usually greater than 5 feet)

Practices to Avoid

- Do not operate equipment if it is disconnected or turned off at the breaker, or if water levels are too low.
- Preferably, have owners demonstrate the equipment to you, if they are willing.
- If the unit smells of chemicals, mold, sulfur or methane, or electrical burning, it may need additional chemical cleaning or repair.
- If there are filters, recommend regular cleaning/replacement of cartridges.
- New owners should be made aware that chemical sanitation is required for safe operation.

Acceptable Practices: Saunas

- Make sure equipment is not damaged or stained, and that the room does not smell moldy.
- Run equipment using normal controls.
- Check heater for safe operation, timer, vents, and door safety.
- Look at equipment while it is operating. Look for wiring hazards.
- Look for temperature rise or amperage draw (220V electric heaters usually draw about 22 amps when heating).
- Look for physical damage to walls, seating, and wood around the heater.
- Encourage installation of grab bars and handrails, and safe operation in general.
- Doors need to open out and must not have locksets, in case of an emergency.

Figure 11.14 Saunas require a slightly different type of evaluation than tubs.

Practices to Avoid

- Do not operate equipment if it is disconnected or turned off at the breaker, or if water levels are too low.
- Do not operate these on your own unless the homeowner is not there. Preferably, have owners demonstrate the equipment to you, if they are willing.
- Do not operate the unit if it smells of chemicals, mold, sulfur or methane, or you sense electrical burning, it may need additional chemical cleaning or repair.
- Do not leave units unattended or run them for an extended amount of time.

Tennis Courts, Play Spaces, Playground Equipment, Trampolines, Putting Greens, Basketball Courts

Description

While these are outside the standard of practice, the inspector may be willing to give an opinion on conditions found and safety concerns. In most cases, the inspector should be familiar enough with the equipment to know what should be checked and be able to provide a meaningful service without incurring liability.

Figure 11.15 You are looking at drainage, damage, safety, lighting, and hazard issues that may not be obvious.

Assessing Existing Conditions

- Look at play areas for settling, heaving, erosion, and uneven surfaces.
- Note drainage issues.
- Note any damaged netting or broken equipment.
- With trampolines and swing sets, all hardware should be tight, with minimal corrosion and no rips or damages in fabric.
- Wood surfaces on swings should be sanded, and swing hardware should look safe and unrusted. Swings should be staked to the ground to avoid tipping.
- Slides should be secure, and ladder spindles should be intact.
- Check overhead wires for safety above all play equipment.
- Pressure-treated equipment may be a concern because of splinters.

Acceptable Practices

- Test for loose hardware.
- Look for loose play equipment, damaged wood or metal, uneven surfaces, and tripping hazards.
- Note drainage issues.
- Note deteriorated fencing, uneven or damaged asphalt or recreational surfaces, unsafe walks, and stairs.

Practices to Avoid

- Do not use the equipment to test it. Do not put your weight on swings, slides, or other equipment.
- Do not fix damages; report any situation you consider a hazard.

Water Features

Description

Water features, both interior and exterior have become a very popular trend. These may include a fountain, a pond, and a waterfall or stream, either in the home or outside. They may be self-contained or be fed naturally. Most use a submersible pump to circulate the water and may include natural plantings and fish. More complicated ones may require additional filtration, aeration and chemical treatment. In some municipalities when a water feature is deeper than 24 inches, they may require installation of pool fencing and water alarms.

Assessing Existing Conditions

- Run the equipment using normal controls. You may have to discuss operation with owners or have them demonstrate.
- Look for leaks, electrical safety issues, and deficiencies.
- Examine child safety issues.

Figure 11.16   Waterfalls, ponds, and fountains are typically rather simple by design. Make sure they are all protected by a GFCI.

- Consider moisture levels if the feature is located inside, and freeze concerns if in a climate where the temperature will go below freezing.
- Water features must be on ground fault protection circuits.

Acceptable Practices

- Look for leaks, safety issues, and proper operation.
- Note any deficiencies in your report.
- Note limitations of your inspection.

Practices to Avoid

- Do not run the equipment if fish or other animals are present, without the owner's help or permission.
- Do not run the equipment unsupervised.
- Make sure you turn the equipment off after the inspection.

Wood-Destroying Organisms

Description

In most states, the home inspector, a pest inspector, or both will search for evidence of wood-destroying insects. Carpenter ants, termites, carpenter bees, and powder post beetles can all do damage to a home, as can fungi. The ability to detect rot, damage, and signs and symptoms of infestation can save the buyer lots of aggravation and expense, if these are found ahead of time.

Figure 11.17   The termite is such a small insect, but it can reduce the strength of a structural member to that of mush. Probing properly and thoroughly can often find the damages quickly. Look under door frames, windows, garages, and damp areas.

Assessing Existing Conditions

- If properly trained, the inspector can often note signs of insects in the midst of probing and checking for foundation deterioration of sills, joists, and lower framing—especially under front and rear entry doors and sliders.
- Carpenter ant frass and termite shelter tubes are very typical in the Northeast. As they can do substantial damage, it is important to note any evidence of infestation, previous problems, and treatment.

Acceptable Practices

- Probing of all wood structural members in the lower sections of the home is recommended. Check all sill plates, joists, and the inside of the box beam, as well as girders and posts.
- Taking soundings (tapping on wood and listening for hollow sounds or rotted wood) is important as well.
- Look for signs of frass, sawdust, and digested material left around carpenter ant nesting areas.
- Look for termite shelter tubes and termite-damaged wood, books, and paper.

Figure 11.18 The right tool can make the job so much easier.

- In crawlspaces and basements, check for infested stored items and debris.
- Wood damaged by powder post beetles looks as if it has dart holes in it. Although they rarely cause structural issues, these insects re-infest the same piece of wood and are typically found in antique homes.
- While not usually a structural concern, carpenter bees will often damage siding and trim in certain climates. Woodpeckers will often follow and damage the wood even more, trying to eat the bee egg cases.

Practices to Avoid

- Try not to do more damage than necessary to already damaged wood.
- Do not damage termite shelter tubes, because they are evidence of continuing activity. These should be removed by the pest control company during the treatment process.

Figure 11.19 Make sure someone is on contract to check bait stations, or you may be looking at an abandoned system.

- When you find bait stations, remember that it may take some time for insects to find the bait. Always recommend frequent reinspections.
- Do not assume there is an ongoing treatment plan just because there is evidence of previous treatment or bait stations. Contracts may have lapsed.

Figure 11.20 Careful reinspection of damp wood is critical to keeping subterranean termites from infesting a home in the Northeast. You should learn all you can about the wood-destroying organisms that are prevalent in your specific area, and the treatment protocols for dealing with them.

Health, Safety, and Maintenance Inspections

Description

In the past few years, health, safety, and maintenance (HS&M) inspections have become a very popular ancillary business for inspectors. These inspections may be requested by homeowners who are not even interested in selling their home. Such inspections help to point out needed repairs, maintenance needs, and safety issues and help homeowners plot out ways to keep their homes operating properly while maintaining their value.

Figure 11.21 From changing filters, to basic maintenance, to knowing how much insulation is enough, many homeowners are clueless and apt to just hope things are okay without checking. Maintenance inspections can save thousands of dollars lost through ignorance, and can correct unhealthy and unsafe situations.

Assessing Existing Conditions

- These inspections are done in a very similar manner to a normal home inspection, with the difference that the homeowner is the client, and he or she can offer history and service information that is often missing or not disclosed in a regular inspection.
- Items that the homeowner already knows are in good condition can be excluded from the inspection and areas of concern can be focused on.
- We recommend that you first sit down with the owners and interview them as to their concerns and needs for the inspection. Following the interview, perform a full inspection while they come along and taking notes.
- Health concerns, previous leakage, heating and cooling levels, and any other concerns can all be discussed—as well as renovations and alterations—solely with the goal of developing a plan of action. With this information, clients can solve house needs and get on schedule to make operating the home more pleasant while keeping up its potential value.

Figure 11.22 This homeowner never even realized that water was entering the home in heavy rain situations.

Figure 11.23 Water entry can do considerable damage and create unhealthy situations, including growing mold, in less than three days.

Acceptable Practices

- Inspect the home and write a regular inspection report, but with the focus of making recommendations that will help the home to become more energy efficient and safer, and offer tips for taking care of any needed repairs.
- The inspection should help clients reflect on what they want the home to be and allow them to evaluate what they are capable of doing and what projects will require professionals.
- The inspection will help clients understand what they need to do, and will help direct them to get the resources they need by referring them to professionals in the trades.
- As clients learn, they better understand what is required and the inspection may clarify why the home has not operated as well as desired, in the past.

Figure 11.24 Most homes need more ventilation and insulation. Clients are often surprised to hear that their home needs improvement.

Practices to Avoid

- Try not to focus on possessions and other distractions.
- When performing a home inspection, we are trying to see the forest through the trees, with the understanding that everything will leave when the owners move. Our worry is that when the clutter is removed, hidden problems will be more blatant, and the new owners will find it hard to understand how these elements were missed in the inspection. In the HS&M inspection, there is no expectation that anything will change, or that one book or possessions in a closet will ever move.
- Always give clients choices, not ultimatums. Let them know that doing nothing, especially if the do not agree with your suggestions, is perfectly acceptable. But that repairing safety issues is in their best interest.

Figure 11.25 Do the best you can. Sometimes it will take more than the inspection to motivate your client into action.

Energy Inspections

Description

The desire to live in a home that is more energy efficient and to reduce energy waste has become a very important topic. Many inspectors have training in both green building techniques and in ways to evaluate energy waste in homes. Some have purchased infrared cameras, blower doors, and "duct blasters" to better determine conditions and help diagnose deficiencies. These inspections (or "energy audits") can range from a rather simple walk through to a rather sophisticated, time-consuming evaluation.

Assessing Existing Conditions

- Interviewing clients will help to determine what they are hoping to achieve with the audit.
- A discussion about the previous heating, cooling, and electrical bills for the home may be a good starting point. Determining previous

Figure 11.26 Blower doors can pressurize or depressurize the home, making it easier to find energy loss.

Figure 11.27 The infrared camera can see water entry and see temperature differentials.

seasonal problem areas within the home may help to focus the evaluation.

- Pressurizing and/or depressurizing the home may help find drafts, leaks, and areas in need of sealing or repair.
- Infrared scans will often show missing insulation and cold or hot areas where heat may be escaping. (Note: Some temperature variation is required for this equipment to be of value.)

Acceptable Practices

- The energy audit should be a thorough evaluation of areas of the home that the client is concerned about, including, but not limited to, heating and cooling, insulation and ventilation, quality of the windows and doors, weather-stripping, pipe insulation, window treatments, water heating equipment, ducting, and condensation issues.
- The inspection can be visual, using instrumentation or not.
- Inspectors should be properly trained and have necessary equipment to properly evaluate the home, based on the scope of the inspection.
- A well-written report should follow, to help guide clients toward reaching their energy consumption goals, if possible.

Practices to Avoid

- Avoid confusion. Inspectors should make sure clients fully understand the scope of the audit, to ensure that they are comfortable with the limitations of the findings. Explain what will be tested. The capabilities and limitations of the equipment should be understood.
- Do not promise quick paybacks or assure tax incentives. Make sure you are clear about any projections on paybacks, government tax incentives, and programs like Energy Star.

Figure 11.28 Sometimes adding good insulating window treatments will give the consumer more energy savings than a replacement window.

Air and Water Quality Testing

Description

Ancillary testing services during an inspection, or as a result of the findings of an inspection, can lead to a recommendation for specialized testing. Over the past decade, areas of concern have risen to become consumer touchpoints. Testing may vary, depending on the desire of the client and the environmental concerns that are important at that moment in time.

The following are often common tests performed and are areas of concern in most real estate transactions:

- Radon
- Mold
- Lead
- Asbestos
- Water potability and quality

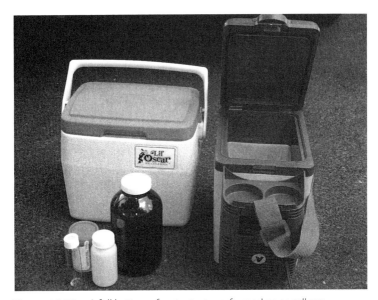

Figure 11.29 A full battery of water tests performed on a well can determine if additional filtration or adjustments are necessary.

Assessing Existing Conditions

- During the process of an inspection, discussions based on conditions found, age of the home, and concerns raised by the client may result in testing or referrals to testing services. Some inspectors will offer these tests, and others may offer referrals for such testing.
- Many times the situation will demand that certain protocols and requirements be met before testing can be performed. The inspector should be sure these parameters are met to ensure accuracy and proper testing results are achieved.
  - Short-term radon air testing takes minimally 46–79 hours.
  - Some states require licensing, certifications, and training for those doing these tests. Know your local requirements and restrictions.
  - Only approved test devices should be used.
  - Closed-house protocols must be followed—doors and windows kept closed before testing and for the entire test, except for normal entry and exit.
  - Test devices should be set in a proper location away from drafts and exterior walls.
  - No burning in fireplaces or use of whole-house fans during the radon test period is allowed.

Figure 11.30 Continuous radon monitors add additional verification and tamper controls, which make for better testing for real estate transactions.

- Findings above the EPA action level (4.0 pCi/L) should be verification-tested before mitigating.
- Mitigation using EPA-approved contractors should be done if testing numbers indicate a problem.
- Long-term testing (which can give a more accurate reading of the home taking into account seasonal changes and weather conditions) is always a good idea, but may not be realistic in real estate transactions.
- Testing for radon in water should be performed following the state-approved laboratories' requested protocol. This will often entail a specific manner of collecting the sample, a particular sample container, and requirements for maintaining temperature or time constraints for the sample to arrive at the lab to ensure the viability of the sample.
- To make sure the sample is properly protected, a signed chain-of-custody record should be maintained.
- To do lead, mold, and asbestos air quality sampling in most states, you must maintain a license to collect and interpret samples. Know your local requirements.
- Air quality sampling usually requires air pump sampling. Take a predetermined grab sample from outside air, then from inside locations, in order to determine the variation and differences.

Figure 11.31 Simple chemical swabs can give the inspector a preliminary evaluation to determine if more in-depth testing is required.

- Contact sampling may be taken by a trained individual or the homeowner and sent to a lab. This usually is done by taping off a sampling area with a template and using wipes to clean that space of whatever residual material is on it.
- Soil sampling requires taking soil from several locations at least 1 foot from the foundation and from approximately the top 6 inches of the soil. A composite mixture would be gathered by the tester or the homeowner and sent to the lab, following state or lab requirements.
- Most air quality grab samples at best only show what was gathered from a particular area at the time of the inspection, and may not be representative of all surfaces in a home.
- Water sampling must follow state and lab requirements, and samples must be collected following their protocols in recommended collection bottles. Autoclaved, sterile bottles may be required for some testing; glass or amber bottles may be required for others.
- Following the protocols, samples should be taken before filtration and noted as such, or after filtration and/or treatment and also noted as such, or from both locations.
- Water should be run at least 10–15 minutes to gather a flushed sample, except in cases of a first-draw sampling.

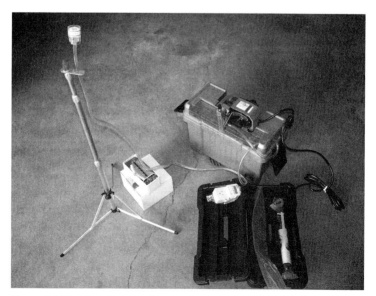

Figure 11.32 Drawing air using a pump onto a small sample Air-o-Cell® can determine the levels of contaminants in the air.

- Mailed or shipped samples should be protected from weather issues and may be required to be iced, refrigerated, or kept from freezing.
- Potability samples should be drawn where water is apt to be taken for drinking.
- Samples for special testing should be noted as to the location from which they are drawn.
- If the integrity of a sampling is questionable, the test should be repeated whenever possible.

Acceptable Practices

- Follow testing parameters required by law, statute, municipal ordinance, lab requirements, or national standards whenever possible.
- Maintain chain of custody and proper documentation.
- Maintain any required quality assurance quality control records and procedures to ensure good testing.
- Maintain ongoing training and continuing education.

Practices to Avoid

- Do not deviate from testing parameters; explain to clients and homeowners what is required, and if there is no willingness to comply, do not test.
- Do not test beyond your certifications or qualifications.
- Do not expose yourself to dangerous conditions without personal protection equipment and adequate training to provide the service.
- Do not place others in harmful situations brought about by testing or testing requirements.

Tank Testing

Description

In the 1980s and until recently, buried fuel tanks were an increasingly worrisome issue when purchasing a home because of the age of the buried tank and the potential for soil contamination. In many states now, it is very difficult to secure a mortgage, or ultimately any type of insurance, if the carrier finds out that there is a buried tank on the property. Even a tank that has been previously tested can develop a new leak and cause contamination that could incur great expense for clean-up. Tank testing is usually a subcontracted process whereby an EPA/DEP-approved contractor will perform soil sampling and follow the appropriate testing protocol to determine weakness in the tank and fuel loss over a period of time. Laboratory samples are usually only submitted in cases where fuel is detected.

Assessing Existing Conditions

- Probably the most important first step for the inspector is to search for and locate any visual and accessible evidence leading to the conclusion that there might be a buried tank.
- Looking for fill pipes, breather lines, and fuel lines may indicate that a tank is or was present.
- Asking previous owners for tank history may establish the existence of a tank.
- Abandoned tanks will require testing paperwork and a certificate explaining the circumstances and the reason for abandonment (usually a hardship).
- Testing and inspecting indoor or above-grade tanks require knowledge of acceptable testing protocols, if more than a visual inspection is performed.
- Tanks above grade inside often can last more than 30 years.
- Buried tanks or those exposed to harsh conditions may not last 15 years.

Figure 11.33   A photo of the tank on a truck leaving the home is priceless when used to calm a nervous buyer.

Acceptable Practices

- Carefully examine above-grade and interior tanks for rust, corrosion, and metal deterioration.
- Examine for signs of leakage or seepage from seams or fittings.
- Look for physical damages.
- Examine mountings and legs to determine conditions that could lead to the tank moving or collapsing.
- Note any deficiencies in your report.
- Note protection of supply lines.
- Note potential for weather to affect oil viscosity.

Practices to Avoid

- Do not bang on or put any undue stress on the tank.
- Be careful not to crimp any supply piping.
- If replacement tanks are to be installed outside, avoid installing them in unprotected areas where wind, heat, or cold will affect their effectiveness and efficiency.
- Interior and exterior tanks that are no longer in service should be protected from accidental filling by sealing or removal of fill lines.

Figure 11.34 Carefully look for oil leaks, corrosion on fittings, and damaged legs. Tanks located in garages should be protected from vehicle damage.

Septic Inspections

Description

Septic systems usually need inspecting to ensure good operation and functioning. In order to evaluate them, the inspector must know the layout of the system, and a proper inspection will include opening the tank cover, checking the distribution boxes, and probing the fields. Many services will pump down or empty the tank to better view the components.

Assessing Existing Conditions

- When the cover is open, the consistency and water levels can be checked to provide information about capacity and maintenance.
- Levels at the distribution boxes will tell which trenches are in use and indicate conditions.

Figure 11.35   If only it were this easy. Once the system is buried and the ground landscaped, it takes a knowledgeable septic person to evaluate what is going on.

Figure 11.36 Opening up the cover, pumping down the water, and checking distribution boxes and fields should all be considered.

Figure 11.37 Sometimes it makes more sense to hire specialists and let others do their job as you watch!

- Checking the tank baffles will tell the inspector if there are concerns in regard to solids reaching the fields.
- Back pressure from the fields may cause water to flow back to the distribution boxes or the septic tank.
- Water or sewage on the yard or at the fields may also indicate the system needs repair or replacement.
- Running some water in the home will show that the piping is connected to the system and that the effluent is reaching the tank.

Acceptable Practices

- Open the tank cover and check baffles and height of liquids.
- Check scum and sludge levels.
- If there is a filter, check conditions.
- Look for damages or leaks.
- Run water to see that lines are operating.
- Open distribution boxes to see if water is reaching the fields.
- Probe fields with a long bar to see how wet they are.
- Look for water breaking out of the fields.

Practices to Avoid

- Do not damage boxes or fields when probing.
- Do not damage tank cover or baffle.
- Do not leave tank cover open and unsupervised.

Chapter 12

Inspector Safety

Inspection Safety Issues

Inspection Safety Issues

Description

We all realize that this business can be dangerous on many levels. We are climbing roofs, checking panel boxes, and crawling in small spaces where an errant nail can scar us or a rabid animal can attack. Many of our insurance policies reflect a higher than normal risk. So I feel compelled to add a short chapter on protecting your health, based on my experiences in the field and some good common sense.

Clothing Safety

- I have always been taught to stay away from synthetic clothing and look for cotton, because synthetics can not only burn but melt and be very dangerous by causing worse burns.

Figure 12.1   Just another day at work … wet crawlspaces, asbestos, rodent droppings, and a chance of electrocution.

- Wear rubber-soled shoes, because these are less likely to slip on a wet surface or roof. And they are less likely to conduct electricity.
- Just as they taught us in high school shop, not wearing rings and jewelry makes you less likely to be hurt by machines and snagged on building components.

Ladder Safety

We carry a 22-foot Little Giant® and an 18-foot Telesteps® telescopic ladder in my truck. We like them in the truck rather than on top of the truck, because this keeps them safe, warm, and dry in most instances. On the top of both ladders we have a small bungee cord attached for windy days. We wrap the gutter nail with the cord to prevent the ladder from slipping or blowing over whenever it seems that the wind is unusually strong.

- Obviously, you should never climb a ladder unless there is someone available to foot the ladder for you. Ask the agent or your client to maintain the ladder's stability while you are climbing, and have him or her wait for you to come down.
- Never raise a ladder without looking up and looking for overhead wiring. Another good idea is to look at the service drop to make sure

Figure 12.2 The proper angle for ladder use will protect you and reduce the chance of a fall.

the gutter system is not charged by a wire lying across the gutters or touching a leader pipe.

▪ Ladders should be angled at approximately 75.5 degrees, for safety. The easiest way to gauge this angle is to place your toes at the base of the rails of the ladder and extend your arms straight ahead of you. If the angle is correct, your fingertips should just touch the rung in front of you.

▪ We recommend that you never allow homeowners, clients, or Realtors® to climb your ladder to better see the roofing. If you do, be prepared to carry them down on your back.

▪ Clean your ladder after each use (if it gets dirty), and lubricate parts that need lube.

▪ When inside the home, placing a towel under the ladder, and/or up against the wall, when the ladder is raised should become common practice. Protect the homeowners and their property.

▪ Never set up ladders in front of doors, driveways, or garages without additional "watchers" to ensure that your ladder is not bumped, hit, or knocked over.

▪ Leg levelers will safely help you adjust for uneven ground without improvising.

Electrical Safety

▪ When opening panel covers:

Make sure the floor and your shoes are dry.

Look to see which breakers are off (if any).

Feel the deadfront cover with the back of your hand to see if there is any indication of an electrical shock hazard.

Look for signs of previous arcing or sparking.

Always wear protective safety glasses.

Use insulated shaft screwdrivers.

Place box cover screws in a logical, convenient place.

Do not allow the client to touch the panel or help you take off or remount the cover.

▪ When closing the panel:

Make sure it is secure and that all breakers that were on are still on.

Look for pinched wires or ones that could be near, or damaged by, the box cover screws.

Figure 12.3 Sometimes you can actually sense the hairs on the back of your hand moving when you touch it to the panel.

- Before setting the ladder, look at service drop and see if wires are touching metal siding or gutters.
- Never test the main breaker. There may be equipment that must remain on for safety, computer memory or security, and telephone systems. Remember, all those digital clocks will need to be reset.

Plumbing Safety

- Don't operate valves. Period. Fight the temptation.
- Don't squeeze traps. What will you do if they implode?
- Look at the connections before you turn on a sink or flush a toilet. Many laundry sinks, darkroom sinks, and utility sinks have been recycled from another room and may only be temporary, with inadequate drains.
- Don't ever test pressure relief valves, because they will open and drip perpetually ever after.
- Don't scrape off corrosion because it may have self-sealed the leak that you could be opening back up.
- When running bathtubs, stay there! This will reduce the chance of leaks or overflows.
- When testing jetted tubs, never run the pump with the water level below the jets.

Figure 12.4 Corrosion is the sign that there is a leak needing repair.

- Never put any weight on tub fillers—they can snap right off.
- Before you turn on a shower, look for possessions in the stall or tub that will get wet! Make sure the shower head and other body-washer heads are not facing you.
- Do not touch sump pumps with your hand or body. A defective pump that is plugged in can kill you.

Roofing Safety

- Always bring your cell phone up with you in case you need rescue.
- Tie off your ladder to prevent it from blowing over.
- Do not allow clients, Realtors®, or the homeowner to climb your ladder.
- Never walk backward on a roof. Watch out for projections, guy wires, and antennas.
- Always climb a roof with the expectation that shingles may be loose or that you could slip. Pay attention.
- When looking at chimneys, do not push against them; a poorly anchored one could fall off the home.
- Make sure the homeowner (or tenant) knows you are climbing the roof. Looking into a skylight might compromise someone's privacy.

Figure 12.5 Examine the attic carefully before walking on badly deteriorated roofing.

- Examining the sheathing in the attic first might warn an inspector to avoid walking on the roof, if conditions indicate rot or delamination.
- If you are going out a second-story door or window onto a roof, will your shoes be too dirty to return without booties?

Fireplace Safety

- Always make noise and jiggle the damper before opening it. This may wake up a sleeping raccoon and warn it not to drop down into the home when you open the damper.
- Don't stick your head in the fireplace till after the damper is open and the soot has fallen. Check your hands for soot as well.
- Glass doors and screens may be poorly attached and fall when you touch them.

Crawlspace Safety

- Always let the Realtor®/tenant, owner, or client know you are going into the crawlspace. If you are hurt, at least someone will know where to look for you.

Figure 12.6   A face full of soot can certainly ruin your day.

Figure 12.7   Hantavirus and other illnesses can be the result of rodent droppings.

- Always carry your cell phone into the crawlspace as a back-up.
- Crawlspaces can be extremely dirty, dangerous places. Wearing a respirator, and protective disposable suits, booties, gloves, safety glasses, and kneepads is important for keeping the inspector safe. Whenever you consider going in without wearing personal protection equipment, you are making a bad decision.
- A good termite probe and gloves may double as protection when you have an animal confrontation in a crawlspace. Remember that, in most cases, making noise can influence an animal's decision to attack or retreat. Make noise entering and moving around the crawlspace.
- Use caution when moving fallen insulation, because it may be used as nesting, and something may be hiding behind it.
- When prodding sill areas for rot and insects, try to avoid hitting unseen wires.
- Look for sharp edges, pipes, and hangers that can cut you.

Figure 12.8   Proper personal protection is vital to staying healthy.

Heating/Cooling System Safety

- Never turn on equipment that has been turned off at the emergency switch, serviceman's switch, circuit breaker, or fuse without discussing why it is turned off with the owner or tenant.
- Make sure whatever you turn on is later turned off and that thermostats are returned to their original position.
- Ducting in attic spaces can be a trip hazard. Look for disconnected ducts or leaky ducts that could have been kicked apart, or are just drafty.
- Do not change valve settings on boilers or hot water equipment.
- Do not test pressure relief valves for operation.
- If you open filters, remember to close the filter cover after checking.
- Stackpipes, vent hoods, and flame shields get hot—try not to burn yourself.

Window Safety

- When operating double-hung (sash) windows, watch your fingers in case upper sashes drop unexpectedly.

Figure 12.9 Read service information on boilers and furnaces. Sometimes the info is very helpful.

Figure 12.10 These can hurt you. The top sash may fall, hitting your fingers.

- Crank casement windows that open out over a deck or walkway can project out and block walks or become a hazard.
- Check for tempered glass near entry doors, staircases, and low-to-the-floor windows, and in bathrooms.

Bathroom Safety

- Check for tempered glass in tub and shower enclosures, in windows in both areas, and around regular and jetted bathtubs.
- Carefully examine grab bars for safety.
- Make sure doorstops are in place, and make sure shower doors don't hit other surfaces that could make the door crack or shatter.
- Look for switches and receptacles that are in damp locations or too close to fixtures.
- Examine heat lights, heaters, and wall furnaces for safety and proximity to combustibles.
- Check toilets for looseness, and check floors between fixtures for weakness.
- Be careful on slippery floors.

Figure 12.11 It is rare that the owner or tenant will disclose any illness, yet you are touching fixtures and surfaces that can harbor germs and bacteria.

- Consider getting regular hepatitis B, tetanus, and influenza inoculations.
- Be careful what you touch, and wash your hands frequently as you inspect.

Closet Safety

- Watch for bulbs too close to combustibles.

Attic Safety

- Do not walk on insulation. Don't assume that there is flooring under it, or expect that the framing will hold your weight.
- Be wary of bees, bats, and other wildlife nesting in these spaces. Make noise when you approach, and expect the unexpected.
- Watch out for flooring, plywood, or planks that are not screwed or nailed down.
- Be wary of potential asbestos and vermiculite insulation.
- Be wary of all kinds of fecal materials in the attic.

Figure 12.12 Bulbs in closets can easily ignite clothing and burn a home down.

Figure 12.13 Attics are great places for hornets, bees, wasps, birds, and bats.

- Never touch a whole-house fan when you cannot see your client in the hallway below. That timer switch is too tempting.
- Watch out for the springs and hardware on pull-down stairs. They can hurt you.

Staircase Safety

- Watch for loose handrails, shaky guardrails, and winder-type stairs.
- Look for enough tread to step on safely and enough riser height to reduce stumble hazards.
- Make sure stairs have 3-foot landings or doors that open away from the stairs.

Other General Safety

- Ask homeowners to take responsibility for their pets. Most animals will feel threatened when strangers are wandering the home. They may bite, scratch, hide, flee into unsafe areas, or run outside, if you are not careful. Give these pets back to their owners to watch.

Figure 12.14 Unsafe stairs can cause serious accidents.

- Ask owners to take pets with them or have them put the pet in a crate or room away from the inspector and client. This room can be inspected first, then the pet placed there.
- Children on inspections are often a major distraction to their parents, but they can also find your tools, play with testers and probes, and get hurt or do damage. Do not encourage them to help you on the inspection.
- Make sure appliances, tubs, saunas, and steamers are all off at the end of the inspection.
- Make sure thermostats are returned to their original settings.
- Over the years, we have opened many window treatments, and raised blinds and shades—and then had them fall off their hardware and end up on us. Be careful.
- When testing garage-door openers for auto-reverse safety, give yourself enough room to get away from the door if it operates in an unsafe fashion.
- With multi-unit homes, look for fire separation and firebreaks. Look for emergency lighting, alarms, smoke detectors and carbon monoxide (CO) monitors.
- Watch for older, unsafe fire suppression systems and antique fire systems that may be dangerous.
- Use your nose testing for gas leaks and mold accumulations.

Figure 12.15 Carbon tetrachloride fire grenades give off toxic fumes. Have these carefully and properly disposed of.

Figure 12.16 A sump pump can be a tremendous asset when a pipe starts to leak or a water heater lets go.

- When outside, watch out for poison ivy, oak, and sumac. Be aware of pesticides and herbicides.
- Exterior paint chips can have lead in them.
- Watch for sinkholes, tripping hazards, and uneven terrain in the yard.
- Garage-door springs should have safety cables.
- Look at deck substructures and support posts before you get on the deck. Make sure ledger boards have bolts, joist hangers, flashing, and proper nails.
- Finally . . . never get between the Realtor® and her next appointment.

Assessing Existing Conditions

- Radon venting from under the slab should only be exhausted at roof height to avoid recontaminating the home.
- Whole-house fans can create tremendous depressurization, pulling exterior air, pollen, radon gas, exhaust, and products of combustion

Figure 12.17 This fan is too big to use just for voiding heat in the attic. Upgrade to a smaller thermostat-controlled fan.

(CO) into the home. These fans should be evaluated for safety and function.

- Dirty filters will slow air movement. Recommend cleaning or replacing old filters.

Acceptable Practices

- Moldy areas that are small can be carefully cleaned by the home-owners. Larger areas should be evaluated by professionals.
- Cleaning cooling and heating ducts can stir up allergens and may add additional odors in the ducting. Freshly "cleaned" ducts may be dirtier than you think. Some of the chemicals and techniques used may increase noxious odors and stir up more allergens.
- Damp odors are a symptom of moldy conditions; use your nose, but beware that you may be exposing yourself to unsafe conditions.

Practices to Avoid

- Do not open installed humidifiers without protecting yourself with a respirator, as these are rarely adequately cleaned and can be very dirty and unhealthy. Opening them may expose the inspector to dangerous levels of germs, bacteria, and mold.
- Do not enter crawlspaces unless you are wearing a respirator and protective clothing to avoid airborne dusts, fecal material, and mold.
- Leaks, drips, and surface standing water in crawlspace and basement areas should be noted, and vapor barriers recommended.
- Wear a respirator and protective clothing to avoid airborne dusts, fecal material, and mold in unfinished spaces.
- Leaks, drips, and surface standing water in crawlspace and basement areas should be noted and vapor barriers recommended.
- Cleaning ducts can stir up allergens and may cause additional odors in the ducting. Freshly "cleaned" ducts may be dirtier than you think.

Figure 12.18 Try to cut down on items that inject unclean moisture into the home.

Figure 12.19 Mold must be further investigated to see if it has grown on other surfaces, not just those that are easily accessible and visible. Look for the source of the moisture.

- Damp odors are a symptom of moldy conditions; use your nose, but beware of unsafe conditions.

Index